P9-CKT-417

ALSO BY TED SOLOTAROFF

The Red Hot Vacuum

A Few Good Voices in My Head

*An Age of Enormity: Life and Writing in
the Forties and Fifties
by Isaac Rosenfeld* (editor)

Writers and Issues (editor)

Best American Short Stories, 1978 (editor)

Many Windows (editor)

*The Schocken Book of Contemporary
Jewish Fiction*
(edited with Nessa Rapoport)

TRUTH COMES IN BLOWS

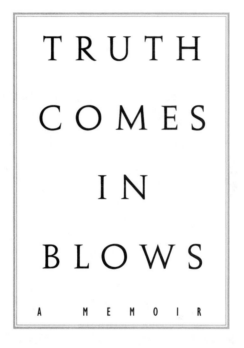

TRUTH
COMES
IN
BLOWS

A MEMOIR

TED SOLOTAROFF

W. W. NORTON & COMPANY / NEW YORK / LONDON

Copyright © 1998 by Ted Solotaroff

All rights reserved
Printed in the United States of America
First Edition

"The Heavy Bear Who Goes with Me" by Delmore Schwartz,
from *Selected Poems: Summer Knowledge*, Copyright ©1959 by
Delmore Schwartz. Reprinted by permission
of New Directions Publishing Corp.
"Preludes" by T. S. Eliot, from *Collected Poems 1909–1962*.
Reprinted by permission of Faber and Faber Ltd.

For information about permission to reproduce selections from this book,
write to Permissions, W. W. Norton & Company, Inc.,
500 Fifth Avenue, New York, NY 10110.

The text of this book is comopsed in Electra with the display set in Nova Augustea.
Desktop composition by Tom Ernst.
Manufacturing by Courier Companies, Inc.
Book design by JAM Design.

Library of Congress Cataloging-in-Publication Data
Solotaroff, Ted, 1928–
Truth comes in blows: a memoir / Ted Solotaroff.
p.   cm.
ISBN 0-393-04679-6
1. Solotaroff, Ted, 1928– .   2. Editors—United States—
Biography.   I. Title.
Pn149.9.S66A3   1998
808' .027'092—dc21

[B]   98-15755
                                                                       CIP

W. W. Norton & Company, Inc., 500 Fifth Avenue, New York, N.Y. 10110
http://www.wwnorton.com

W. W. Norton & Company Ltd., 10 Coptic Street, London WC1A 1PU

1   2   3   4   5   6   7   8   9   0

To Sandra, Bob, and Leah

Does truth come in blows?

—**Saul Bellow**
Henderson the Rain King

The individual is steeped in something more general than himself. By this reckoning, our parents furnish us not only with those habitual gestures which are the outlines of our face and voice, but also with certain mannerisms of speech, certain favorite expressions, which, almost as unconscious as our intonation, almost as profound, indicate likewise a definite point of view towards life.

—**Marcel Proust**
Remembrance of Things Past

ACKNOWLEDGMENTS

I'd like to thank Hyman Enzer, Marcia and the late Louis Posner, Gina Weiss Zucco, and my sister, brother, and aunt for their aid in recovering and piecing together my story. A number of friends have helped me in writing it: Aaron Asher, Hayden Carruth, Nessa Rapoport, Philip Roth, Lynne Sharon Schwartz, Maura Spiegel, Sam Toperoff, and the late Richard Tristman. I'm also grateful to Gerald Howard for firmly editing it and to my wife, Virginia, for her keen eye and ear and otherwise for more than I can say.

Earlier versions of material in Part I, Part II, and Part III appeared in *Salmagundi*, *Tikkun*, and *The Threepenny Review*, respectively.

CONTENTS

WHAT'S IN IT FOR ME?

1 IN THE LAST two years of his life, I came to look after my father. We had been estranged for many years, though "estranged" isn't quite right for we were mostly strangers to each other by my eighteenth year, and yet remained tensely connected across the long silences of the four decades that followed. He was in New Jersey and I in Manhattan, half an hour away, but we could have been at opposite ends of the continent, seeing each other at a family event every year or two, as guarded and aware as two successful people might be who had once been master and servant.

He was living in Livingston, a well-to-do community at the pastoral end of Essex County, to which he had come thirty years ago with a new wife, his fourth, to take his climactic place as a self-made man. Self-made and self-unmade. For the unregenerate "peasant" (the term that he often used about his mother, whom he despised) had gone there with the successful glass distributor, shrewd investor, versatile talker, and quondam bon vivant whose motto was "The best is good enough for me." For ten years or so the better-behaved Ben Solotaroff seemed to prevail, mainly because, as my mother said, he had finally married a woman he couldn't walk over. The widow of the county bailiff and a summons server herself, Debby was the reality principle in a designer dress. From what we could tell, she managed him by a shrewd mix of creature comforts and strict expectations, which had even produced the sight of him docilely grilling chicken and hamburgers at a barbecue for both families. But then he had gotten into one of his "spots" at The Shop, the office and warehouse in Elizabeth where he had never been able to keep office help, except for my mother and me. His latest "girl" had walked out; he had no one to answer the phone so that he could get out to do business. Unlike his other wives, Debby refused to help him out, "even for a few days." Their respective lines were drawn, suddenly but for good, each of them having a rock-bottom principle at stake—business-is-business versus marriage-is-not.

In the marital cold war that ensued, one of my father's main weapons was the peasant in him. After he sold the Standard Plate Glass Co., he loaded up the basement with desktops, mirrors, and other items that were left over and parked in his driveway a big side-paneled glass truck. It remained unsold for the next two years, a daily affront to the house pride of Debby and to her relationship with their neighbors. The truck had been the beginning of the end, which was still going on twenty years later. Here was an estrangement with zero ambiguity. Debby spent seven months in Florida and the rest in the Livingston area, where she occupied a bedroom in their house and cooked and put up a week of his meals so that he couldn't divorce her for desertion, and conducted her life entirely elsewhere. It was as though the gods of marriage, in retribution for his previous derelictions, had put him in an unbreakable, miserable wedlock, Debby being as determined to outlast him as he was her, for the sake of his million-dollar estate. I doubted that he had run into any woman as tough and determined as Debby since his mother.

But the struggle over whose way of life would prevail in their home he had finally won decisively, and he had driven her from the field. Over the years, the spacious brick-and-cedar split-level house took on an unkempt, vacant look, like a well-to-do drunk who has given up appearances. By mid-June, the lawn of the two-acre corner lot would be knee-high in grass and weeds. It would continue to grow until his neighbors once again prevailed on the Board of Health to make him cut it.

My brother-in-law Hy, the family *mensch*, was our main contact with Ben, as my sister, brother, and I referred to him, since he was more a character to us, our own old Karamazov, than a father. A B-25 pilot in World War II, Hy was about halfway in age between Ben and me, his oldest child, and had brought him partway back into the family. In recompense Ben had made Hy the trustee of his estate and loaned him twenty thousand dollars to make the down payment on a house, one of the bursts of largesse that would come over him like rain in Death Valley. Around the time he turned eighty, his strong body finally began to act its age. After Ben had a hip replacement, Hy visited him every two weeks or so to do whatever chores and cleaning he would permit and to give him a massage. But Hy lived halfway out on Long Island, two hours from Livingston, and also had lost some of his phenomenal goodwill when, after making the final payment of the loan, he received a note from his father-in-law demanding the nine percent interest on it. Though Ben eventually backed off from his demand, it left a fair amount of scar tissue on the relationship.

One day in the spring of 1990, Hy called to let me know that I could be of use in helping Ben finally accept the fact that he needed a housekeeper or, preferably, a retirement facility. Hobbled by poor circulation and arthritis and often mired in depression, he was less and less able to look after himself. Also he seemed to be driving his Cadillac from one body shop to the next; always a recklessly aggressive driver, he was now a recklessly uncertain one.

I didn't think that he'd listen to me for a minute, but he had become enamored of Virginia (my fourth wife), a beautiful, gracious woman who had a way with him, played the market as successfully as he did, and, as he said, "drove like a man." With her influence I might get somewhere. Also Hy's tone reminded me that I, not he, was the firstborn son.

And so I phoned Ben and said I'd like to come out.

"You don't say," he replied.

I steeled myself to be warm and calm. "Hy said you might like some company, so I thought I'd spend Saturday with you."

"When's *he* coming?"

"He can't for a couple of weeks. I'm the relief pitcher. I'll see you on Saturday, okay?"

"Suit yourself. But if you're coming, come on Friday so that I can get to the bank. I've been laid up."

I pointed out that I worked on Friday, and said that I'd come early enough on Saturday morning for him to get to the bank.

"I don't get up early. I don't sleep at night." He added an exclamation mark by hanging up.

I took Friday afternoon off, which I almost never did, even in summer when in New York publishing the weekend begins after lunch. As I drove out to Livingston, the strangeness of being away from my desk on the day I got the most done there connected up with that of the situation itself, of being a son again, which I hadn't been since my mother's death almost twenty years before and the intense period of mourning that had followed. And not only a son but *his* son, a role that fitted me like a glove I had long outgrown.

He was still in his bathrobe when he opened the door. I hadn't seen him in eighteen months and was startled by the change. The robe was bunched around his formerly burly body. He had lost maybe thirty pounds and seemingly a couple of inches; his face, which had still been ruddy and handsome, was wizened now, its color bad; he was literally so down in the mouth that his cheeks seemed caved in. Ben Solotaroff abruptly reduced to a bent, weak old man with a shuffling walk. Also the well-appointed spacious living room I'd last visited — Debby was in residence and had brought in a cleaning woman — was now like a trope of his condition, a reclining armchair with a week's newspapers scattered around it facing a big new TV set, the blinds still drawn on the bright spring afternoon, the rest of the room and its furnishings receding into dustiness and disuse.

We hardly spoke as I drove him in my car to the post office and bank, he giving me instructions for the turns as though I were taking my first driving lesson. Then I trailed after him while he slowly shopped for bargains at a Pathmark, choosing a loaf of bread, a pound of tomatoes, a brand of soup like someone on food stamps instead of the investor who had just deposited four or five dividend checks. After we got back he showed me step by step how to use the washing machine and dryer and let me do a little cleaning in the kitchen and bathroom.

I stayed calm and collected throughout, preserving the mature adult I'd need to come across as when I delivered my little speech about his changed situation and the plans Hy and I felt he needed to begin to make. I wanted to take him to a nice local restaurant for the occasion, but he chose a diner five miles away, where he listened to my carefully chosen words as he usually did — barely. He said he had no interest in making any change. As I was driving him home, I hesitated at an intersection and was about to make the wrong turn when he corrected me. "You really were going to turn right, weren't you?" he said with a smile, as though I had finally done something that gave him pleasure. At that moment my rage broke free and I wanted him dead. Still simmering, I drove back to New York, wondering what I could accomplish besides putting myself, after all these years, back under his thumb to remind me how it had felt growing up there.

However, like him, I prided myself on getting things done, so I phoned his doctor, who agreed that the time had come and gave me the names of several good retirement communities and senior citizen residences. Over several Sundays, Virginia and I managed to get Ben to look them over, he lagging along behind us at each visit like a teenager shopping with his parents. This one, in a converted mansion, was too confining; that one, which offered him his own apartment, was too spread out. One was too Jewish and another too Gentile ("I like kosher-*style* food"). When he dismissed a seemingly enlightened and congenial place by saying, "It's full of old people," we gave up.

Next, Hy and I arranged for a private geriatric agency to provide the help he needed to continue living at home. I drove out to attend the consultation, and ended up answering most of the social worker's questions, while Ben, slumped inside his bathrobe, glared at both of us. After she'd left he said, "Neither of you understand a goddam thing about my situation."

I phoned Hy and said, "He's going to have to get even worse before anything happens." I was glad to throw up my hands and let him stew in his weakness and stubbornness. But a few weeks later he called to say in a feeble voice that he felt terrible, that he couldn't get out, that he had hardly eaten in three days.

I called his doctor and drove out the next day to take him to his office. After examining him, Dr. Zauber said, "Your main problem isn't physical, Ben. There are two million people in Essex County but *you* have to be alone. It's bad for you in every way."

Bending to doctor's orders, he said he'd look around on his own and quickly found a brand-new residence—"out in the sticks but pretty nice." The Sunday afternoon that Virginia and I were to go with him to dine there and meet with the management, he called to say that he wasn't feeling well, couldn't get moving, would I come a little earlier and give him a massage.

A massage? The thought was like a quarter falling from my pocket into the middle of a lake, a small thing but it went down and down and settled in the muck at the bottom of my mind.

Normally I like to give a massage. My hands, which are clumsy with a wrench and ignorant with a spark plug gapper, become deft and intuitive with muscles, tendons, and joints. But my father had never asked this of me before. Hy had given him a number of massages. But that was different: Hy wasn't his son.

As Virginia drove us to Livingston, I tried to understand what was about to happen and why I felt so queasy about it. There was the sin of Ham, Noah's son, of seeing his father in his nakedness. Until now, I had thought of it as just another of the primitive taboos of the Bible. I had seen my father naked many times, without thinking twice about it. As a small boy I had followed him around the YMHA during his Sunday-morning workout and could still see the lurid brightness of the massage room as Doc, bulging and looming in his white T-shirt, pushed and pounded on Dad's ruddy body, getting the blood up. Those Sunday mornings were chief among the few occasions of male bonding I'd experienced with him. Why should I now be feeling the force of that injunction, for the breach of which Ham was punished so harshly through his own son?

The injunction, of course, was part of the patriarchal slant of the Old Testament: thou shalt honor the dignity of thy father even when, like Noah, he is in a drunken stupor. In this case, the father would not be drunk but aged: a shrunken, rusted version of the imposing man I'd known all these years. I didn't want to look upon, much less handle, that waxy skin, those pathetic loins. I wasn't touched by my father's loss of his force; in some ways I welcomed it, it made him less difficult for me to be with. But I didn't want to put my hands on his body.

When we reached his house, rang the chimes, and waited, I was hoping hard that the delay meant he had managed to get himself going. When he finally shuffled to the door and opened it, he was still in a bathrobe, a short one, his veiny, whittled thighs exposed. Whatever my compunctions, he had none.

He greeted Virginia with a vestige of his charmer's smile, and then turned to me. "Where you been?" he muttered. "I'm supposed to be there in an hour." As he often did these days, he looked both angry and forlorn.

Virginia used her gentling way with him. "Don't be upset, Ben. We'll get you there."

"I'm not upset, dear. I can hardly move. This one here was supposed to give me a massage."

"Well, stop grousing and let's get started," I said. Being able to
talk back to him now was my main compensation for these trips
and services.

I followed him into his bedroom. He removed his robe, slowly lowered himself across the unmade king-sized bed, and there was his
nakedness.

"Start around the hip," he said. "I had an artificial one put in a year
ago, so take it easy. There's some oil on the night table you can use."

It was Johnson's baby oil. I put some in my palm and began to
slowly knead around the hip socket. "How's that?" I asked.

"A little gentler, for Chrissake," he said, but his voice was more
good-natured, the complaint half in jest.

Like much that is significant in life, what I had anticipated so
strongly was not what came to pass. As I carefully pressed my palms
and fingers across the top of his buttocks to the base of his spine and
upward along the column and then back, I did not see any wrinkles
at all; the skin of the lower torso seemed as smooth and the flesh as
tender as an infant's. I could hardly believe my eyes or hands. He was
like a blown-up version of one of my sons when I would take him
from the bath, then oil and caress that delicious skin.

"How're you doing?" I said. He made a little ooing sound of pleasure in his throat. He extended his arms, turned his head to one side,
and closed his eyes. "Now a little higher, Ted," he said.

I straddled him to get a better purchase, then pressed my palms on
up the vertebrae and into the soft muscles under the shelf of the
shoulder blades. The oo sound became interspersed with a deep
hum of contentment.

Inspired, I worked my way, now with fingers and now with palms,
up and over the shoulder blades and into the deltoids of his once
beefy shoulders. After kneading them, I moved down and away to the
stringy biceps and then up to the tender neck. Cupping my hands, I
eased the tendons. I concentrated on the task, fending off the memory of how broad this back had been, how these muscles had lifted his
side of a plate glass window as though it were plywood and laid it on
the cutting table. I did not want the anger and shame that came with

the adjacent memories of the beatings these shoulders and arms had inflicted. I wanted this ooing and humming gratitude to continue, my fingers to go on gentling into his neck and his neck into my fingers the closeness that had finally, strangely come to us.

2

SUNNYVALE MANOR WAS a bright, white two-story building with Colonial touches and a big parking area in back. The office looked like the front desk of an upscale motor inn and the lobby like one that was booked solid on this Sunday evening, because of the visiting families. The residents, mostly women, were well-dressed and alert-looking, and there was not a wheelchair in sight. The atmosphere among the couches and armchairs of the lobby had a settled feeling and a mild sense of mortality: all these comfortable guests whose reservation was for the rest of their lives.

The owner/manager, who looked like a retired contractor himself, took us in hand ("Just call me Vince. We don't stand on formality around here") and led us into the spacious restaurantlike dining room, complete with puffy linen napkins that matched the beige tablecloth, individual menus, and sweet-faced young waitresses and busboys. All and all, it looked like the best prospect yet.

We were soon joined by Hy and my sister, Sandra, who had come from Huntington to participate in what we called "the big push." After a few minutes at the table it no longer seemed to be that; it had become something else, something remarkable. Ben came out of his shell and took over the conversation, joining the affable Vince Stefano in explaining the place to us as well as asking most of the questions. It wasn't just a shift of mood. It was a physical thing, as though an invisible magic wand had touched him and turned him back into the man he'd been, who liked to say, "I know how to make an impression." His handsomeness had returned to his face; he even seemed to have taken on flesh inside his Hickey Freeman suit, a soft gray worsted, so that it fit him. His pale blue shirt, its French cuffs set off by small gold-and-onyx links, and his subtly checkered silver-and-gray tie gave him the quiet gleam of a retired banker. His voice was both firmer and warmer—that of a man who chose his words, his comments and questions rounded by self-assurance. Before long, Vince was explaining to him how he'd financed and built the place.

It was a startling change but not a surprising one. I'd seen my father at The Shop, an important customer or supplier on the way, turn himself with a wash and a necktie from a coarse glazing contractor into a well-spoken businessman; or, in the course of a visit to my mother's family in Manhattan, from the grump behind the wheel to the center of the conversation at the dinner table. A few years ago he'd visited us in Amagansett. His arthritis had begun to get him down, and when we went off to a lawn party, he said he didn't feel up to it, which was a relief to me because of his tendency to hold forth and set everyone straight. But Virginia had coaxed him into going. We tried to stay close to him—Virginia so he wouldn't be alone, I to minimize the embarrassment—but we soon got separated in the heavy social surf, and when I located him he was talking to Shana Alexander. I walked over to cut in but saw that she was now doing the talking. They were still at it ten minutes later. When I subsequently thanked her for her feat of patience, she said, "That was the most interesting conversation I've had here. Where did you get such a charming father who knows so much about the market?"

After dinner, Vince showed us the room Ben would have. He said he'd want to come back to take some measurements since he'd be bringing in a desk and filing cabinet for his investment work. Also he'd want his own phone installed. "Anything you need, Ben," said Vince, who by now seemed ready to offer him a partnership.

The next week continued to be upbeat as Ben went about pricing furniture, moving his three bank accounts, even talked about putting the Livingston house on the market. The morning came when Hy and I were to help him move. We found him sitting inertly on his bed, staring at enough pairs of shoes fanned around him for a window display. "What am I supposed to do with all these shoes," he grumbled. "That place isn't right for me."

"Come on, Ben," said Hy in his unflappable way. "You've told me yourself you can't wear most of your shoes anymore. You just show us the ones you can use. We'll find a place for them and for all your clothes."

"What use would I have there for twenty suits and jackets?"

I was both exasperated and touched. He looked like Lear after his daughters had taken away his retinue. I knew what those shoes meant to him—most of them no doubt Ballys that he'd gotten at a good price, emblems of both his status and shrewdness. Leaving behind his shoes would be like my leaving behind my books when my time came. Hy's firm gentleness got him moving, and once he began to supervise us his mood improved. By the late afternoon he was off looking at office furniture and Hy and I had taken his clothes, files, and other effects to Sunnyvale Manor and put them away. Then, rubbing our hands at each other—Ben, at last, off them—we had a celebratory drink. As it happened, it was New Year's Eve; there would be a party at Sunnyvale— what better way for Ben to ease in among all those widows?

But the next day when I called him he said the party had been "chintzy," his room was freezing at night, and his bed was hard as a rock. Less than a week later I received a phone call from Vince Stefano, who told me that my father's behavior was completely unacceptable and unless he stopped criticizing everything and humiliating one of the other male residents he would have to leave. Ben didn't return my call, and the following day, he had already moved out. I reached him at home. In a fury, he berated me and Hy for pushing him into that "half-assed joint," said that he'd lost most of his deposit, that Hy was no longer his executor, and that both of us should be ashamed of ourselves.

Furious myself, I said, "I'm ashamed all right. I'm ashamed of you. You've brought this on yourself by your obnoxious fucking behavior."

"What've you got to be ashamed of? You've never given a shit about me."

"What're you talking about . . . ?" I began as he hung up. But if he'd waited five minutes I wouldn't have known how to handle the curve he'd thrown me.

3 NOTHING STAYED THE way it was between us now for very long, and in a few weeks I was going out to Livingston again to help him get through the winter. The sweet rapport of the first massage did not return. I continued to give them but they were now just

part of the routine of doing what he wanted. Some visits went better than others, but I usually felt diminished during them: the figure I was in New York, even the person I'd been for the forty years since I'd sprung myself from our relationship, counted for nothing here; I was back to being the teenager stuck in The Shop.

In order to stop floating glumly through the hours and the errands, to get something of my own back, I hit on the desire he'd once mentioned to tell the story of his early life. I'd heard many of his anecdotes about it a dozen times, an aspect of his obliviousness, but I figured it would give him a lift to tell them for the record and give me a piece of own ground as an editor to help him fill in some gaps and make some connections.

Also I thought there might be some significant history to unearth. I'd been trying to understand my father probably ever since I'd started to try to understand anything, and since it appeared to be a lifelong project, any new information and insights were welcome. Also, having turned sixty, I was at the beginning of the self-commemorative impluse, of the what-has-it-all-meant question. I'd even begun to write a memoir of my career, starting as a graduate student at the University of Chicago in the 1950s. But it wasn't going well, my heart wasn't in it, my mind wasn't haunted by the material.

What it was haunted by was Eliot's line that "the lengthened shadow of a man is history." For part of the self-commemorative and self-scrutinzing desire is to view your life as a part of the great human parade, as marching in the ranks of the cohort that most identifies you to yourself and makes your life seem less ephemeral and insignificant because your cohort gives it an historical status. In my case, a resonant one. I was an American Jewish intellectual, of the increasingly fabled New York wing. But to become its kind of editor and critic, I'd first had to become the American and the Jew that the intellectual would tie together. Moreover to become a writer, to become anything worthwhile, I'd had to squeeze the slave, as Chekhov put it, out of myself, drop by drop. It seemed premature and superficial to tell the later story until I had taken on the early one. So the unfelt prose of my memoir— a kind of higher gossip—was telling me. Meanwhile, after these months of unemployment in Livingston, my imagination was saying, "You didn't come out of nowhere. You had a grandfather much like yourself and a father you've been battling in yourself all your life but who is the connection between you—three generations of typically emancipated Jews, most typical, perhaps, in their disconnections."

My grandfather, David Solotaroff, had been a *maskil*, a man of the Jewish Enlightenment, and a member of the First Aliyah, (immigration) to Palestine during the 1880s. Before that he had been a gymnasium student and an early Zionist activist in Odessa, a writer of Hebrew poetry, a reader of the Russian classics. In time he spoke seven or eight languages and studied the parallels between the Bible and the Koran. Not only did his rich blood flow through my father to me but he had even named me, three years before he died, asking that my birth name, Lawrence, be changed to Theodore Herzl.

This much I knew from my mother, whom he had drawn close to in his last years, two gentle souls in a family of contentious loudmouths. I wanted to learn anything else I could about this obscurely distinguished forebear, self-made in the way that I was, from his son, who'd had little to say about him over the years, other than "My mother never gave him a minute's peace" and "He was a gentleman and a scholar who knew everything except how to make a living."

The next time I visited, I left him with a copy of Irving Howe's *World of Our Fathers*, telling him that I wanted to write a personal essay on the subject and could use his help. "I'll see how I feel," he said. Two weeks later he'd read the book. "It's interesting," he said. "But it didn't have much to do with us. We weren't your usual immigrants."

"Tell me about it," I said.

He was still in his pajamas but looked more alert and well-meaning than usual.

"My grandfather's name was Benzion," he said as I set up a minirecorder on the coffee table between us.

"That's very appropriate," I said. "It means son of Zion."

He shrugged. "I thought you wanted to hear the story," he said. "He was a *padroshik*, a big contractor, on the railroad. He had something like seven, eight hundred men working for him and maybe a thousand versts of railroad he did work on. He handled the sheet metal, carpentry, plumbing, and painting for the stations, and he also repaired the tracks. He was in a very good position, since his partner was the governor of the province. My father was his oldest son, and was raised in silk stockings. When he was thirteen they sent him to Odessa so he could study in a regular Russian school and then go to the university."

He went on to relate that when the pogroms broke out in 1881, after the assassination of the Czar, the governor dispatched four Cossacks to guard the road to the Solotaroff estate in Bogapolya, about a hundred miles from Odessa. Nonetheless, Benzion Solotaroff was sufficiently alarmed to move his family and relatives to Palestine. "Because of his connections, he was able to get his whole fortune out, something like five hundred thousand rubles in gold. He was even able to get out his furniture, his pots and pans, and bedding, and not only for himself but for the whole *mischpocha*. They all went to Palestine. He bought property in Rishon LeZion and planted grapes there. But they didn't know a thing about irrigation. Everything dried up and they lost their land. Rothschild bought them out and they ended up working for him, digging up the roots of the vines they'd planted."

The light outside inched through the drapes at my father's back, dust motes circling in it like these memories of a dim past, dim and improbable. Ben's account of his grandfather was news to me but sounded less like family history than a family romance—the riches-to-rags story I could almost have predicted of the megalomaniacal Solotaroffs (other than my grandfather), their way of dealing with their immigrant status in America—not lowly but fallen. It was not uncommon for Jewish immigrants, however poor after they arrived, to say they came from the wealthiest family in the *shtetl*, but the Solotaroff's account was a whopper.

Even as the family's fortunes continued to decline, its distinction remained on tap to enrich the story my father went on telling. Benzion and David, along with his three younger brothers and sister, remained in Palestine for another fifteen years, becoming charter members and landowners of the colony of Hadera. "Hadera was mostly swampland and they all came down with malaria. My father, who spoke French pretty good, was sent to Paris to persuade Baron Rothschild to take over the colony and provide the barges and other heavy equipment they needed to get the place running properly."

In Paris, David met a young nursing student, Bathsheva, who had come there from Bessarabia with her family. They were married in Jaffa the following year. David and Bathsheva, I thought, fact embroidering fantasy. My father went on, "After a year or two of nursing the people in Hadera, my mother caught the eye of Baron Rothschild. He sent her to Paris and Vienna to receive the best training available at the time for a midwife. She already knew a little French but then she had to learn German to go to Vienna."

Meanwhile, David stayed in Hadera with their first child, Marion, and he helped plant groves of eucalyptus trees as a last-ditch method to drain the swamps. Finally the colony had to be abandoned, and David and Bathsheva ended up at Metula, another Rothschild colony in the mountains near Lebanon, where life was almost as hard as it had been in Hadera. "After two years there, my mother decided enough was enough and they all went to New York, including two of my father's brothers who never amounted to much."

My mind spinning from all this furniture I'd been given from the attic of the Solotaroff memory, I went back to New York. In the Columbia libraries, I looked through the two major Jewish encyclopedias but found no Solotaroffs or variant spellings among the prominent early settlers in Palestine. I then read a good deal about the Rothschild colonies in Palestine and the Zionist movement in Odessa. I took out Simon Schama's biography of Rothschild, which contains a first-rate account of the early settlements, and brought it with me on my next visit to Livingston. "You can read all about the Solotaroffs here," I said. "Though none of them are mentioned. The only Jew who came to Palestine with anything like five hundred thousand gold rubles seems to have been Rothschild. But maybe it will bring to mind some other stuff you were told."

I assumed he'd be interested, but he wasn't. He hardly opened the book. Meanwhile, I'd mentioned my quest to an Israeli writer, whose wife, an archivist, put me in touch with a colleague at Rishon LeZion. She quickly located and interviewed a surviving relative there, a cousin of my father's, who as a boy had known Benzion.

"Your grandfather was a tinsmith," I announced on my next visit. "He settled in Zichron Ya'acov, which was also an early Rothschild colony. As far as your cousin knows, your grandfather was always a tinsmith and never a wealthy man, much less the partner of the governor of the Odessa province." I handed him the letter I had received from the archivist.

My father didn't like to be corrected, particularly by me, so I expected him to be doubly annoyed by my research. But when he finished the letter he smiled and said, "Well, that's the story I got from my father. I always wondered what happened to all that money."

"I've been trying to figure out what really happened," I said. "I think maybe your grandfather was a foreman or a subcontractor for the railroad, which would have enabled him to send his oldest son to Odessa to the gymnasium. Also, Bogapolya was mostly a Jewish town. It doesn't exist anymore, but it was probably an important railway junction, which could have been why the governor protected it from the pogrom."

"Could be," said my father.

"There was a lot of bad feeling among the colonists at Zichron Ya'acov because Rothschild and his French administrators were very autocratic, which may be why the family went to Hadera. But Hadera was a real hellhole. Rothschild did take it over, but they still had to close it down until the eucalyptus trees drained the swamps."

"That's where my father and his brothers got malaria."

"Half of the original colonists died of it. Ahad Ha'Am, a famous writer, visited Hadera toward the end and said it was a place of utter desolation, that the abandoned shacks looked like mourners and the ghosts of the dead seemed to be hovering there, whispering to each other. Did your father ever talk about Hadera?"

"Not much. None of us were interested in that stuff. The property in Hadera didn't amount to much. It was sold in the 1930s but we couldn't even get the money out until after the war."

"But that's where your parents spent their first years together, where your sister Marion was born. It's a very famous place, sort of like the Valley Forge of the first immigration."

"I told you my mother wasn't there much. She was in Paris and Vienna learning to be a midwife. She had to leave my sister with my father."

"That's pretty unusual. Marion must have been a baby then."

"Well, that was my mother. She never let her family stand in her way."

As I was leaving he went into the bedroom and came back with an old manila envelope. "I don't know anymore what's in here, but you might want to take a look."

Among the documents, which mostly had to do with the 140 dunams (about forty acres) in Hadera, was a diploma from the University of Vienna awarded to Bathsheva Zolotarev. Also a notarized letter signed by my grandfather, *"colon à Hederah,"* that give his wife *"l'autorisation d'aller à Paris en vue d'étudier la profession de sage-femme."* Also a document in a beautiful German script signed by some twenty other colonists that attested to my grandmother's good character and requested that she be assisted in her studies. So, that much of the story was true.

There was also a photograph of their wedding. Looking older than his twenty five years, David, a small man with a serious, upright bearing, is wearing a stylish morning coat and a fez. Alongside him looms Bathsheva, four or five inches taller, her full figure packed into a long white dress, her curly dark hair framing black eyes that seem to blaze even in the grainy photograph—a figure of coarse energy who dominates the picture but is somewhat aloof as though the whole thing were someone else's idea. It looks like the marriage of a scholar and a gypsy, which in certain ways it proved to be.

Yet, as he'd told me, my father had gotten the tales of the Solotaroffs as Russian Jewish gentry from his father. So this studious little fellow with a taste for the exotic, expressed by his fez and his bride, whom I'd always excluded from the Solotaroff *mishigas*, was likely an extravagant liar. I pored over the photograph, particularly his face, looking for signs of mine. Far from disaffecting me, the revelation of his tall-tale-telling made me feel closer to him—another high-strung Jewish intellectual who was trying to make his life a more dramatic place to inhabit and talk about. Also he was not the first Solotaroff I had met, beginning with myself, who had enhanced his past.

I also studied Bathsheva: all that energy and strength and willfulness had sustained her to the age of eighty-eight. After my grandfather died she had lived with a succession of widowed, well-to-do men in the euphemistic role of housekeeper. The chief family story about her was that when she was getting ready to move to California in her late seventies, my mother had twitted her by saying, "Bathsheva, maybe you'll meet a handsome fellow on the train." To which she'd replied, "Rose, I'm not looking for romance anymore. I'm looking for security."

When I came to Livingston the next time my father was waiting for me, freshly shaved and already dressed. Even the living room looked cleaner, though it may just have been that he'd picked up the newspapers. "Let's get started," he said. "I've got a lot to tell you about my father and me."

He fixed me again with his look that said, No interruptions.

"When I was thirteen we moved to Roselle because my father couldn't make a dime in Yonkers and my mother was getting tired of supporting the family. So she got her brother Shia to take my father in as a kind of half-assed partner for a thousand dollars." He paused and drew his fingers across his lips, a gesture he used when he was in his element and fully enjoying himself.

"Shia was the black sheep of the family. He could hardly read or write but what he couldn't do with his hands wasn't worth doing. He'd buy a house cheap that was falling down and then him and a couple of *schvartzers* would fix it up as a two-family and he'd rent it out. By this time he had about twenty pieces of property and he needed someone he could trust to collect the rents and handle his books."

I knew what was coming and half tuned out as he told about being a street kid at thirteen who got in with some "rough customers" in Roselle and was caught stealing. Because his father couldn't control him, his mother had gone to her brother, who came to the house, grabbed him by the neck, threw him in the truck, and drove him to "the Port" in Elizabeth, where he put him to work for Sam Myron, a young glazier who needed someone to mind the shop when he was out on a job.

While he was retelling this with his usual relish, I was still back with his family in Yonkers. Uncle Leo, who had married my father's sister Sophie when she was still a teenager, had told me that he'd never known a family less in touch and more unhappy with each other than the Solotaroffs. It was mainly Leo who had given me my sense of the Family Solotaroff—one-third Chekhov, two-thirds Dostoevsky, with a dash of Bruno Schulz.

I imagined their shabby flat over a bakery in the Italian immigrant section of Yonkers. In the parental bedroom Bathsheva is getting ready to go out again, whether to deliver another baby for a pittance or to assist the surgeon "who wouldn't operate without her," or maybe primping, on her way to a wedding or another of her "affairs"—the social kind in which she is famed for her exuberant dancing but possibly the other kind as well. In the kitchen David sits at the kitchen table, grammars and texts, his Zionist correspondence, and one of his beloved Russian novels scattered about as he broods about his position in the family and tries to ignore the tumult. Marion, the oldest child, without whom the family would hardly have existed at all, is screaming at her renegade sister, Ethel, to help her with the housework and Ethel is talking a blue streak back. Meanwhile, Leo's Sophie, a piano prodigy, high-strung to the point of snapping, is attacking a passage in a Liszt piece in a frenzy of frustration because her hands are too small and the pressures on her and inside her to succeed are too intense. And then there is Benny, the youngest, who doesn't talk to his carping mother at all and barely to his sisters and is waiting until his mother leaves so that he can raid the refrigerator and then sneak out to run with his rough customers.

Meanwhile, back in Elizabethport, a relationship was growing between the bachelor Sam Myron and the unparented Benny, who took to the glass business like a young Cossack to his horse. Along with imitating the ways Sam handled a glass cutter and putty knife, Benny was intrigued by Sam himself. An orphaned immigrant, he and his sister had raised themselves. Then he'd gone into the Army and made sergeant in Panama. His stories of knocking around Central America and the United States as a soldier and journeyman glazier fascinated his young helper. Sam, in turn, responded to the boy's quick mind and curiosity and started him reading books by Burton Holmes and other travel writers. Impressed by all these changes in his son, David told him to invite his new boss home for a Shabbos meal. "Sam was completely enthralled. He had never met anybody like my father, someone who was so intelligent, who he could talk to about anything and everything. Sam knew Russian and Polish and Slavish and my father could talk to him in those languages and also talk about languages he'd never heard before."

After Benny went back to school in the fall, Sam asked his new friend if he would like to go into partnership with him. Sam would handle the outside work, David the retail glass and shade business, and Benny would help out after school. There was some space in the back of the shop that wasn't being used, so David brought in an armchair, a lamp, and a samovar, along with his books and journals and correspondence to keep himself occupied between customers. He also began to make acquaintance with the intelligentsia of Elizabethport—whom he invited to come by in the late afternoon for a cup of tea and some good conversation. Sam was delighted to find his shop occupied by such distinguished talkers. When he was called away on a job, he'd say, "Please, don't say anything interesting until I get back." Benny was less impressed. "They'd sit around for hours solving the problems of the world. Then the next afternoon they'd solve them all over again."

I asked him if he remembered what they talked about, but he waved the question away. "When war was declared, Sam was one of the first to get called up. The company he trained was one of the first to be sent to France, and Sam was one of the first Americans to get killed in action."

His voice had slowed toward the end of the litany and now his storytelling machine stopped. A fugitive feeling from the past had broken loose in his memory and set him brooding, staring silently into the event.

Then he went on. "It was like losing a member of the family. He'd listed my father as his next of kin and the Army sent him the Distinguished Service Medal Sam had gotten posthumously awarded. I don't know what happened to it. I had it for a while."

I knew that Sam had been killed in action but I hadn't heard about the medal before. Also Ben's wistful expression made him look like someone who barely resembled the father I knew. Normally, his affect about his past was meager at best; the only feelings his memory seemed to activate were those of vanity and blame as well as a little nostalgia, mostly about how cheap things used to be. His sense of himself was almost all ego and almost no conscience, so that, like a mythological figure, he lived in a kind of perpetual present, the events and feelings of the past either radically eliminated or reconfigured to accord with his ongoing success story. As he had once told my brother, "When something happens I don't like, I get rid of it."

We sat there in silence—my father moved by the death of a man who must have seemed like his real father and I bemused by this outcropping of feeling, this blood from a stone. But was it? It felt like a sorrow of my own boyhood. Perhaps this was really why I was here, why I was doing this taping—to learn sympathy and empathy, *rachmones*, for him, as my mother used to say, and to figure out the person my father had been when he wasn't being my father, which he wasn't most of his life, though he had seldom taken more than a day off from haunting mine.

It began to dawn on me that my interest in my grandfather was mostly a construct, that the sense of kindredness was an autobiographical and historical conceit to make both of our lives appear more interesting, while much of the real stuff of my story was sitting right in front of me, buried in this man whom I'd thought I knew all too well but perhaps, in crucial respects, hardly knew at all.

Meanwhile he had snapped the memory away and gone on. At fourteen, he'd become the "outside man" who did the jobs that kept the business going.. His parents had moved to a small flat in Elmora, the new, uptown Jewish section of Elizabeth, and he'd started Battin High School. At noon on Wednesday, he would be excused so that he could go into New York to pick up the week's order of window shades from the factory there.

"My father would give me ten cents carfare for the trolley from the Hudson Terminal all the way across to Delancey Street on the Lower East Side, where the shade factory was. But Canal Street was such an interesting place in those days that I'd walk. You could see people from all over the world—Chinese, Italians, Armenians, Gypsies, even some Arabs and Indians. You could look into their shops and stalls and some of them would be wearing their native outfits, so it was practically like taking a trip around the world."

As he continued, I thought of Sam Myron, the traveler, and the

Burton Holmes travel books that my father had often mentioned as his favorite reading in childhood.

While they were making up his order, he would walk around the Lower East Side, which gave him a chance to see the Old World ways that he and his family had mostly given up. These were the *pruss* Jews, the "peasants" in his mother's contemptuous term. There was nothing exotic about his description of Delancey Street and Hester Street—its pushcarts and hole-in-the-wall shops, its vile, packed tenements that looked like the housing version of steerage, the shouting and haggling in the streets—it was a place of "*mishigas* and *dreck*," craziness and shitiness, "that I wanted to get as far away from as life could take me."

The other afternoons after school he would install shades and replace broken windows. He did this on foot, carrying the glass in a box slung across his back, a bag of putty in one hand, his tools in the other. Sometimes his route through Elizabeth took him past the high school or the Elmora neighborhood where his Jewish classmates would be hanging out. They took to taunting him as he went by, as they were doing in school. With his ragged clothes and his tendency to be unprepared because he'd fallen asleep over his homework, he was an embarrassment to the high marks makers among them— something else I could relate to—as well as to others who were already being dressed to succeed.

"One day one of them passed a remark about me and one of the teachers overheard it. He said to them, 'You should be ashamed of yourselves. Here's a young fellow who's helping his people by working after school. What do you do after school? Fool around with the baseball or football?' But they kept ragging me. I should have punched one or two of them in the nose, the sons of bitches. The only thing I liked about that school was going to the library and taking out books to read on my own. There was a hell of a novel I found there by a Spanish writer, Ibiñez. It was called *The Four Horsemen of the Apocalypse*, and it taught me about the war in Europe. That was my high school. I didn't even finish the tenth grade." The last words were again weighted and spaced by hard feelings.

This, too, was new. In the past he'd always said that he'd had to quit school to help his father. He took off his glasses and wiped them on his shirttail, a gesture he used when he was upset.

When he resumed, he told me that his father, seeing him struggling in school and the business itself going down the drain, had brought in a new man, Hymie Korn, "a regular glazier and a regular *gonif*. I'd had my suspicions before, but now I could see for myself what Korn was up to. I even discovered the garage where he kept the glass he was stealing from us. So I went to my father and told him what was going on."

Again he stopped, took off his glasses, and wiped them. "I . . . could . . . never . . . tell . . . my . . . father . . . anything," he said, his voice slowing and hardening even more, putting a deep, reactivated bitterness between each word that he was telling himself more than me.

In all the years and all the stories I had never heard him speak harshly about his father, who had seemed to dwell in the only forgiven area of his family memories. Early on this hadn't made much sense to me, since he seemed to revere his father for the same qualities he was trying to knock out of me when he caught me reading at The Shop. My resentment was still on tap, and I said to him, coolly, maliciously, "You mean Korn went on working for him and you didn't."

But it was just another of my jabs that didn't land. "He told me he wanted me to learn another trade that had more money in it. That's what he said, but I knew he was in a bad fix. He'd taken it on himself to pay Sam Myron's mother and sister for his share of the business, but instead of doing it out of profits, he'd taken out a loan for the full amount and was barely meeting the payments. Anyway, he got me a job with an electrician who was wiring a lot of houses and stores in Elizabeth. Later I found out that he paid Leboff the ten dollars a week that he paid me."

"Even though he was having trouble meeting his bank payments?"

My father flapped his hand, a Ben Solotaroff gesture, marking still another example of human foolishness.

"Anyway, it didn't last long because I couldn't stand the way the guy worked. Instead of removing the floorboard and running the cable through the joists behind it, nice and neat, he'd break into the walls, wiring any which way that was fastest, and leave behind a big mess. So one day we had it out and I punched him in the nose and that was that."

He was back in his narrative groove again, his father's betrayal of him returned to the file of obliviousness where he kept the experiences of being knocked down and of knocking down others. "By then it was almost summer," he went on, "and I'd heard you could make a lot of money in Atlantic City. Also I wanted to get away. We were living in this dump on Magnolia Avenue and I had no home life to speak of anyway."

"You mean because your sisters weren't there, had left home?"

"I mean because my mother was there. She was the world champion *nudzh*, which in case you don't know it means a pain in the ass."

"But she'd provided for the family too. Your sister Sophie told me about how she would take the four of you shopping at the big market on Friday afternoon, then cooked and baked for Shabbos."

"That's true. She liked to shop for the family. She was a mother on Fridays but couldn't wait to get out of the house on Saturday. Also she liked to shop so she could flirt with the butcher, the baker, the butter-and-egg man."

"You once told me that when she was delivering a baby for the poor families in Yonkers, she'd always leave a loaf of bread and a bottle of milk for the mother."

"That's true," he said. But the admission was too much for him. "I'll tell you about my mother," he said in his once-and-for-all tone. "Nothing you did could ever please her."

A silence followed. When he spoke again it was with the full-bore bitterness with which he'd talked about his father and Hymie Korn.

"One time she sent me out to buy a pound of tomatoes. I ran downstairs to the grocer. What does a kid of eight or nine know about tomatoes? I gave him the order, paid him, and brought them upstairs. Well, one or two had a soft spot on them and she yelled at me as though I'd brought back a bag of rotten ones. When she gave me the whole bag to take back I threw it on the floor and ran out of the house. And that was the last time I ever wanted to do anything for her."

The room was almost dark; so caught up had we been for the past hour that neither of us had thought to turn on a lamp. I had come there hoping to find out more about my grandfather's struggle in America and to be bored by and indifferent to another retelling of my father's self-aggrandizing stories. But now it was turning out that his early life, if you reversed the parents, wasn't all that different from my own. As though sensing the change in the weather between us, he said, "That's enough for today. Let's have a drink. I've learned to make a pretty good Gibson by practicing on myself." The self-irony also seemed new.

There were two more taping sessions. The first took him through his next four years of working, hustling, and bumming his way through America as a rolling-chair pusher on the boardwalk in Atlantic City, a dishwasher and pastry chef's helper, a carnie, a door-to-door seller of "medallions" (the plastic casing for photographs of loved ones) in the coal towns of Pennsylvania, an oiler on a tanker that took him to California, a farmhand, a timekeeper for the Union Pacific, a furniture mover, and an electrician's helper in Berkeley. After that came his early years as a contractor, when he took his father's window glass and shade shop into plate glass replacement, storefronts, and industrial glazing. "If I saw something going up where you could stick a piece of glass, I was right there."

These last sessions brought out not only the energetic raconteur but his better nature. He would thank me for coming, say that he knew it was a *shlep* for me and he appreciated my assistance. Once we even ventured a parting hug, the more touching for our mutual awkwardness. It was the first time I could remember him embracing me.

One morning he called in particularly good spirits. I figured another of his shrewd market plays had panned out and he wanted to brag about it to Virginia. Instead he started talking about a recent collection of my essays that I'd sent him.

"I've been reading that *Few Good Voices in Your Head* you gave me last year. You want to know something? When it comes to understanding writers and how the process works, I think you're a fucking genius."

I had two responses, one flashing after the other: a stunned joy ("At last!") and a wry reflection ("This is about forty years too late"). When I'd begun publishing regularly he'd said that I used too many "dictionary words," and that was it for the rest of my writing career. He'd shown a little more interest in my editorial positions at *Commentary*, the *Sunday Herald Tribune*, *New American Review*, and various book publishers, but mainly to get a take on the business side of them, about which he then spoke with his usual authority.

My dual response created a high-amp circuit that kept our relationship alight and ponderable in my mind for days. What mainly occurred to me, and moved me, was that his phrase "fucking genius" expressed his own struggle to come closer, his share of the recent diffident hug, and that this effort didn't come out of nowhere, that a positive feeling for me had been working for years toward the surface, climbing the long slope of his anger, contempt, and jealousy. Out of the blue, he had offered my third wife the tuition for a year of graduate school, and ten years later, my oldest son ten thousand dollars to pay off his college loans, both of whom he hardly knew, having been an even less interested grandfather or father-in-law (until Virginia came along) than a father.

His "fucking genius" words also brought back to mind a curious letter he had written to my brother, a literary critic and English professor, some years back, after one of their tiffs when he'd barged into Bob's vacation house in Maine. He wound up a surly defense of himself by writing,

> I went to a Brandeis book sale in W. Orange last night which I will list below what I bought. You know everytime I get an annual note from you, I wonder do you type it in the dark and do you have a chicken walk across it. Say hello to the better half, kiss the children for me especially Jacob who I fear is my image. I edit all my letters, so I will say with all my Love,
>
> Dad the Editor (Half Ass)
>
> Great Critics—Smith and Parkes
> Claudius the God—Graves
> Julius Caesar and the Grandeur That Was Rome—Victor Thaddeus
> Diplomat Among Warriors—Thomas Murphy
> The Ginger Man—Donleavy
> Augie March—Bellow
> The Collector—Fowles
> Conversations with Stalin—Milovan Djilas

P.S. Did you read Fowles The Ivory Tower? I did when first published. I am determined to make Ted and yourself eat your Words.

Neither Bob nor I could remember ever high-hatting him intellectually, so we'd regarded the final remark as a pure projection of the "Half Ass" editor. Now, in my softened mind, the list had a poignancy that competed with its aggressiveness. I'd reviewed *The Ivory Tower* in the *New York Times Book Review,* and he must have read the review and then gone out and bought the book. The list was one that Bob or I might have chosen at a benefit book sale: whether he'd read the books or not, they spoke for the native curiosity and acuity that had caught what I was trying to do in the essays of mine he'd read, which, though hardly of genius caliber, were attempts to understand the literary vocation.

Was I now bending over backward to see him in a better light because he had finally praised me? No doubt—but perhaps no more than he'd had to do to change his attitude toward me and remove his blinders. And even if this new estimate of him did not, any more than his of me, square with objective reality, well, there was also subjective reality—the soft facts of life as well as the hard, *rachmones* as well as reason. And when there was a competition between the two, my Jewish soul had been taught to choose *rachmones,* the primal Jewish virtue. There was also the hard/soft fact that we were father and son, so a little pride in the other, particularly exaggerated pride, what we Jews call *naches,* was natural as well as long overdue.

4 DURING THE LATE spring, summer, and fall, his wife, Debby, was in residence, and though they were like Israel and Iraq, Debby cooked and froze his dinners each week and brought in a cleaning woman, who also did his laundry. So since he was feeling better in the warm weather, I took most of the summer off. In September, Sandra, Hy, Virginia, and I took him out for dinner on his birthday, and he once again rose to the occasion, showing us his higher comportment, good spirits, and even gratitude as well as his renewed appetite by consuming two small lobsters. So I was knocked sideways about a month later when Debby called and said Ben was worse off than she had ever seen him, that she was going back to

Florida soon, and that I'd better make another arrangement for him before they had to carry him out.

Both Hy and I respected Debby. Much of her apparent grasping-ness came from Ben's stinginess; her callousness had grown over what had been a patient understanding of him. At times, as now, we'd commiserate with each other about trying to do anything for him. "I know what he says about me to you," she said.

"It's probably no worse than what I imagine he says about me to you."

"He doesn't say you're trying to poison him."

"No, he saves that one for his wives. That's what my mother used to hear, that she poisoned his coffee every morning. Don't take him literally."

"I don't take him any way. But it must have been very hard having such a brute for a father."

"Well, as one of my novelist friends said, he's a deep brute. That's made it interesting."

The next visits, though, weren't interesting; his crabbiness and haplessness had returned with renewed force, as did my coldness. There was a moment when he was paying for a prescription at Shop-Rite, slowly handing over the money as though at gunpoint. Watching from twenty feet away, I saw a miserable old man, exuding self-isolation and lovelessness, his character twisted by money, stand-ing defenseless before the bar of moral justice. This was his true nakedness, and I quickly turned away.

The only person who got any rise out of him was Virginia, the one family member he asked about. Sometimes when I phoned him I'd say, "Virginia wants to say hello," though she didn't because of the half hour he usually took up to discuss his and her portfolio and plays. But by then he had stopped answering the phone for a day or two at a time, and I needed to give him an inducement. Talking stocks with her seemed to be the only thing that brought him out of his moribund mood. It was winter again, he rarely left the house and hardly slept, so after the third or fourth call I'd begin to fret. Once when I finally got him I began to lay into him. "I'm not some nui-sance caller," I said. "We're concerned about you. You've got to pick up the phone."

"What's in it for me?" he said.

Was it clinical, terminal depression talking or the last vestige of the man with a high-speed self-interest calculator in his head that he'd always kept turned on? I decided that it was probably a combination of the two—despair drawing out character. "Character is fate," I said to her. "We're seeing that in action."

"I think what we're seeing is a frightened old man who probably wants you to be with him but can't bring himself to ask."

It was an interesting possibility, but I was in no mood anymore for new insights. "Yes," I said. "And underneath that is the Ben Solotaroff who loves to keep people dangling, particularly his family, especially me. It's the last refuge of a self-important man."

So I tried to take a hard line, to say what's in it for *me*, other than letting him put me over a barrel again, so that I could hate him less guiltily. Also, being with him came at a price, sometimes activating a nastiness in me which I would inflict on Virginia's gentle nature. I even had almost blown the marriage apart in a prolonged burst of fury after she criticized my driving as we were returning from seeing Ben. She wanted me to help him but she also dreaded my visits.

Finally, I went out to talk to him, prepared to ring the bell for five minutes until he came to the front door, prepared to make him promise to pick up the phone when it rang more than ten times. But the back door to the basement of the split-level was unlocked when I tried it, which was unusual. I let myself in and called ahead. There was no answer. I went upstairs, fearing what I might find—my father lying murdered. A mugger had followed his Caddy home from the mall and done him in. "Well," I said to myself. "Be careful what you wish for."

He was sitting in front of the TV, staring at the Financial News Network program, the sound turned off. "How's the market doing?" I said, my relief prompting a show of cheerfulness.

"Funny you should drop in," he said, still gazing at the screen or into space. "I was just thinking about your mother."

"You don't say," I said,

He spoke slowly, the words spaced by reflection. "You know something? Virginia's more sophisticated than her, but deep down they're a lot alike."

"In a few ways," I said. Had he been reading my mind?

"They even look a little alike."

"A little." This, too, was surprising news from him..

"Your mother was a beautiful woman when I married her," he said. Then he said, "The biggest mistake I ever made was walking out on her." He was still not looking at me, as though he were talking to the world or to himself. "I've told Sandra I want to be buried next to her."

Oh, Jesus, I thought. He all but put her there and now he's crowding in again. A spurt of disgust mixed with rage at the utter wrongness of it went through my blood like an electric current. I visited her grave every year or so to commune with her, to bring her up to date. How could I do that with him listening in?

"She was the one who really loved me." He took off his glasses and finally looked at me. His eyes were bright with tears. "She would have cut off her arm for me," he said. And then he broke down.

I'd heard both statements before, always together. I'd derided the first and loathed the second because of what cutting off an arm said about him and, more troubling to me, about her. Coldly, I watched him weeping, surely for himself.

He put his head in his hands, exposing a bit more of his neck. Its tenderness, its vulnerability, caught my attention, got to me. My feelings for him were like a high-speed elevator, either inert or else shooting up to rage or down to pity. Whether I wanted to give it or not, some *rachmones* was in order. I went behind him and took him by the shoulders. "It's okay," I said. "Let it out. Let it all out." I tugged his robe back a little, slipped my hands in, and began to massage the soft hollows above his heaving shoulder. You poor obtuse son of a bitch, I said again and again to myself.

After that visit, he was a little better about answering the phone, but still a whole day of calls could go by without his picking up. I got the phone number, just in case, of the one neighbor who still spoke to him. Then, toward the end of February, a second day went by and then most of a third. I called Mrs. Montello and told her the problem. She called back ten minutes later to say that the living-room lights were on but my father didn't answer the door.

An hour later Virginia and I drove into his driveway. I wanted to enter through the back door, to which I had a key, but Virginia, a stickler for considerateness, said, "Maybe he's just been sleeping a lot. Let's try the front door." I, who was not and was upset, my elevator now speeding between dudgeon and dread, reached for my key to the house and discovered I hadn't brought it. Cursing both my father and myself, I plowed up the slope of the lawn through last fall's leaves to the front of the house. The door only offered a view of the foyer, and there was no answer to several minutes of ringing. "I'm going to call the police," I said.

"Let's try the back door again. I think we can break the glass and open it from the inside."

"Look, he's either dead or in need of major help. And even if he isn't or doesn't, a police call will get his attention once and for all."

"Let me try," she said.

So we trekked back down the slope to the back door, the upper half of which was glass-paneled, but the bolt inside was out of reach.

"I think I can climb in," she said.

"No, you can't. For Chrissake, there's hardly two feet of clearance."

"I'm going to try. Just break the glass." After I'd done so and we'd picked as much broken glass as we could from the molding, Virginia took off her coat and spread it over the still-jagged bottom molding. Hiking up her skirt, she slid one leg up over the coat, and with a kind of limbo action, lowered her leg to the floor while angling the rest of her body past the other dangerous edges. My fifty-eight-year-old wife—I was so bowled over I forgot for a moment why we were there.

But, having unlocked the door for me, she was already moving through the basement. I moved more slowly, trying to prepare for a range of possibilities. By the time I reached the stairs up to the second level, she was beginning to come down them. "He's there," she said.

He was lying on his back on the carpet, completely naked, even his eyes naked without his glasses, staring in frozen amazement, or horror, his mouth gaping in a death rictus that looked like a feral snarl. Then the odor hit me, not heavy but already distinct enough, and I turned away. I didn't feel anything other than a kind of repugnance at this ugly, stinking corpse who had been my father but could have been anyone. When I glanced back again, Virginia was kneeling beside him. She closed his eyes, then raised his arm and gently slipped off his wristwatch as though she were preparing him for bed. "His legs look like a boy's," she said, settling into a sitting position beside him.

We talked about how he might have died naked in his living room but I kept my distance, hardly looking at him. The death I had wished for to regain my freedom from him and to enable his money to do some good in recompense for the harm he had done in handling it had come to pass. The rest was just a corpse I had to do something about. I called 911, then I called Hy to tell him and Sandra and ask what funeral home to call. When I returned, Virginia was still sitting there, still attending the body. Where was all that feeling coming from? And for my father?

I noticed his familiar rimless glasses lying on the rug. I picked them up, and then, as I held them and gazed at them, a tenderness of my own welled up, a sudden wind of feeling, bringing rain with it. I stood there, beginning to weep over the glasses, which unlike his corpse were producing my father who had died, the man who was almost blind without them. They were telling me about the chink in his heavily armored being that had led to the vulnerable, virtually invisible and unreachable Ben who had wept in this room a few weeks ago, who had now and then been able to push his vanity and shriveled feelings in a generous direction, and who had suffered the loneliness and bitterness they had produced. His presence in me, and it was a presence, distinct and potent, was that of my father as a much younger man whom I would watch shave and wash in the morning when he would take off his glasses. This presence also came from Virginia's words about his boy's legs, which brought to mind what I'd learned about Sam Myron and about his father and Hymie Korn and about the high school boys who derided him, and about his absent or hectoring mother—all of whom he had gone on the road and hardened himself against in self-interest and imperviousness. After that his vulnerable side didn't have a chance and shrank into a knot that very seldom came untied. But it was now untying inside me, enabling me to begin to mourn him.

The eulogy I gave at his funeral was an effort to view his life on his terms, that is of the self-made man out there in the world rather than the imperious one back with us in the house. But doing so only raised my terms and their impacted relation to him more fully into view. Who was this man who, even in death, could play my spirit like a pipe? How had the holes been put in that he'd fingered? How had I managed to keep him from breaking it, as he had tried to do? Most of all, given my bitter memories of his business, which had cost me part of my youth, why had I taken away an old glass cutter I'd found in the basement of his house, and put it in the jar on my desk that holds pens, pencils, and felt markers, the tools of my trade?

PART TWO

THE WEISS BOY AND LITTLE BENNY

1 ONE OF MY early memories is of my three Weiss uncles coming back from the fields in the early evening at Cream Ridge, a hamlet in central New Jersey where my mother's family owned a hotel and farm. They were husky men, their meaty shoulders and arms bare under their overalls. When they picked me up I breathed in the rank odor of their armpits, the dry brown smell of the dirt dusting their skin, the sharp green smell of the tomato plants they handled. I would burrow my face into their necks and take a lick. They smelled and tasted male and I couldn't get enough of that.

The one who usually picked me up was Moishe, the youngest, whom I called Uncle Mush because the word tasted like he did. He called me Butch McDevitt and Little Bondit, which was Yinglish for rascal. Uncle Jack and Uncle Harry, who had young children of their own called me Little Benny because I looked like my father and because I was hungry for attention.

Mush was also called Gil, the name given to him by Toni Warren, a Yiddish actress he had met in the winter in Lakewood, where the family had another hotel. He was going to be either an actor or a lawyer and raised pullets to save up money for college. I helped him in the chicken yard, where I raked the feathers and the shit into a pile, shucked and scraped the chickens' corn, carried water to the drinking trough. For doing that, he gave me rides on his horse. One time he had to wrestle Brownie into the stable and shouted, "Get in there, you son of a bitch!" I knew the expression; my father often used it in talking about his head glazier and other people he didn't like. But now it was thrilling rather than nasty. Son of a bitch! I said it over and over. It wasn't just a "dirty word" anymore, it was what men said when they were doing something hard.

Another of my chores was holding the hose and watering the two tennis courts every evening, while Mush dragged a huge broom that smoothed them out or pushed the heavy, rusty roller filled with water. Then, like my grandmother Regina decorating a cake in the bakery of the hotel, he would lay down the straight white lines of powdered lime that turned them back into courts.

I was at the courts on a hot afternoon with my aunt Leah, the next-youngest to Mush and his pal in the family. She often looked after me when my mother was in Elizabeth because my father needed her in The Shop. While Leah was playing on one court, I drifted over to the other and saw that the back line needed marking. I got some handfuls of lime out of the big bin Mush kept nearby, dumped them on the court, and patted them straight. The smell of the lime reminded me of him, and I took some of it in my palm and began to lick it. It didn't taste like him, it tasted like the unripe grapes in the orchard. Soon I was retching and rolling around on the court, my stomach in the grip of a fiery fist. Screaming "Green grapes," I was rushed to the nearest doctor, five miles away, nervy Aunt Leah at the wheel, getting me there in no time flat because I'd gone into shock.

Such was my love for Mush, the first positive man in my life. At the hotel, he and my aunt Fan, who was the local schoolteacher, organized activities for the children who stayed there with their families. He had two sets of boxing gloves with which he taught the boys to spar. He said I wasn't old enough but I kept after him until he laced the gloves on me and paired me with one of the smaller kids. Eager to show my stuff, I lowered my head and charged. I got socked, began to cry, and ran to him. After he pried me off his knees, he knelt, looked me in the eye, and said, "You're a Weiss boy and the Weiss boys don't cry. And they always keep their heads up when they fight."

"You're a Weiss boy" lodged in my mind for good, on the same active block but across the street from "Little Benny."

That same summer, when I was four and he twenty-two, Mush took me for a walk with Toni Warren, who had come to visit him for a few days. (Later on I learned that she was married at the time and her visit was clandestine because my grandfather, an extremely pious and strict man, would never have allowed such a *shanda*—"scandal" only touches its odious hem—to take place on his property.) Toni was the first woman I'd seen whose hair came all the way down to her waist. I thought that Jacob's Rachel, whom I was learning about from Aunt Fan, must have looked like Toni. Mush, who had wavy hair, a big but well-angled nose, and velvety eyes, was said to look like John Barrymore if John Barrymore had been Jewish.

Walking in the fields, we came to the old shed that my mother had fixed up when she was a girl to get away from everyone and to read. Mush lifted Toni and me up onto the roof. It now had a hole in the middle of it, and we sat on the edge, watching the Cream Ridge sky put on its show of sunset through the tall stands of pines that bordered the fields. Then some of the "college boy" waiters came with Aunt Leah, who was in charge of them, and some of the other "younger crowd," and they sat up on the roof with us. Mush kept his big arm around me so I wouldn't roam around and fall through the hole, and they told jokes and harmonized songs like "Down by the Old Mill Stream" and "When the Moon Comes over the Mountains." The star-crammed sky shone down and the bliss and security I felt under my uncle's wing carried me up into little kids' paradise.

Uncle Harry and Uncle Jack were the farmers; Uncle Mush was the Mr. Everything. When he wasn't helping out his brothers during the harvest or tending to his chickens, he was fixing things, like the pump for the swimming pool or the engine of the tractor. He had his own Nash roadster and a police dog named Laddie that rode in the rumble seat when he took me with him to Trenton almost every morning to buy supplies for the hotel. At night he put on his dressy slacks, suede shoes, and thin, flowing white shirt and became the social director of the Belfane, the name of the hotel. He was in charge of the hayrides, the movie excursions to Hightstown, the midnight weenie roasts, the horseshoe tournaments, the bingo games. He and his sisters, particularly Fan, who had a college education, were responsible for the readings, concerts, short plays, sketches, and skits performed by the guests, the staff, and actors from the Studio Players, the drama group Mush belonged to in nearby Trenton. The "cultural evenings" were what made the Belfane special; people came there year after year because it had a "serious crowd," guests who brought their brains and talents well as their bathing suits and dancing shoes. Later on I learned that George S. Kaufman and Heywood Broun had been guests there.

Mush also put on the big show in the dance hall on Saturday night, for which he brought in a professional comic, singer, or other entertainer. Lying on my cot in our room in the Old House where the family lived during the season, I would try to stay awake in my happiness at hearing the music and bursts of laughter and applause and especially the drumroll and cymbal crash when a new act was starting. All of which reassured me that the guests were really enjoying themselves. In my four-year-old mind this meant that "business was picking up"— a concern that was all around me the summer of 1932.

I wanted Cream Ridge to pick up because I was having, literally, the time of my life. I was the second grandchild in the Weiss family and the first male, so much was made of me. The hotel was like one great lap to nestle in, and also, not being Mush's nephew for nothing, a series of scenes for my own little star turns. Grandmother Regina and Aunt Belle, who were in charge of the kitchen, would sit me on a stool at the pastry table and let me play at being their helper. Aunt Fan would bring me into the office, sit me down with a pencil and pad, and admire my drawings. Aunt Leah and her boyfriend, Eddy Van Dam, would take me around with them as their practice child. Then there were the waiters and one or another of the guests to applaud my efforts to catch or hit a ball, to swim, to ride a horse. I became almost professionally adorable from all the attention and my desire for more. Even when I misbehaved, the baby ham in me would go stand in a corner and mutter, "I've been a bad boy," which got me more smiles and hugs.

These Cream Ridge summers, particularly the halcyon one of 1932, came in the nick of time. The following summer almost all of the guests were gone, my uncles couldn't market their produce, and the family was too worried to pay much attention to me. My mother was there the whole time, but she was more distracted than usual. She now had Sandra, my baby sister, to take care of, which made her happy. But each time my father came for the weekend he would be angry with her and embarrass her. Then toward the end of the summer there was a big blowup with my uncle Jack, who told him the family was "fed up" with his criticism and advice, and he stopped coming to see us. Mom said he was being sued by a bank and couldn't get credit and this made him impossible to deal with. She didn't cry, she smiled more than ever and tried to be cheerful, but already sensitive to her moods, I know she was unhappy because her mind was so often elsewhere.

One afternoon when she was in this mood we went to the pool by ourselves. I jumped into the shallow end to splash around and teach myself to swim. She sat nearby in a beach chair. I lost in my play and she in her thoughts, neither of us noticed that I'd gotten close to the ledge where the floor of the pool dropped away. The safety rope across the pool had been removed, and when I tried to put my feet down I couldn't. The next thing I knew I was under water, the ghostly ledge a terrifying foot or two away. I somehow thrashed close enough to get my foot on it and propel myself to the surface and scream to her. When Mom reached me I was standing on the ledge again, but both of us had come very close to drowning, because she couldn't swim.

After she calmed down a little and stopped blaming herself she said, "Please don't tell anyone this happened. I don't want to give your father and the Solotaroffs any more ammunition."

I knew what she meant. Soon we would be going back to Elizabeth, where she had to "tread on eggshells," because our life was very different, as different as the peacefulness of Cream Ridge from the fights in our house, as different as the hearty Weisses from the baleful Solotaroffs, as different as my soft, dreamy mother from my harsh, impatient father.

2   MY MOTHER'S AMBIGUOUS personality is perhaps best captured by a photograph of her at the center of a small group of young women taken when she was about nineteen. She was the family beauty and this immediately comes through, not only from her striking looks but also in the way the other women—the two in the foreground, Belle and Fan, are her older sisters—become a kind of court; or, better, the ordinary flowers in a bouquet that set off the single, lovely rose (which happened to be her name). Stylishly turned out with her boyish bob, she does not quite hold her place at the center but seems to recede from it into her own space, her brooding eyes making her look both melancholy and sultry, both of which she proved to be.

Another of my early, primal memories is of sitting next to her on the piano bench while she played classical melodies and shared her reveries with me. The most vivid one accompanied Schumann's "Traumerai." It

is about a mother and a little boy whom she dearly loved, "the light of her life." But one day the boy became very ill. No matter what medicine the doctor gave him or all of the mother's alcohol rubs and cold compresses they couldn't stop him from burning up with fever until he "passed away." Since she loved him more than anything else in the world, she didn't want to go on living herself. But then she discovered that if she played this song of Schumann's the soul of her son would come down from heaven and sit beside her on the bench.

This memory lies next to those about the composers whose lives she would tell me about as she played their music. There was Bach with all of his children to support, and Mozart who was even poorer, and Schubert who was the poorest of all and had tuberculosis besides and died very young. And then there was delicate Chopin, who coughed blood when he performed, and stormy Beethoven, who became deaf, of all things. Nor did the painters, prints of whose work we had in the house, fare any better what with Rembrandt's debts and Van Gogh's torments and Toulouse-Lautrec who stopped growing as a boy and Renoir's arthritis. From all of this I came to believe that artists were noble, unfortunate people who often lived in a dark, unhealthy place called a garret, and that beauty, like love, had something very sad about it.

Yet if I picked up my mother's sadness, I received her pluck as well, for she came in layers of wistfulness and willingness. Withal, she was a robust woman who had been raised in a country family that was used to adversity and believed life's problems would give ground if you did your best. So, she was either rushing off to The Shop or daydreaming by the window, hanging wallpaper or playing one of her pensive pieces, lost in a novel or doing the laundry, making dinner and nursing my baby sister, more or less at the same time.

She had been her mother's favorite daughter, inheriting her kindness, her quietness, as well as her love of music. The fifth of seven children, she was the odd one out, the others bonding in pairs, Harry and Jack the farmers and providers, Belle and Fan the managers, Moish/Gil and Leah the cutups and rebels. The Weisses were the only Jews for miles around and had mainly each other for companionship. Rose grew up companioning herself, accompanied, when she could, by her busy mother.

Her great regret was that the family had moved, when she was five years old, to the country. Regina Weiss, her mother, had made a name for herself and a good living for her family as a young designer for Russeks, a leading department store, and then as an independent dressmaker in Yonkers. Had the family remained there, Rose thought she might have had the musical education that her sister-in-law Sophie, who also grew up in Yonkers, won for herself at the Third Street Settlement school in Manhattan and then at Juilliard. At Cream Ridge, piano lessons went the way of the other amenities that her mother's needle and sense of fashion had provided and that her father's improvidence had taken away. A presser who had scorched his lungs and whom her mother had set up as a small grocer in Yonkers, David Weiss was every inch a Litvak—pious, authoritarian, abstract. He decided that a farm in the Jersey Pine Belt was the solution to his severe asthma and to his lack of control over his sons in Gentile, pagan Yonkers.

The farm he bought was on choice land in New Jersey horse country. Its large, even opulent house had two kitchens in which to keep kosher—a bargain to be snapped up at a 1906 depression price. But the Weisses knew as little about tomatoes and corn and chickens as the Solotaroffs knew about tending vineyards. One of the indelible images in the family memory is that of "Poppa" in his skullcap and city clothes, standing amid his 160 acres, a manual in hand, instructing his two older boys to plant each of the crops in an adjacent row as though they were growing a vegetable garden.

Year by year the family sank further toward poverty. Jack and Harry improved as farmers, taught by Gentiles whose influence David had been fleeing from, particularly an erstwhile Hungarian peasant named Gus who soon made himself indispensable and was willing to work for little more than Regina's Hungarian dishes. But farm prices remained depressed and the family reached the point where they were taking in workers from a nearby highway project for ten cents a night and feeding them for fifty cents more. Regina was also feeding her husband's cronies from Yonkers, whom he would invite to make a Shabbos *minyan* and study Talmud. Ever resourceful, Regina saw that there might be a business in all of this cooking, a better one than from their crops and chickens. By the time the road was finished she was offering a kosher Sunday chicken dinner with a Hungarian touch that soon caught on with the Jews of nearby Trenton, who, taking to the road like other Americans, made it a feature of their Sunday drive. Then came the salesmen and other travelers during the week to and from Trenton. So it was that Regina, as aptly named as Bathsheva Solotaroff, rescued her family by taking it into the boardinghouse, the country inn, and eventually the hotel business.

My mother's account of her girlfriend before the family got on its feet again led me to think of the early Cream Ridge as barren and isolated and nearly as cold as Siberia. Aunt Leah's account of them is of robust country life with a few early years of hardship thrown in. But Leah still gardens and wisecracks at ninety; my mother was made of more sensitive stuff, and her memories of the early years were of a Gorky-like setting of highway workers tramping mud through the dining room and up the stairs, the Talmudists filling the parlor with their loud arguments and heavy cigarette smoke, the water for washing frozen in its pitchers, the Gentile children in the one-room school-house putting dead mice in her overshoes.

Her good memories didn't begin until her mother had saved up enough money sewing for the ladies of nearby Allentown to buy her a piano, which came with the ten lessons that were to be her musical education. Around that time her sister Fan, who had managed to commute to Rutgers and become a teacher, sent the family a sub-scription to the Harvard Classics. The first was *Père Goriot*, which Rose would read to her mother at night, after the boarders and family had beed fed, the two of them sitting beside the big cook stove, the only warm place in the house. In the spring they swept out and whitewashed an old shack in the fields and brought in a broken-down sofa and chair, some pictures clipped from the rotogravure, and pine boughs and field flowers. During the week Rose would retreat there, joined on Shabbos afternoon by Regina, and the reading went on.

When Rose was fourteen, her sister Fan returned to Cream Ridge to teach in the local one-room school house. She made her literary sister, who was beginning high school in Allentown, her main pupil. "Fan was as strict as Poppa. She was always after me about my writing because I used too many flowery words. But she made a real Latin scholar out of me. She had only two years of Latin herself, so the Cicero and Virgil we studied together. Two country girls sitting by the stove in the kitchen translating Latin poetry until we couldn't keep our eyes open." Sometimes when my father called her a "stupid hick" or worse and left her weeping, she'd say to me, "I won a New Jersey state prize for my Latin essay. He can't even write a grammatical sentence."

After high school, she became a bookkeeper in Lakewood, a nearby winter resort town where the family had a small hotel, helped out summers in the large, successful one it had built in Cream Ridge, and continued her solitary way through classical music by imitating the gramophone performances of the masters. The Harvard Classics led her to the Brontë sisters and Jane Austen and George Eliot. Tentative in most things, she had strong musical and literary opinions. "I never liked *Madame Bovary*, she's too vain and stupid. The book I liked from that period is *Germinie Lacerteux*. It's about a lovely French seamstress who is worn down by her later life, a little like me, I guess."

Beginning when I was five and continuing ever after, I'd listen to her tales of Cream Ridge and Lakewood, coming to know them almost by heart. The one that most interested me was about a man named Philip whom she had almost married. He was a widower at thirty-one, without children, whose family was the largest real estate broker in northern New Jersey. "He came to Cream Ridge every weekend that summer. After I finished in the dining room on Saturday night, he would be waiting for me in the lobby. We didn't go to the shows in the casino. Instead we'd walk down by the pool and sit in beach chairs and talk. He had no background in music or literature, so he was very impressed by mine. I didn't know that much but I could always put it on. He said I was his invitation to culture. On Sunday afternoon we would go to the casino by ourselves and I'd play for him. He'd sit and listen and never take his eyes off me. He was a businessman, but he was the opposite of your father in every way."

Which was what I was mainly waiting to hear, the point at which I would join in her story of the might-have-been, even after I realized there wouldn't have been me. "So he wanted to marry you."

"He said that he wanted to help me to get the serious musical training I had always craved and also a college education. He didn't propose, he was a shy man, but I knew I couldn't accept his help without marrying him."

"But you didn't love him."

"I was confused. I was twenty years old and hadn't had a serious beau before."

"So you went back to Lakewood to talk to Fay Rabinowitz."

Fay was two years younger than Rose but more sophisticated. She, too, was a tall, striking brunette. "Fay had style and I had taste, so we complemented each other. We were both dying to get out of Lakewood but I had more patience because of my music and reading, which she admired me for. She said I brought out her serious side."

"Fay was for Philip."

"She said he was right for me. She took me for long walks along the lake past the Rockefeller and Gould estates as though that would influence me. But I just wasn't in love with him. I didn't know enough. I still had a young girl's heart."

The following winter the young handsome smooth-talking glass contractor arrived at their Lakewood hotel to cash in on the coincidence that his mother, the midwife, had delivered Rose in Yonkers. Soon he was talking of dressing her in gowns from Paris. "Just buy her a good cloth coat from Klein's and I'll be satisfied," Regina said. Less than a year later she was heard to remark, "Tonight I have married my gentlest daughter to a bear."

During the early years in Elizabeth my mother was often at The Shop as the bookkeeper and the fill-in office worker. It was not that she was a businesswoman—far from it. She loved to stay at home with me in our small house on Boudinot Place, a block or two from The Shop, the command center of our lives. Boudinot Place was a spavined, derelict street that went back to the Revolutionary War, but my mother had made our cottage pretty, furnishing it with pieces from the Cream Ridge Belfane, and prints which she framed herself at The Shop, and brightening the house with flowers and plants that she grew from the moldy soil in back. As she would later say, these were the happy years of the marriage, the three or four of them, and I have a memory of being taken into my parents' bed on a Sunday morning and romped with, and another of the three of us playing catch in a park, memories that seem so incongruous that they are more like dreams.

After they married, Dad had four good years, building the Elizabeth Glazing Co. from scratch with the $4,500 he received as a settlement for his share of the family business after his partnership with his sister Marion and her husband had turned into another Solotaroff snake pit. Using the prowess and contacts he had developed, along with an iron nerve in kiting loans, he had positioned himself aggressively on the inside of the building boom of the late 1920s. But then in 1933, as he was putting up his own building, the Depression and the banks finally caught up with him, and drove him into bankruptcy. As he used to say, "I was sitting on top of the world and then all of a sudden I was on my ass but good. It's something you never forget."

Nor did we. Three months later he was able to open his door as the Standard Plate Glass Co. A smart chancery lawyer had enabled him to get back on his feet, but with creditors chasing him and scarce business to chase after and to collect on, he was henceforth a man on the run, ten hours a day, often six and a half days a week. His sudden fall from prosperity, his three months of humiliation and frustration as a shrewd operator who had nonetheless expanded into the teeth of the Depression and lost everything, his anxiety as a man who had barely escaped ruin, hardened his heart all the more about money and tightened his fist around it.

The firstborn of an increasingly unhappy marriage, I led a precocious emotional life from the time I was five as my mother's comforter and sometime confidant. The early mornings when she had to ask Dad for extra money (he left her a dollar a day) were usually when my services were most needed: she sitting at the kitchen table in tears, my father shouting that he should have his head examined for marrying her, that money ran through her fingers like water. Then he would deliver his parting shot, "I can't even get out the house in the morning without you poisoning my coffee," and slam the back door behind him.

As soon as I'd hear his car start, I'd get up from my bowl of Ralston, run to her, and put my hands on her eyes, which in a minute or two would make her stop crying, and then stroke her hair. I'd ask her to "make the sun come out on your face." Smiling, she would pull me to her, gaze at me, and say, "What would I do without you? What sense would any of this make?" Then she would calm us both down by telling me, "Money makes your father crazy. He can't help it. It's in the Solotaroff blood. He's more to be pitied than scorned." Or she might explain, "He's very overextended at The Shop. Once he gets back on his feet he'll be nicer to us again. We have to try to understand him." Or, if she had been driven beyond her reassurances and had only resignation left, she'd say, "The leopard can't change his spots."

Trying to understand him was to be our main project. With no one else to talk to in Elizabeth—she was slow to make friends there because of The Shop and because of her shyness—my mother would sit me down in the kitchen while she cooked or have me trail after her as she did the housework and tell me her stories and explanations, the steady overflow of her full, perplexed heart.

"We met when I was being born," she would say, "Mrs. S. delivered me when she was two months pregnant with him. That's fate for you," she'd add, as though the coincidence of their meeting, as it were, *in utero* dictated everything that followed. In her less fatalistic mood, she would say, "I married him because I knew he would give me beautiful children."

In telling me about their courtship, she would usually bring up the two events that seemed to form the crux of her decision. On one of his visits to Lakewood, Dad had gone outdoors too soon after taking a shower and caught a cold that turned into a case of galloping pneumonia. She and her mother had helped to nurse him at the hospital. "It got so bad he had to have a pipe inserted into his lung to drain the pus. We didn't think he'd make it. Mostly he was unconscious, but after the worst was over, he kept telling the doctors and nurses that he had never had anyone care for him like we did. He was like a lamb. I would sit by his bed and read to him, or he wouldn't let go of my hand, he would just look at me and call me his angel."

This account of how she had fallen in love with him tied in with her reiteration of the different person he could be when he didn't have The Shop to worry about. But this view of him would be countered by the story of the bathrobe. When my father was convalescing at the Weisses' hotel, he would come down to breakfast and sit in the lobby in his bathrobe. "We were very polite people but it became so embarrassing that my brother Jack tried to talk to him. Your father said the guests found him so interesting he couldn't understand what Jack was complaining about. So I knew I had my work cut out for me. But I'd say to myself, *Amor omnia vincit*, which means love conquers all."

As if I didn't know that and disbelieve it by the time I was six. Such was the usual tenor and direction of our discussions: from pain to memories to acceptance to nowhere. They would go on for many years but I didn't lose my taste for them. They felt like the main reason I belonged there.

The one area of my parents' life that was compatible was the one I saw just enough of to preoccupy and upset my child's mind. Before I knew what they were used for, I would find a crumpled, pale rubber

finger sitting on top of the toilet tank. Then, around the time I found
out what it was, it was replaced by a rubber disk, which confounded
me all over again until one of my eight-year-old friends wised me up.
By then I was emerging from a period in which I'd intensely disbe-
lieved the explanations about what parents did in bed and where
babies came from, grasping whatever straw of other possibility could
take away the queasy thought that soon that night or afternoon my
father would be ramming that fat thing of his into my mom.

There was more to this than standard oedipal dismay and trembling. I was being raised in the middle of a very sexual and bad marriage. Along with the paraphernalia that was left in view, there was
Dad's special nice look, the chuckle in his voice which I had known
ever since I was a small boy. He and I would get back from the Y on
Sunday morning and after lunch, Sandy and I would be sent out to
play, knowing they were having something they called a "matinee."
From the lighter mood in the house afterward, we knew, before I
understood why, that a "matinee" was what made Dad the different
person he could be for a day or two.

My mother was a chaste woman in her mind and speech but a
careless one in the way she exposed her body while walking around
half-dressed or sprawled in a chair or on a couch. Dad would sometimes growl, "Button your blouse," or "Close your legs for Chrissake."
In his other mood, though, he might say, "You're looking pretty *zaftig*
over there." Her immodesty in this respect seemed part of her dreamy
negligence, but it may also have been her semiconscious way of
keeping in view one of the few sources of pride he left her with and
her one negotiable asset with him. But, as in other ways, I was seeing
more than I wanted to, and was glad when Dad snapped at her for it,
and, in time, was doing so myself.

3   SOME OF THE peaceful times with my dad were in the early
morning when, if he was in a good mood, he would take me
into the bathroom and I would sit on the toilet seat and watch him

shave and wash, brush his teeth, and then brush his hair with his two "military" hairbrushes. He wore the singlet undershirt of the times and had the same broad meaty shoulders as my Weiss uncles. But Dad didn't pick me up as they did or even say much to me, except to go into the fine points of shaving close without cutting himself or brushing his teeth with vertical strokes from the gums down instead of sideways as most people did. Even then, he didn't seem to be talking to me as much as to the mistaken world at large. I was there as his audience, a lone little courtier at the ablutions of the Sun King.

The most interesting part was when he finished shaving and took off his glasses. Then it was as though all that I feared in him would go away with his glasses, which he could hardly see without, and there would be something younger and softer about him as he scrubbed his face, ears, neck, and armpits, then lowered his face to the bowl and splashed away the soap. His face streaming, he'd put out his hand for the warmed towel I would whisk off the radiator. Then he would pat his cheeks and armpits with talcum powder, slap his cheeks with witch hazel, put his glasses back on, and become my father again.

Once or twice a month in those early years he would take me to the YMHA on Sunday mornings, his only consistent respite in the week. Leaving me at one end of the gym to find something to do, he would go off to play paddleball with his cronies. By the time I was six or so, I had an eye for athletic performance and could tell that Dad was slow and clumsy but hit a low, hard, accurate shot. When their hour was up, I would trail after him to the weight room, where he and his friend Gabe would work out with Indian clubs and with the big medicine ball. Then came the best part—the pool. I'd splash around in the shallow end while he glided up and down with his peculiar sidestroke, his big, naked body rising and falling in the water like a pink porpoise. He loved to swim. It was the one sport he had learned as a youth, after he had left home and was working in Atlantic City.

Then we would catch up with Gabe and the other men in the steam room. I would have a towel wrapped around me just like the men did, and it was here that they would pay attention to me sometimes and call me "Little Benny," as Uncle Jack did. When they asked me a taunting question, such as, "Has he got you working for him yet?" I'd give a smart-aleck, Little Benny answer—"No, he's raising me to be a lazy bum like you."

The best thing about these Sunday mornings at the Y was that I could tell Dad liked to show me off, and, in turn, I felt most like his son, his flesh and blood, my nervousness and fear of him put away for those two hours like the clothes we wore the rest of the time.

With a father who seemed proud of me and at one with those beefy, half-naked, wisecracking Jewish men in their prime, just like my uncles at Cream Ridge, I was grounded in what unity I had between being my father's son and my mother's, between Little Benny, the rough-and-tough wise guy, and the Weiss boy, who didn't cry and always kept his head up.

It is a spring afternoon, and I am at the playground of Abraham Lincoln, the elementary school for the Jewish end of Elmora, the main residential district of Elizabeth, to which we have recently moved. Two or three older boys are doing a stunt on the big swings. Standing up and pumping in longer, steeper arcs, they jump off, throw their arms wide, and drop like birds to the ground.

I am there by myself; my mother is in our apartment on the other side of Grove Street with my baby sister. I'm supposed to be playing in front of our building but I like to roam. I'm not allowed to cross Grove Street by myself because of the traffic, but I have anyway. I have to mind my father every minute, so I hardly mind my mother at all when he isn't home.

A year before, when we were still living on Boudinot Place, I had taken myself for a walk three blocks away to Broad Street. I had a quarter in my pocket which Uncle Mush had given me. In 1932 money was what my father and mother mostly talked and quarreled about, and suddenly I had a lot of it, enough to go to a movie by myself for the first time or buy a malted and Baby Ruths. As I headed up East Jersey Street to Broad Street where the Regent Theater was, I felt myself getting taller and braver until I was at eye-level with the grownups, as though I was Jack, the quarter was my magic seeds, and East Jersey Street was my beanstalk. Though I soon became lost amid the waves of people on Broad Street and had to be taken home by a policeman and was given a spanking I wouldn't forget by my father, what I remembered more decisively was the delicious feeling of being "a big kid," a feeling I wanted more than anything else to experience again. And here were these boys doing really big-kid stuff.

So when a swing became free, I asked one of them to give me a boost, and once seated on the swing I managed to pull myself up to a standing position and began to pump. My five-year-old legs and weight didn't take me very high, but they took me high enough so that I remember the thrill of jumping out into space.

That is all I remember. For I had gone high enough to be knocked unconscious when I landed directly on my face. As my mother was to tell the story, over and over in the years to come, I was carried home by two of the playground supervisors. When she had gotten over the shock of my black-and-blue face glazed with dirt and blood, she called my father. "I should have just taken you to the emergency room myself," she would say in her wistful way. My father was annoyed by her calling him up at The Shop, where he had more than enough "aggravation" already. He ordered her to stop being so hysterical, to clean me up, that he'd take a look at me when he got home. When he arrived that evening he found out that I'd been on the playground by myself and went into one of his tirades about my mother being as dizzy and incompetent as the day she was born, about his never getting five minutes of peace even in his own home. After he took a look at my nose he declared that my face was too swollen for a doctor to be able to tell anything, that it would just be throwing money away, that we'd see in a week or so when the swelling went down.

But after a week it was hard to tell if the swelling had gone down, because my nostrils were still thickly distended and the bridge was still a large bump twisted to the right. My mother had become so alarmed that she stopped being intimidated. "I just picked you up and took you to Dr. Gittelman myself. He couldn't understand why we had waited so long with a nose that looked like that." The upshot was that the fracture, which could have been straightened before, had begun to set and nothing could be done now until I stopped growing.

And so at the age of five I received the odious wound that doesn't heal, which is said to be the source of an artistic temperament. Certainly it was to make me self-conscious and sensitive—as sensitive as a boil. For the patch of ugliness in the middle of my face that I was henceforth to carry around became even more prominent when it burst forth with the rest of me in adolescence.

Among the Weisses, it was all along a source of outrage and commiseration, not only for me but for my mother, since my aunts and uncles regarded it as Exhibit A in their case against my father's "heartless" neglect and miserliness. As for my mother, I would often catch her eyes lingering sadly on it or sense the implicit reference to it when she would praise me for my beautiful smile. When I was young she would stand me in front of a mirror and push the tip of my nose center and upward. "See," she would say. "That's all it will take when the surgeon is able to straighten it. Then you'll have an aquiline nose again like your father's."

As for my father, I couldn't tell if he included my appearance in his general dissatisfaction with me. He seldom if ever mentioned my nose as such, but he was mightily irritated by my night cough, the most persistent of the respiratory problems it was to breed. Usually when I was awakened and tried to cough away the phlegmy tickle in my throat, my mother would come with a glass of water and the little blue bottle of Vicks that opened my "poor passages" a bit. She would sit with me as the water and the pungent salve did their work, the fumes turning breathing into a trip to the mountains where the air was piercingly cold and pure. But then my father would call her back to bed and I'd lie there, and soon the phlegmy tickle would be back in my throat that I must try not to cough away too much or too loudly. For if I did, the chances were the next trip would be made by him and then anything could happen because he needed his sleep and if he needed it badly enough, he'd grab me, shake me, bend me across his knee, and yell, "Cough! Goddamm it, cough it out of you once and for all." And then my mother would be back, imploring him, "Please, Ben, be sensible. He can't help it."

For the most part, though, my nose complex was as much a spur as an embarrassment and threat during my boyhood years. As children do, I worked with the givens. I was a big sturdy boy for my age, with energy pouring into me from both sides of the family. I also had an angry father who always seemed to be fighting with creditors, competitors, workers, customers, his family, my mother. Also I had my Weiss uncles who'd had to fight the Gentile farm boys all the time. Uncle Jack had even won five dollars at a fair by staying on his feet for a round with a professional boxer. So, already having the role models as well as the nose and irascibility of a fighter, I became one.

I couldn't stop the big guys from teasing and abusing me, but let any-one my age or size try it and I was ready to fight—glad to fight, given the hot rage and shame that were always on tap.

This pugnaciousness came on strongly when I was seven, the year I hooked up with Bruce Brown, a roughneck two years older, who was as untethered as I was. One Saturday afternoon he treated me to the movie *Kid Galahad*. Played by Wayne Morris, the Kid is a Jewish boy's ideal of a Gentile, a big blond friendly farm boy from the Middle West who is taken under the wing of a big-city fight manager who, as played by Edward G. Robinson, could be nothing but Jewish. A natural boxer rather than a puncher, the Kid makes his way to a championship bout, but his manager is coerced by the Mob into throwing the fight. He does so by instructing the Kid to slug with the champion, which gets him repeatedly knocked down. He is down for what may be the count when Edward G. Robinson, overcome by his conscience, signals the Kid to come up boxing, that is, jabbing and dancing away. Slowly the Kid's head clears, his left hand begins to land, the tide of the bout turns, and he wins the championship on points. So, at least, I remember it, and I remember it much more vividly than I do any other film I saw as a boy. It not only gave me a boxing style for the rest of my youth but also a way of dealing with defeat and abuse.

The movie also gave me a manager. From then on I was the Kid and Bruce, the best fighter in the fourth grade, was Edward G. Robinson, who trained me to dance and hit. Bruce also got me my fights when my nose or bullying wasn't doing so. By the time I was in the third grade both of us were banned indefinitely from the Shelley Avenue school playground at the lunch recess.

For a few days the punishment felt like a reward. We signaled to each other from the telephone poles a block apart we had to stand next to, and I was confirmed as the sidekick of the toughest kid in the fifth grade and was as notorious now as he was. As my classmates would go by on their way back to school, I would receive the tributes of my buddies as well as the wary glances of the other boys and the disgusted headshakes and shrugs of the girls. All of it added up to the attention I craved.

I remember that telephone pole more distinctly than I remember

Bruce. For it became the home base of the wretched two weeks or so that followed once my bravado dissolved into envy and shame. The tough guy who did his talking with his fists turned into a lonely, self-hating outcast, the sense of a streak of ugliness within me connecting up with the one in the middle of my face. It was during those two weeks that Little Benny and the Weiss boy began to get to know each other.

4 PEOPLE THINK OF Elizabeth as the place to roll up the car windows as the New Jersey Turnpike passes through a fuming exhibit of the Industrial Age, petroleum sector, its neolithic catalyst crackers smoking away by day, luridly lighting the night, its storage tanks looming for miles on either side of the highway like a promise to the motorist that this noxious place will never let America go dry. But this area was nothing like the Elizabeth I knew as a boy. By the time I was six, my parents had completed a Chinese checkers jump westward from a little flat in the Port, the industrial immigrant crotch of the city adjacent to the refineries of Bayway, to Boudinot Place, in the midst of the business district, to Grove Street in the dense, shambling second-generation Jewish end of Elmora, and on to the suburban Gentile end, where the sky was not smoky all day. On the other side of nearby Magee Avenue, part of the western boundary of the city, the farmland and deep woods and swimming holes of Union began.

Gentile Elmora, where I was to grow up for the next ten years, was one of Dad's positive provisions for his family. Its society ranged from the respectable working class to the professional and executive one, anchored in its privileges and prestige by the Elmora Country Club, which not even the few wealthy Jews among us were allowed to join. Some streets like Harding Road and Coolidge Road featured spacious Colonials and Tudors set back from their proud lawns and shade trees. Others, like Keats Avenue, where we lived, were lined on both sides by bungalows and modest Cape Cods, set close to each other and to the street, hunkered down like a team making a goal-line stand, protecting the ten yards of grass and garden in back.

Their blue-collar and frayed-white-collar households were tenaciously hanging in during the 1930s, managing to meet the rent or mortgage payments, put food on the table, and maintain the more visible proprieties on a reduced shift at Singer Sewing Machine or General Aniline, a dwindled plumbing or grocery business, a temporary job as a delivery man or a Fuller Brush salesman that went on for years. On Keats Avenue, times were difficult but not wretched, a place of tightened belts rather than empty stomachs, of children in oversized rather than ragged clothes, of a householder painting the porch in the middle of a workday afternoon rather than sitting abjectly on it.

Now and then I would see such men. They would come into The Shop when I was stationed in the front on Saturday afternoons in case Dad had to go out or was busy in the back. I could tell they weren't customers by the way they looked around and hesitated before they started talking. They weren't like the hoboes I'd see along the Jersey Central tracks who'd tell us to go home and swipe some potatoes and they'd show us how to make "mickies," as though we didn't already know from imitating them. The hoboes either looked dangerous or jovial—clowns in real rags and busted shoes who had just been riding the rails and would be doing so again, figures of adventure rather than poverty. The men who came in The Shop leaked desperation from the moment they opened their mouths and said something like "I see you're helping your dad out."

They were usually shaved and wore clean clothes, but that only made them seem more pathetic when they then asked me if they could talk to my father or even told me, a nine-year-old kid, what they could do, what they'd be willing to take for a day's work, even an afternoon's. They looked like my father did when he'd put on his sheepish act to try to get out of a ticket from a cop or state trooper for speeding or running a red light. But these men couldn't drive away from their embarrassment and futility. I knew if I got my father, he'd take one look at them and say, "I've got nothing," and if they started to talk, he'd say, "Get out of here, I'm a busy man," which would only make them feel worse. So I would tell them he was out even if he was in the back, and watch them go next door or across the street or just look around as if they were lost.

Like the song "Brother, Can You Spare a Dime?" they made me realize that the primary task in life was to "make sure"—to make sure that this could never happen to you—a realization that would last well into adulthood and stamp most of my generation with its imperatives and caution.

In the atmosphere on Keats Avenue of hard workers contending with hard times, our family could have fitted in, but we didn't. Though I was an active kid on the block who got into the marble and knife and baseball-card games in the one empty lot, the touch football and roller-skate hockey in the street, the games of kick the can and ring-a-levio we played through the long summer hours after supper, I sensed early on that I didn't fully belong, that unlike the other kids who were in and out of each other's houses, my relationship with them stopped at the door. If I went into one of their houses for a glass of water or to get a school assignment, the parents would look at me in a special way, as though they had just finished an unpleasant conversation about me.

For a time I thought it was because I was Jewish. When I roamed the neighborhood looking for a game or at least a catch, or hung out at the playground and ball field at the Shelley Avenue school, one block over, it was as someone who with a few words could suddenly be turned into an outsider and occasionally a despised one. Most of the best athletes in the area went to St. Genevieve's, ten blocks away, but, during the summer hung out at the Shelley Avenue playground, where they were the mainstays of its teams in the city playground leagues. They were older than I was, except for Shrimp Ward, the youngest of the three Ward brothers, who were already a legendary fighting team in the youth annals of Elmora. I tagged along with the group whenever I could, in a half-daze of awe and curiosity.

Once when I was nine or so, I was sitting with them on the iron steps that led up to the school auditorium, and the talk turned to the upcoming fight between the champion, James J. Braddock, and Joe Louis, the young heavyweight sensation. For George Tiernan, Miles Gilson, Tommy Hopkins, the Ward brothers, and the others, the only question was what way Braddock would win, and they decided he would outlast Louis, that "the nigger didn't have half the heart Braddock had." I was for Louis—he was such a lethal presence in the ring, stalking his opponents like a big cat ("It's only a matter of time," as fight announcer Sam Taub would tell us), and outside it he was so quiet and modest ("a credit to his race," as Harry Balogh, the ring announcer, would say when he introduced the fighters). Also I was already an avid reader of the *New York World-Telegram*'s sports section, where Lester Bromberg, "the dean of the boxing writers," had decided that the Brown Bomber had too much firepower for the slow-moving champ. So, nervous but eager to contribute the savvy opinion, I gave them mine and Lester Bromberg's.

As they say in boxing, it was like walking into a buzz saw. The suddenly incredulous and contemptuous faces turned to me; then came one remark after another like a series of slaps. Jim Ward's "A voice from the peanut gallery" was the kindest one. "You're saying you're for a nigger against a white man?" "That's because he's a Jew-boy." "They're all nigger-lovers. "Yeah, him and his Lester Bromberg." "Yeah, what do sheenies know about fighting?" "All they know is . . . ," followed by a smirk and a thumb rubbing the next two fingers.

I slunk away, one of the rock-bottom moments of my boyhood. I stayed off the playground for several days, which for me was like Huck Finn staying away from the river. Along with the humiliation I had a lot to wonder and brood about. Two years before, I had been in Sam Felber's candy store, where the few Jewish men in the neighborhood would drop in on their way home or on Sunday mornings to buy cigars, pick up the newspaper reserved for them, sip an egg cream, and schmooze with Sam. That day a dark impressive man had been sitting at the soda fountain as I was making my penny-candy run, and I could tell that he and Sam were talking about me. "I hear you're a Jewish boy," he said. Then he asked me questions about what made me Jewish besides my parents being so and why anyone would want to be, what were Jews good for. I didn't have any good answers but I knew when I was being baited, and so I said, "I'm a Jew and proud of it. So you can just shut up." This became a big item in the family, because the man was Judge Henry Waldman, probably the most distinguished Jew in Elizabeth. He had told the story around town and it had gotten back to my father, who, for a change, seemed pleased with me.

But I hadn't told the St. Genevieve guys to shut up. I didn't want to get into a fight with any of them, because the Irish were in another league when it came to fighting, but it was more than that. In the two or three years since I had snapped back at Judge Waldman, I had lost my pride about being Jewish. Instead of being the part of me that made me feel like a Weiss, it was now the part that made me feel depressed to be a Solotaroff.

What most troubled me was Billy Herlihy's gesture of rubbing his thumb against his fingers. That wasn't like having to deal with the accusation that the Jews had killed Christ, which was way in the past and you could say the Romans had done it. But the idea that many Jews cared only about money was hard for me to deny. It was even in many of the jokes Jews told. The Weisses didn't care that much. I mean, Uncle Jack cared and Aunt Belle cared, but money wasn't the only thing they cared about, because Jack was said to be a very good husband and father and Belle cared about the whole family and was always there when they needed help. Most of the family cared about the stock market, but that was different, that was gambling, sporty and American, a foot in the Gentile world of Wall Street and the big corporations. That wasn't what Billy Herlihy meant or what was really Jewish in my nine-year-old mind.

What was really Jewish was the Solotaroffs' obsession with money. It was my grandmother Solotaroff always wanting to know what my mother paid for something, whether a chicken or shoes or a train ticket, and telling her what she herself had paid, which was always less. Why pay $1.10 to take the Pennsylvania Railroad to New York when you could take the Jersey Central and save thirty cents (it also took almost an hour more because you had to cross the Hudson by ferry). To Mrs. S., as my mother called her, the world was a vast version of the basement of Klein's, New York's cheapest department store—bargains everywhere if you knew how to look. That my mother didn't was about the only thing that Dad, his mother, and his sister Sophie agreed on. He, too, was just like them. When he bought himself a good suit or an expensive tie the first thing he'd tell anyone was how little he'd paid for it. Some Gentiles were penny pinchers too, but they didn't talk so much about it.

What I hated even more was that his practice of giving Mom only a dollar a day for "household expenses" was such a handicap and humiliation. It put us on a kind of Home Relief in which he was the government. He paid the monthly bills and did the big food shopping. Any incidental benefits such as for clothing, transportation, or entertainment had to be appealed for. Or stolen. When Sandy began to take piano lessons, Mom every week would have to extract the two dollars from his wallet while he was sleeping. On Saturdays when I would have to stay in The Shop, I would tear up the invoice for at least one piece of glass I had sold and pocket the dollar and change as the "allowance" I'd never been given.

Worst of all was the terror bred by money. We never knew when Dad would explode over a window left open during the heating season or a hole in my shoe sole from "all that running and jumping *you* have to do," or the Friday chicken Mom could have gotten cheaper if she'd gone to the market later in the afternoon. Every week there was bound to be one prolonged "scene" over how was he going to meet a payroll when he had a wife who had never learned the value of a dollar and kids who thought he was made of money, while Mom implored him to "at least close the window, Ben . . . the neighbors."

Every spring a particularly black mood would come over him. He would stop giving Mom any money at all until finally she would say that he was no husband or father, that this was not a life, that she was taking the children to her sisters in New York, and he would shout, "Good. I can't wait to wind this up." Then there would be a day or two of stark silence between them—Mom weeping or talking to her sisters or both, he staring coldly all through dinner, as though wondering what we were still doing there, Sandy and I and later Bobby (who came along when I was eight) bent over our food as though we didn't deserve to eat it. At bedtime I would try to reassure them that the storm would blow over, that it was just Dad's spring fit again. Then I'd lie awake for hours, hoping to hear the quiet conversation begin downstairs that meant there would be no divorce (as shameful as being evicted), and I wouldn't have to leave Shelly Avenue playground.

About four years after we came to live on Keats Avenue, Dad was laid up for a week by a cut from a piece of plate glass that had fallen on his foot. The cut had become infected. He wanted to rest it on a board while he soaked it in hot water and Epsom salts, but he couldn't find one small enough to fit across the basin. So when I came home from school to change clothes he told me to go to one of the neighbors to borrow a saw.

In a hurry to get back to the school playground for a softball game, I went three houses down to the Hinkels'. I knew that Mr. Hinkel was home because he had lost his job as a foreman at General Aniline and was repairing people's appliances and cars in his garage. So he was sure to have a saw. On the other hand, he didn't like me. He was a rugged blond man with the hard blue eyes of a cop and he had a way of slightly shaking his head when he looked at me as though he had my number. His daughter Helen was in my class; she was tall and pretty and the fastest runner our age on the block as well as the girl who got the most valentines. Sometimes we walked home from school together and talked seriously. She'd told me I was nice when I wasn't showing off. So when she came to the door and took me back to the garage, I relaxed a little and asked Mr. Hinkel as politely as I could.

"What do you want it for?"

I said that my father needed it to saw a board. "He has to soak his foot a lot."

"Well, you tell that loud-mouthed old man of yours that I wouldn't give him the sweat off my balls. Tell him he don't belong in a decent neighborhood. Tell him to go back to Jew-land so we can have some peace and quiet around here."

I was as humiliated by Helen's pitying look as I was shocked by her father's words. I hadn't realized that the neighbors did actually hear what went on in our house, that my mother's concern about them was more than another of her futile ways of controlling my father's rampages. In my nine-year-old mind the drama of my parents' fights, his terrible threat "to wind it up right now," was so upsetting that anything outside it at the moment hardly existed. But now I knew this wasn't so, that the neighbors as well as the walls (we children) had ears, and I walked away in a daze of shame.

I tried Mrs. Elsesser, our next-door neighbor, who said her husband didn't like her to lend out his tools and told me to come back after supper. Mrs. Palumbo, on the other side, said she didn't have a saw.

I went home and told my father that no one would lend us a saw.

"What do you mean, no one would lend you a saw? Who'd you ask?"

I told him. I didn't tell him what Mr. Hinkel had said.

"You went to three houses and that's it? That's all the houses in the neighborhood?"

I shook my head and then stood there in the hot glare of his scrutiny.

"It embarrasses you to ask? Is that what you're saying?"

"Sort of."

"Your father is in pain, he has men standing around at The Shop and you're too embarrassed to help him. Is that it? Are you too embarrassed to eat? Are you too embarrassed to wear the clothes I buy you?"

"People don't like us in the neighborhood," I said, coming as close to the truth as I dared. "I think it's because we're Jewish."

"Is that so. I've never seen any sign of that. Now you go and borrow a saw and don't come home until you do."

I tried several other houses, to no avail. It was as though saws had become as precious on Keats Avenue as the family car. I thought about asking people who lived too far away to hear Dad's scenes and know about the divorce talk, but then they wouldn't know who I was. Meanwhile the guys were probably choosing up sides by now on the Shelley Avenue playground, and so I ran there, thinking that I would have a better chance asking one of the kids who lived near the school. Then I could get the saw between innings and run home with it. But in the intensity of the game I forgot about my errand. I wasn't my mother's son for nothing, and by the time I remembered it again, the game was almost over. All too soon I was walking home by myself, walking toward his belt, already hearing his voice saying, "Here's something you won't forget."

I grew up in two different households that formed around my mother's passivity and father's imperiousness—the one with hardly any boundaries, the other almost all boundary. As in his life generally, Dad drove fast and braked hard, so we always knew when he arrived in the evening from the automotive anthem of engine rumble, brake squeal, and slammed car door. I imagine, though, we would have known he was home if he had floated down by parachute, so alert, wary, and fine-tuned were we (including Bobby by the time he could talk) to Dad's arrival and his mood, on which the next hour or two of our home life would depend.

Most of the time he would arrive like a boxer returning to his corner at the end of the fourteenth round, only to be sorely hampered by the incompetence and blitheness of his crew. My mother's problem was that he expected dinner to be on the table by the time he washed up, but there was no telling when that would be. Though he phoned when he left The Shop, he would usually make a stop or two, and after work he seldom met a conversation he didn't prolong. So, he often found that the meal was "cooked to death." Then, unless he fell asleep on the couch, he was off again, often to the drug store of a friend, Lou Holtz, who stayed open until ten and "happens to be one of the few people in Elizabeth I can have a decent conversation with."

The only sustained time he spent with us was on our occasional Sunday-afternoon excursions. After he got back from the Y he was usually in a good mood. If he was in a really good mood, he'd bring back a coffee cake with roasted pecans on top or an almond ring. Then he'd often send us out while he and Mom "took a nap." In the afternoon, if it was nice out, we'd get in the car and go on an excursion to Watchung Reservation or some other park or, in hot weather, to Lake Hopatcong or Budd Lake. He'd be like a different person, relaxed and pleasant and one of us. He'd even join us in our car games.

The good time would usually last through Sunday-night supper—kosher specials, with mustard that came in twists of glazed paper, Heinz vegetarian baked beans, potato salad, and coleslaw. Then Dad would often send me out to the drugstore for a quart of hand-packed Breyer's ice cream, and Mom would pass the plates of it around as we settled down like a normal family in front of the big Atwater Kent radio for the Sunday-night comedy shows. When we laughed too loud, Dad would say, "Quiet, vipers," but that was part of the evening fun.

Food was another positive link that connected him to us. He did the big shopping in bulk, buying oranges or grapefruit by the crate, potatoes by the twenty-five-pound sack, canned soup and toilet paper by the carton, loafs of American cheese and two-foot salamis. Two or three times a month on Saturday night, after he had closed The Shop, he and I would drive to the Big Bear, the first supermarket in the area, and fill up two or three shopping carts—all manner of staples and produce, meats and delicatessen, and sometimes even an extravagance or two, a basket of persimmons, a block of halvah, a chunk of smoked sturgeon. When we got home he'd say, using his affectionate name for me, "Teedle, bring all that stuff in the house," and I would go to work on the big brown bags piled in two tiers in the back, and then the crates and cartons in the trunk, while he would horse around with my mother, showing off the quality of his choices, the bargain prices he had paid, the benevolence he was bestowing.

However, the refrigerator and food closet would often be bare before his next shopping, and Mom would be hard put to piece out our meals on the dollar dole, for he always expected meat or fish for dinner. Like time, food was money, his money, hence it was also a source of prerogative and control. The cream at the top of the bottle of milk was skimmed for his coffee. He would take the tender part of the steak, the breast of the chicken, and then push the platter over to Mom to cut up what was left. "Eat bread, kids," he'd say. "Don't fill up on meat."

When I was ten or so, I came home ravenous from the playground and found a cold chicken leg and thigh in the refrigerator. I tore off a delicious piece and then another, until there was nothing to do but finish it and dispose of the evidence, hoping that my mother would forget it had been there. Which might have happened, except that the leg had been put aside for Dad's dinner. He arrived home, the discovery was made, the investigation opened, the chief suspect called into the kitchen. I put on my innocent face and waited for him to try to break me down. But he didn't. Instead he put his arm around me and said in his gentle voice, "I don't care about the chicken, I just want you always to be truthful with me." So like a little George Washington I began my confession. He removed his arm and suddenly slapped me with all his force, sent me reeling, and shouted, "If you ever steal food in this house again, I'm going to break your spirit for good."

Some of the lights I saw then were never to go out. I didn't stop loving him when he was in his good mood or hoping to please him or trying to understand him. A child of a domineering father doesn't have much choice in these matters. But I was shocked into a different attitude toward him. Up until then I had viewed him as a sort of grim, intimidating natural force, somewhat as primitive people viewed their storm god, a presence who had to be deferred to and placated and obeyed, even though it didn't do any good when the dark clouds gathered and the wind began to howl. That was the way the world was. Just so was our family. There were nicer men, like my uncles Gil and Mickey, Leah's new husband, but they weren't my father, they didn't have his headaches and pressures and responsibilities. They didn't have to meet a payroll every Friday. They weren't aggravated to death six days a week. I went on believing that. But I also began to believe that my father was not just singularly harassed and moody and terrible-tempered but that for some reason I didn't understand, he was out to get me, would even "break my spirit," and from now on I had to protect it against him.

Which was hard to do. One Saturday afternoon in December while I was by myself at The Shop and poking around in the plate glass racks, I discovered a cache of presents—an unassembled boy's bike, a football, a doll's house, a Monopoly game. We didn't celebrate Hanukkah at home and usually didn't have much in the way of Yuletide joy. Whether we would get Christmas presents was an anxious, last-minute thing; that is, it depended on whether Mom would prevail upon Dad to go shopping on Christmas Eve. Even when she did talk him into it, the present was usually an article of clothing, except for one year when he bought me a Philadelphia Flyer sled and Sandy an expensive doll, so carried away by his largesse that he woke her up to give it to her.

But now here in its carton that I couldn't prevent myself from opening was a blue-and-white Columbia two-wheeler with balloon tires, the present I wanted more than any other, being the only kid my age on the block without a bike. I took out the frame, the handlebars, the tires, even the oily chain. Then I put them back and tried to press the staples on the top into place. My cup was running over. That Dad had actually planned this for me, probably all by himself— it was as though my family had suddenly turned a corner and headed in the direction of the other families on Keats Avenue, as though my sister and little brother and I would now be like other kids, our home life a happy one. Mom was wrong, the leopard was changing his spots right before my eyes.

The following Monday, Dad came home from The Shop in a fury. Had I been messing around with a box that had a bicycle in it, a box that was none of my business? My high hopes came down with a crash, my joy replaced by a familiar feeling of misery, the misery of the *schlemiel*, the screw-up, he reduced me to by his glare. Then he was on me, hands flailing. My mother wailed, "Not with your fists, Ben. For God's sake, not with your fists." Overwhelmed, I went down to the floor for mercy, but he continued to pummel my shoulders and back as he shouted, "I don't have enough with that sneering son-of-a-bitch anti-Semite. You have to give him a stick to hit me with. My own good-for-nothing son. You didn't know it was Frank's? Well, now you know, now you'll know to keep your clumsy hands off things that don't belong to you." The hard blows rained down until my mother finally flung herself over me.

It was the worst beating he was to give me—real bruises that hurt for days. My mother wouldn't speak to him, slept on the living-room couch, and went about the house with a new resolute look. To see her so firm and angry with him, so tender with me, was almost worth the beating. When I told her about finding the presents and thinking they were Dad's, that too moved her. She said that Frank Weisskopf was a thorn in my father's side but that was no excuse for behaving like a wild beast.

From being at The Shop, I knew that Frank Weisskopf derided my father, called him Benny instead of Boss, but that Dad couldn't let him go because of the union. Also Frank was a crackerjack glazier who he could put on a job and know the work would be done right. What I hadn't known was that Frank Weisskopf was an anti-Semite. Because his name was similar to that of my mother's family and because his grizzled face was as dark and his hair as curly as my father's and mine, I had assumed he was Jewish too. Instead, he was an anti-Semite. In 1938 anti-Semitism was turning black with a red armband and swastika, a fierce salute and heel click. An anti-Semite was the worst thing a person could be. And I could even understand why my father would be so angry if I'd given Frank the chance to come at him, since I knew what it was to have a Gentile giving you that special sneer.

Yet if Frank was as bad as the Nazis, he was also a good father who saved up on a worker's pay to bring happiness to his children, a happiness I had experienced for a weekend when I thought the Christmas presents were my father's. Maybe, then, Frank wasn't a real anti-Semite but someone like Mr. Hinkel who didn't like my father and blamed the Jews for him. In any case, I envied his children, as I did Helen, because they had a father who really cared about them and even in the Depression tried to give them a normal life.

5 I AM SIX years old, toward the end of the first grade, and am catcher for the Blue team in one of the Field Day softball games. The other boys are all second-graders; catcher is sort of a non-position, you just throw the ball back to the pitcher, and if there is a play at home the pitcher takes over. But in the last inning with us one run ahead, the pitcher fields a grounder and throws it home. The ball comes whizzing at me on my left, my awkward side. I somehow make the cross-handed catch, the first one in my life, tag the runner out, and we win. The older boys crowd around me. I feel a rush of body pride, a sense of the heroic. I've made a big play and am hooked on athletic prowess for life.

By the time I was ten the Shelley Avenue playground was my true home in the way that The Shop was my father's. It was where I took the skills that were most important to me as well as my passion, determination, and imagination, and freely enacted them. On the playground I was my own person, not my mother's exalted little ally or my father's incompetent loafer.

Once spring settled in, I played two softball games a day, one after school and then back again after supper, when some of the fathers and older kids came out to play. The level of the game would rise, and instead of being the captain or else the first or second chosen, I was just glad to play, a rookie on his way up the ladder.

The evening game started around seven-fifteen which was when Dad came home. If he wasn't there by seven I could usually wheedle my mother into letting me eat early, but otherwise it was an agony. Eating was the one thing in the house Dad did slowly, delib-

erately, and there was no getting up from the table until he was finished with the main course. Nor was I allowed to show any impatience—though of course I did. My mother would intervene. "Ben,
he's jumping out of his skin, let him go." And depending on his
mood, he would say something like "He can learn some manners
for a change," or "All right, go. Go play with your ball. Learn some
more how to be a bum."

One evening I looked around from my intent fielding stance to see
my father, of all people, wearing his nice-guy smile as he stood on the
sideline, looking to play. It got even weirder when they put him into
the game. "Play short," one of the fathers said. I could see that Dad
didn't even know what he meant. I was on the other team, so I could-
n't run over and position him.

If only they had put him in right field. The first grounder went past
him while he was still bending down. All the envy I had for the boys
whose fathers put on a glove and played catch with them turned
upside down and became acute embarrassment. Dad couldn't do
anything right. At bat he had no timing and he chopped down at the
ball. Worse yet, he threw like a girl. Also he kept calling out dumb
things he thought ballplayers still said, like "Slide, Kelly, slide."

But the ball field, as it often did, was to stand me in good stead.
Until then, I'd taken my father's physical dominance for granted, just
as I had his dominion. That evening on the ball field he was stripped
of his aura as "the lord of the manor" (my mother's phrase) at home
and The Boss at The Shop, and became a fat, foolish, slow guy who
couldn't field or hit or talk baseball talk; the sort of person I would
have scorned if he were a kid. It was too physically dangerous and
emotionally dissonant for me to scorn him, but having seen his feet
of clay in this situation, I was able to take one of my first steps away
from living at his knees.

Around this time, I began to develop a fantasy that my real father was
Lou Gehrig—the peerlessly modest, well-spoken, stalwart first baseman of the New York Yankees. I played first base in a right-handed
version of his stance, my knees slightly bent, my mitt held open and
low, and even smiled slightly as he did in the photograph I had pasted
to the wall of my bedroom. At the plate, I cocked the bat high and

back, tucked my chin into my shoulder, angled my front foot slightly toward the pitcher in what I took to be his stance. For a few days I even tried to turn myself around and bat left-handed as he did, but I couldn't develop any power or timing and stopped when he told me in one of our conversations that I should wait until I was older.

The following year, my attachment to him was even stronger. For he was no longer hitting his massive home runs, dependably fielding his position, and extending his phenomenal record of consecutive games played. Instead he was fighting a paralyzing disease, one that was so rare and devastating that it seemed to have been reserved for the man called the Iron Horse.

I was eleven that summer, the age at which a boy feels that he has two bodies: the child's one he still mostly inhabits, that can throw and hit only so far, run only so fast, coordinate hand and eye only so much; and an idealized one he is beginning to grow into, hints of which appear in those charmed times when he is "on" and he out-performs himself. The images of these two bodies stay in touch by means of certain studied movements and mannerisms that we called "form"—the first baseman's stretch, the shortstop's throw on the run, the batter's complete follow-through, the baserunner's hook slide. The boys who had too much of it, whose style often exceeded their performance, were called "Joe Form." I was one of them.

That summer I tried to make my form more like Gehrig's, less flashy and "big-time," more sturdy and consistent. I also tried to emulate his renowned positive spirit that was being tested by his disease. When I lost out at first base on the summer playground team and was put in left field, Gehrig and I told me to stop bellyaching and play the position. Our team made it to the district finals, and my steady fielding took me from left field to short field to third base. In our final game I handled all but one of the chances hit my way, and I heard one of the older spectators say, "That kid at third just makes the plays"—high praise for someone fighting the nervous showoff in himself.

Why did Gehrig become my hero rather than, say. Hank Greenberg, who was also a first baseman, a power hitter, one of the aristocrats of the game—and Jewish to boot? Proximity had something to do with it: Gehrig was in nearby New York, Greenberg in remote

Detroit. Also Gehrig was a college graduate—rare at that time for a baseball player—and of Columbia no less, the bailiwick of my autumn hero, the quarterback Sid Luckman. That Gehrig was the son of immigrants and yet Christian also made him compelling. Like President Roosevelt he didn't entirely belong to "their" world and served as a mediating figure in the uncertain part of my identity that lay between being American and being Jewish.

But mostly it was Gehrig's character that got to me. He was the spirit of the ball field and of its values such as team play, fairness, consistency, that were taken for granted there and emulated and that I was otherwise growing up at home without—indeed with their opposites. It is little wonder that sports in general and baseball in particular displaced home and school as the center of my life.

In a dream many years later, I came upon myself as a boy, sitting on the back steps of our house on Shelley Avenue. It is night; I have come back from the evening game but I am still wearing my first baseman's mitt and gently socking a softball into its pocket. "Short to second to first," I hear the boy who was me saying. "Second to short to first. First to short and back to first. There's nothing as beautiful as a double play."

6 CREAM RIDGE WAS lost in 1934 because the family couldn't meet the $140-a-month building loan. Two pieces of the yellow wicker porch furniture came to us, a touch of brightness in the household, a spot of warmth in my heart. The couch and chair made me feel that we came from somewhere besides Elizabeth, the territory of the Solotaroffs, which the Weisses seldom visited.

Every few months, Mrs. S., my only living grandparent, blew into our lives from nearby Linden, less a guest than an occupying force, roaming through the rooms picking up this, poking into that, inspecting for laxity and extravagance. Mom was nice to her, as she was to everyone, but the visits left her muttering about the overbearing Solotaroffs. So too with Dad's sister Sophie, who would come from

New York to see her sister Marion and stop by at our house. A small, pretty women with wild, wild eyes and the personality of a threatened cat, she would give my gifted young sister a kind of master's piano lesson and all of us a hard time as a more vitriolic version of her mother.

The Solotaroffs who haunted me most were the ones I didn't see. Marion and her family lived only ten blocks from us, but she and my father were not speaking, as they had not been since she and her husband had driven Dad out of the family glass business. Marion had two sons, some years older than I. Eugene was said to be in and out of insane asylums; the younger son, Sidney, was a top-flight cross-country and middle-distance runner whose exploits at Jefferson High I would follow closely in the sports pages of the *Elizabeth Daily Journal*. That I had one cousin who was crazy and another who was a star athlete living close by, as well as an aunt Marion and an uncle Kibey, none of whom I had ever seen, was part of the dark dizziness that lurked in the corners of my mind when I thought of being a Solotaroff.

Which I did a lot in those years of the middle thirties when the Weisses were dispersed in Manhattan, Brooklyn, the Bronx, and Lakewood, and struggling to find new livelihoods. Their remoteness from us was such that the deaths of my two grandparents on that side barely registered on me. But there was the shining interval around 1937 when Uncle Mush, now Gil to everyone, came to live with us on Keats Avenue and work for my father. That this should come to pass was another indication of the desperation of the times.

Gil was no longer the Mr. Everything he had been at the hotel and farm. He had tried various schemes to save the property, including renting it out to bootleggers during the off-season and planting acres of string beans in August in the hope he could get a premium price for them. But the state troopers had discovered the still, and the first frost the beans. After the property was gone he drifted here and there, hoping for an acting career, waiting for something to turn up. He and my father couldn't have been less alike—the go-getter and the easy-goer, Jonas Chuzzlewit hires Mr. Micawber.

As Gil put it, "Ben is paying me fifteen dollars a week and all the glass I can eat." Dad's reason was that he could pay Gil below the union scale because he was family; that his brother-in-law, who was "mechanically inclined," would learn the glazier's trade; and "at the proper time" (one of Dad's favorite expressions, used to keep us dangling), Gil would become the foreman of his storefront crew. This was not how Gil saw his future, which was bathed in footlights rather than by the naked bulb hanging over the cutting table at the Standard Plate Glass Co. As the difference in their intentions revealed itself, Gil took to working off his boredom by sharpening his comic skills and entertaining Frank Weisskopf and the apprentice Zeke. His most famous stunt was to climb one of the twenty-foot-high plate glass racks and swing to the next one in what he called his "Tarzan in the glass business routine."

One Saturday when I was at The Shop, Gil took my father's overcoat and hung it from the top of the rack. Dad was in the midst of the one-man relay race that was his day, and his frustration at not finding his coat so that he could "run out" to wherever he had to be was so severe that I felt sorry for him. When Gil pointed to where his coat was, Dad shouted, "I told you I never wanted to see you climbing that rack."

Gil said, "I heard you. I did it when you weren't looking."

"Well, get the fucking coat down."

"You just told me again you didn't want to see me climbing."

"You get my coat down right now or you're through here."

And so it went, the beset king and jester. It only lasted several months, but during this time that Gil lived with us on Keats Avenue, it was almost like being in a different family. At the dinner table he drove the usual strain right out of the room by his wisecracks and his stories about The Shop and Cream Ridge. My mother looked younger and freer, laughing at and joining in his stories. Sometimes even my father would get into the act, though the next night he'd sit there glaring, an outsider at his own table, and mutter, "very funny," at Gil's antics, finish the meal quickly, and go back downtown. "You coming?" he'd snap at Gil, whom he would drop off at the Maskers, the semiprofessional theater group he had joined at the YMHA. As M. Gilbert Weiss, he soon was playing starring roles in popular plays of the day, his performances praised in the *Elizabeth Daily Journal* and the *Newark Star-Ledger*.

Sometimes when Gil came home from The Shop, he and I would go out on Keats Avenue in the autumn dusk. Though he'd played tackle in high school, he had an "arm," and he'd send me out for bullet passes and long, floating ones that I would race under and try to catch over my shoulder. He told me I had very good hands for a nine-year-old and my confidence soared, so that I was making catches in our touch game in the schoolyard and our neighborhood tackle games over on Byron Avenue on Saturday morning that I would have been lucky to hold on to before. He made me feel inches taller, two steps faster, harder to tackle. "That's my boy," he'd say when I told him of my touchdowns. I was a Weiss boy again.

After Gil stopped working for Dad, he lived for a time elsewhere in Elizabeth, drove a laundry truck, and continued to act and direct with the Maskers. One evening he called and asked to speak to me. He said that he was in a play and they needed someone to play a boy about my age.

The next week I went with him to the Y and tried out for the part. It was a small one, but the read-through was transforming. I felt as I had when I walked to Broad Street by myself. I was taking a giant step into the world of adults and of serious theater. A few of the actors and actresses sat in chairs on the bare stage, and as they read through a scene, the others would listen and the director or someone else would ask a question or make a suggestion. I was seeing real stage acting for the first time—someone turning himself or herself completely into someone else, making that new person come alive before my eyes.

I started to read my lines with "expression," as we did in school plays but the director stopped me and said, "Don't try to act, Teddy. Just be natural." So I did, and he and the striking young woman who was playing my mother said I was doing fine, and by the end of the evening I had become part of the cast.

It thrilled Mom that I was in a play with Gil and the renowned Maskers. During the next week we read the play together, she playing the mother and the other characters in my few scenes, helping me to memorize and express my lines naturally and accurately. Whenever we were this close before, she was in one of her sad moods or I was sick. Those evenings of sitting at the dining-room table and reading with me were a new kind of bonding. They brought her out, as though I had suddenly been given a more focused and clever mother, while I was a more mature boy than the one so madly caught up in sports and resentful toward her whenever anything at home got in their way. Instead I was giving her the same kind of joy that she got from listening to Sandy's playing.

When Gil and Fay, the young woman who was playing my mother, dropped me off after the second rehearsal, my father had already gotten home from his evening rounds. He was furious when he jerked the door open. "I'll speak to you tomorrow," he said to Gil, almost slamming the door on him and Fay. Mom was sitting in the living room; she had her beaten expression and my father his hate look, so I knew there had been another fight. "Do you always have to be so rude?" she said.

"That's all you ever think about. You and your fucking manners. Rude? I'll show you rude." He picked up a small, transparent blue swan from the piano and threw it against the wall. "That's rude. You want to see more rude?"

She stiffened but said nothing. When he got his way, she withdrew even more, as though silence were her only recourse, numbness her only defense. "As for you," he said to me, "you can forget about this crazy play business. I'm not going to have any ten-year-old running around Elizabeth at all hours the night. I can't even get you up in the morning as it is."

"I'm eleven now," I said, wanting to say something, wanting to hold on to this new joy in my life, though I knew it was as shattered as the glass swan.

"You want it too?!" he shouted, raising his hand. "Any more of your back talk and I'll smack *you* against the wall. Now get up to bed where you should have been two hours ago."

"It's only an hour past my normal bedtime," I said, my despair making me brave.

"And what about your homework? When were you planning to do that?"

This made no sense at all. He was hardly ever home in the evenings, much less involved in my schoolwork. He didn't even look at my report card except for the behavior marks. "I did it before I went," I said.

"When did you do it? During your basketball after school? While you were listening to your radio programs? You think life is a big bowl of cherries, don't you? Well, I'll tell you something. You're going to suffer. Someone with your character is going to suffer and suffer."

That was one of the things he'd say to me, part of his fault-finding litany. "I'm already suffering," I said. "You're making me, for no good reason."

He shifted to his slow, patient, aggrieved tone. "Did it ever occur to you to ask permission from me to be in this play?" He turned to Mom. "Did it ever occur to you that I might have some thoughts on the subject?" The question was rhetorical, as were almost all of his questions. "I'll tell you why you didn't," he said to me. "Why should you when you've got a mother who'll say yes to anything you ask for, who you've got wrapped around your little finger? Now get upstairs and get to bed so that you can get up for school. The subject is closed." After I had reached the top of the stairs, I heard him say to Mom, "You can tell your brother that I'm not raising a son to be a theater bum like him."

I learned from Gil that he'd told my father they would schedule the rehearsals so that my scenes would come first, that he'd see that I got home at a reasonable hour. But my father wouldn't even listen to him. "You've got a hard old man, Teddy," Gil said. He looked straight at me, sharing an understanding, making it stick. "Don't let him get you down."

7   AT THE BEGINNING of the sixth grade, the final one at the Shelley Avenue school, Ned Sprague appeared in our midst, all the way from Lincoln, Illinois. God had been lavish with Ned: he was smart, handsome, and a powerful, graceful athlete. As self-possessed and sensible as I was high-strung and grandiose, Ned let the world come to him and say hello, and within a few days we were all competing to be his friend.

For me, Ned had an additional glow: he was the nice Gentile, the wholesome paragon of the American heartland that my favorite author, John R. Tunis, had created in Jim Wellington from Waterloo, Iowa, who makes his earnest, democratic way through the elitism he encounters at Harvard. Jim has a sidekick, Mickey McGuire, a plebeian quarterback with the right stuff from Boston, who teams up with him to set the stuffed-shirt cliques on their ear. *The Iron Duke* and its sequel were the 1930s' answer to the Frank Merriwell novels.

Along with his prowess, Ned had the Tunis virtues of modesty and poise. On our six-man touch football team that represented the school, he was content to play end, though he threw a football ten yards farther and more accurately than I, the quarterback, did and was faster and shiftier than our running back. Our relationship began as a passing combination. Ned caught virtually anything that came his way, and this helped to steady my arm and aim in the games with other schools, I became the Cecil Isbell to his Don Hutson of the Elmora elementary school league, scoring touchdown after touchdown like our Green Bay Packer counterparts. Not Sammy Baugh and Don Looney of the Philadelphia Eagles or, closer to home, Eddie Danowski and Jim Lee Howell of the New York Giants, for I was doing the casting and the spell of the Middle West had descended upon me.

Until then I had rooted for Columbia in its struggle each year in the otherwise ultra-Gentile Ivy League. (We didn't have the term WASP yet and had to make do with "Gentile" for the pale, upper half of Christendom and "goy" for the dark, lower one.) Columbia's quarterback was Jewish, the great Sid Luckman. Also it was on the Upper West Side of Manhattan, where my aunts Belle and Fan lived, and hence, like Schrafft's Eighty-Sixth Street, was Jewish by association. The idea of a Jewish quarterback at Harvard was hardly plausible; at Yale and Princeton (me or even Sid Luckman calling the signals for Clint Frank or Hobey Baker?) virtually unimaginable. Yet for all the personal fit and gain of rooting for Columbia, it remained an embarrassment in my neighborhood, where the guys from St. Genevieve and the "Fighting Irish" of Notre Dame formed a seamless predomination. To my mind, which was the stadium in which all of these ethnic implications were playing, I needed a stronger team to represent me, one that could stand up to Notre Dame. So for a few weeks I joined Ned and rooted for Navy, which was a football powerhouse back then that played Notre Dame every year. But knowing that I had as much chance of going to Annapolis as to Princeton, my new loyalty was somewhat vicarious and halfhearted.

One Saturday afternoon that fall, grounded by my chronic bronchitis, I tuned in Bill Stern's broadcast of a Michigan game. Bill Stern was a cross between Grantland Rice and Walter Winchell, combining the dramatic details and imagery of the former ("the Galloping Ghost" and "the Four Horsemen" were but two of Rice's coinages) with the melodrama of the latter, America's Town Crier. Stern gave his college football broadcasts an epic spin — "And here on a golden Ann Arbor afternoon, before a crowd of ninety-eight thousand partisan fans, the two greatest halfbacks in the game, Niles Kinnick and Tommy Harmon, will duel for the supremacy of the Big Ten." Tommy Harmon came from Gary, Indiana, which seemed a lot like Elizabeth. Also Benny Friedman, the other famous Jewish quarterback, had played for Michigan. That afternoon the Michigan Wolverines became my team. I lay in bed drinking hot tea with lemon and honey, my chest tingling with Vicks Vapor-Rub, and made up my own lyrics to the ringing Michigan fight song:

> Hail to ye fields and forests
> Loudly proclaiming weather,
> Hail, hail, oh hail, oh hail,
> The man from Michigan.

Which I continued to sing to myself, year after year. My seemingly idiotic version came from the heart. Even more than Ned Sprague's Illinois, Mark Twain's Missouri, Booth Tarkington's Indiana, Michigan loomed in my imagination, its pioneer roots clinging to its name, taking its central place in the America that rolled westward through the amber waves of grain and the fruited plains that we sang about in school assembly. Perhaps for every American farm kid dreaming of the Great White Way of New York, there was a New York or New Jersey kid like myself dreaming of the fair fields and forests and intense weather of the American heartland.

In the years that followed, the Middle West became the cynosure of my imagination of American life. By the time I was twelve I was reading my way to Sauk Center, Minnesota, and Niles, Michigan, and Winesburg, Ohio, as well as Hannibal, Missouri—hungry for information and otherness. From the crisp social fiction of Sinclair Lewis to the aching moral tales of Sherwood Anderson, from the sentimental idylls of Booth Tarkington to the stunning satires of Ring Lardner, from the Chicago of Bigger Thomas to that of Studs Lonigan and Upton Sinclair, the teachings of Nick Adams to those of Nick Carroway—I read on and on into the society of the Middle West. From the wide literary coverage and the vividness, variety, and glamour of its authors, it became what was most American for me about America.

Ned's father was an unruffled sales manager for a candy manufacturer and allowed him an unlimited supply of the firm's candy bars. For this reason and others, I contrived to moor our friendship at his house, and we would often end up there after school and on weekends, where we would work on our pass plays. Ned lived on Coolidge Road in a handsomely furnished, spic-and-span Colonial that seemed to me the height of Gentile style. His room was furnished in a nautical way with a captain's bed and chest and with a banner and pennant on the wall from Annapolis, to which he hoped to win an appointment. Hanging out with him on his bed, reading comic books or listening to *I Love a Mystery* on Ned's own radio, I felt wafted out of my life and taken into one that I had only read about in books like *The Iron Duke* or seen in movies like the Andy Hardy ones. Several of my schoolmates lived in expensive houses with bars and Ping-Pong tables in their pine-paneled "finished basements," and one of their fathers even had a "library," but that wasn't the same as the spare refinement of the Sprague house, where each piece of furniture, like each of the three people living there, seemed to exist in its own calm, confident space.

The spirit of its charmed atmosphere emanated from Ned's mother, a slender, fine-featured woman who looked more like a high-class actress such as Katharine Hepburn or Greer Garson than one of our mothers. She often wore a print scarf tucked into a blouse or a cashmere shawl, with the same casual stylishness as their home housed its furniture and ornaments and paintings. Several of the paintings were done by her, delicate still lifes or landscapes of farm country, most of them in watercolor.

I asked her if these were like the paints we used in school.

She said they were, more or less.

I was bowled over. "It's like Albert Einstein doing long division," I said. Then I realized that it was a dumb thing to say and said so.

"I think it's a very clever as well as flattering remark," she said. Then she said that she liked the way I talked, that I had an interesting imagination.

Her name was Grace, which was just right, too. She was the first mother I'd known who said I could call her by her first name if I wanted to, which I tried to do but couldn't.

The pleasure I had in being there was sometimes a tense one. My elation in quickly becoming Ned's best friend at school gave way in his house, particularly downstairs, to a sense of being out of my element. Just as his mother's beauty reminded me again of his handsomeness, in whose aura my nose became even uglier to me, my skin even swarthier, my hair even unrulier, my ears even bigger, so his home and mother made my own house, despite Mom's efforts to decorate it, seem more shabby and she more unkempt and awkward.

I dealt with this sense of inferiority, as I often did, by upward slanting, exaggeration, and lies. In the course of conversation with Mrs. Sprague, my father became an industrial glass contractor, my mother a classical pianist and the Elizabeth representative of the Metropolitan Opera Company, my sister a prodigy who had already performed at the Mosque Theater in Newark, my aunt Sophie a virtuoso who regularly gave concerts at Town Hall. Carried away, I cast my uncle Mickey, a cigar store clerk and voice student, in major performances of *Rigoletto* and *Pagliacci,* and sent my uncle Gil from the Maskers to the Broadway stage: a whole festival of the performing arts in one family. Mrs. Sprague listened to it all and then she said how much she would enjoy meeting my family, particularly my mother.

The previous year we had moved to a somewhat larger and nicer house on Shelley Avenue, but it didn't begin to stack up to the Spragues'. The thought of Grace Sprague making her way through our messy living room and of Mom in one of her torn housedresses, paint or wallpaper paste on her hands, making one of her out-of-nowhere remarks sent me plummeting from cloudland to earth. I'd so far managed to keep Ned away from our house, but how long could even that last? Mrs. Sprague said that she'd like to know about subscribing to the opera series in Newark. I said that I would tell my mother to call her and changed the subject as soon as I could.

I stayed away from the family cultural achievements after that, hoping that Mrs. Sprague would forget about her request. But when she said that she'd been hoping my mother would call her about the opera season, I had to deliver the message. I hung nervously on the edge of the phone conversation that followed, vastly relieved when my mother handled the details of the subscription plan (she was selling tickets for her Hadassah group) with efficiency and even aplomb. "I think you'll particularly like the *Carmen*. They're sending out . . ." as she mentioned two or three of the prominent members of the New York company.

I was pleased but not entirely relieved, since they ended up calling each other by first name. "Grace Sprague, seems like a lovely person," my mother said. "I'll bet she does something"—meaning something artistic.

"She's very busy," I said. "She paints all the time."

Of course, this doubled Mom's interest, and she pressed me about her style and subjects. "I'm glad you've made a friend who has such a talented and cultivated mother," she said. I heard her desire to be introduced to Mrs. Sprague dangling shyly in the wings.

"They're not like us," I said. "I mean, they're really Gentiles."

"Don't worry," she said, going from dim to bright in one of her flashes of wit. "I'm not going to invite her to a mah-jongg game."

We were not observant Jews, except in a loose dietary way. My mother bought kosher chickens, plucked but with the feet still on them, for our Friday-night meal. We did not eat bacon, ham, pork, or shellfish—known as *trayf*—or drink milk or use butter with meat. At Passover we duly changed from bread to matzoh, even though we seldom had a seder. That's as far as kosher went at home, and it left me with plenty of latitude outside it. Pastrami, corned beef, and rolled beef were always kosher; salami and hot dogs were kosher if you were in a Jewish home or neighborhood or at Ebbets Field; bologna was *trayf*, unless proven otherwise, so-called luncheon meat was really *trayf*. Though I had devised my own dietary laws, they were strict enough to keep me from buying a hot dog at Ruppert Stadium or having a malted with my salami sandwich. Like the local superstitions to Huck and Jim, those I believed were all the more formidable.

One evening Mrs. Sprague asked me if I would like to stay for dinner. My heart leapt up and then tumbled around in uncertainty.

She asked if something was the matter.

It was hard to get out, since it came with a thick tail of embarrassment. I had never felt more Jewish than at that moment. Or wished more that I wasn't. But there was no way around it, so I asked what they were having.

They were having Swiss steak. It could have been worse. It could have been pork chops or Virginia ham. I had no idea what Swiss steak was. If it was just plain sirloin (Dad sometimes brought one home), I could have managed but Swiss steak sounded as Gentile as the Swiss Family Robinson.

Mrs. Sprague waited with the expectant expression I seemed to elicit in her, somewhere between sympathy and amusement at what this strange boy would come up with next. I didn't want to bring kosher into it, didn't want to admit to that kind of difference, which seemed to me, in the Sprague home, so foreign as to be un-American. Which must have led directly to the excuse I came up with. I blurted out that my parents didn't like me to eat foreign food, so that I'd better say no. As soon as I'd said it, I felt my face burn with shame; I realizing that I was not only a transparent liar but also a disloyal Jew.

In her gracious way Mrs. Sprague said that perhaps I could stay another evening for dinner, and I got away as soon as I could. The shame continued to burn for a time and then cooled and hardened into the resolution never to hide being Jewish again. The next time Mrs. Sprague invited me for dinner I said that it would be better if I didn't have meat because of my religion, and she said she was planning tuna fish croquettes, which were no less exotic to me than Swiss steak and tasted wonderful in their cream sauce.

Friday afternoons Ned wasn't available because he went to dancing class at the Elmora Country Club. I didn't understand why he would go in for such a sissy sort of thing, and he set me straight by saying that a lot went on there that the dancing teacher didn't know about.

He said that if you knew how to dance you could get to feel a tit or even get a girl who didn't mind or even liked it if you had a boner. Did I want to try it? He could bring me as a guest who was seeing whether he wanted to join the class.

There was a lot to think about. The word around the neighborhood was that Jews weren't even allowed inside the Elmora Country Club. We asked Mrs. Sprague about it, and she said that it was unfortunate but probably only applied to being a member and that one's family didn't have to belong to the club for one to go to the dancing class there. She liked the idea of my going with Ned, which gave me heart. She said that the two of us savages could use some civilizing, which made us smile at each other, since it was our newfound savage interest in tits, which some of the girls were growing right next to us in the sixth grade, and what we called "boxes" that was drawing us there. Also I had a longstanding curiosity about what it was like inside the Elmora Country Club, having poked my nose every summer through the screened fence along the woods in back to watch the club tennis matches and sometimes a county or state tournament being held there on a Saturday and Sunday afternoon.

Mrs. Sprague asked if I had a dark suit and black shoes and a red tie, since they were required for the boys in the class. I didn't. I had a blue corduroy suit, and my only pair of shoes were brown. She said that Ned had a suit he had outgrown that might work. I tried it on; the jacket fit but the pants were too short, since we were almost the same height. I took the jacket home with me.

I thought my mother would be thrilled at the idea of my going to dancing class with Ned Sprague at the Elmora Country Club, but when I told her about it and what I needed to wear, she looked at me askance, "Why do you want to mix with all of those rich Gentiles?" she said with unexpected asperity. "You don't belong there."

This being what I was struggling not to tell myself, her response threw me into a fury. Since I couldn't afford to lose my temper with my father, I freely came down with it on my mother, never more my father's son than when I thought she was trying to cross me. I shouted at her that my father wouldn't let me be in a grown-up play, my mother didn't want me to learn how to dance or go anywhere that Gentiles did. What a pair of parents to be cursed with.

When I blew up at my mother, it often didn't seem to register. Her driftiness would move in, as though the point I was making had no possible substance or even connection to what had just occured. It wasn't a contemptuous silence so much as an oblivious one, which made it all the more provocative, until I would use the last of my anger and petulance to storm out of the room à la Dad. Five minutes later I would be back, needing to know that she hadn't been hurt by my outburst, that her obliviousness wasn't lasting, that she had returned from where she went to evade my "Solotaroff temper."

I said that I wouldn't go to the dancing class if she didn't want me to. She said that she wouldn't stand in the way of my having a new experience, but she hoped it wouldn't turn me into a snob. The night before the class I showed her Ned's coat. She said she didn't like the idea of my wearing another boy's hand-me-downs, and besides it clashed with my blue corduroy pants, and she couldn't afford to buy me a matching pair. The upshot was that I went to the dancing class in my corduroy suit, a maroon tie of my father's, which my mother decided was close enough to red to count, its hanging tail tucked into my pants ("Just keep your jacket buttoned") and my brown shoes polished a mottled black.

The ballroom of the Elmora Country Club was as bright, full of flowers, and daunting as a funeral home. The teacher, Mrs. Pease, was an older woman with a stiff air who wore a lot of face powder and whose glasses had the same Gentile gleam as the rest of the room. When Ned brought me over to her, she gave me a long disapproving look and said I needed to wear a dark blue serge suit in the future. When she then asked me if I'd had any dancing lessons, I said that my cousin Marcia had taught me a little. "Is your cousin a ballroom dancing teacher?" I said that she was just my cousin but very graceful. "Well, you can watch for a while," she said. "We don't have a partner for you, so you can just watch until we do."

She then had the class form two lines, the boys facing the girls, who all wore white dresses and black Mary Jane pumps. At her word, the boys stepped forward until they were directly in front of the girls and then bowed. Then Mrs. Pease said, "Dancing position, boys and girls," and they moved their corresponding hands until the palms touched while the boy placed his other hand on his partner's waist and she placed hers on his shoulder. It was about as sexy as a first-aid demonstration.

I sat on one of the chairs along the wall and watched the class practice the box step. Then, all the more conscious of my wrong clothes and shoes, my swarthy complexion and bulging nose and everything else that made me feel out of place, I stood up and began to practice the step by myself. Mrs. Pease appeared to have forgotten me as she clapped her hands and swung her arms. I caught Ned's eye and began to mimic Mrs. Pease's gestures as she counted out the beat. Then some of the others began glancing in my direction, a few of them amused, the others not. Whenever Mrs. Pease seemed about to turn in my direction I would go back to practicing the step by myself. When all of that got boring I began to add little flourishes like snapping my fingers or pushing my knees together and rotating my palms. I missed Mrs. Pease's next turn. She walked over to me with a fresh supply of disapproval and said that since a partner for me hadn't come, I should go home, and that my mother could call her. I got out of there and walked around for a while, waiting for Ned, fondling the wave of approval he had given me like one of the girl's breasts I hadn't touched.

Ned and I went from football to basketball to softball that year like Frank and Joe Hardy solving one "case" after another. Our winning passing combination moved indoors during the winter and Ned became the dominating pivot man and rebounder teaming up with me, the ball handler and set shooter. In softball, we both hit over .400 in the interschool games, and we made up a flashy short-to-first combination. I was so successful that year that I even began to think I wasn't that bad-looking. Basking in Ned's view of me and particularly his mother's, I began to approve of myself in a way I hadn't before, to think that my differences from them made me interesting rather than inferior.

The last and climactic athletic event of the year for us graduating sixth-graders was Field Day. Ned was captain of the Red team, I of the Blue. We would run, throw, high-jump, and play softball against each other, and I hoped to win at least one of the events, lead the

Blues to victory, and go forth from elementary school in a blaze of glory. Two days before it was all to happen, though, I came down again with bronchitis. The next day I kept taking my temperature and swallowing aspirin until it had dropped down to a little over 100. The following day I wasn't well, but on the other hand I wasn't as sick as I'd been the day before, and after running around the room a few times, I convinced myself that I could compete.

Mom had begun her morning piano playing, so it was easy to slip out of the house. But by the time I reached the school my weakness had returned and I was coughing a lot. After a while the school nurse came over, put her hand on my forehead, led me to her office, made me lie down, and telephoned my mother. Two days later my temperature climbed past 105, my chest felt like it was full of hot water, my lips were stuck together, and I could put my tongue through the roof of my mouth.

I had lobar pneumonia in both lungs and a strep infection in my mouth and throat. I don't remember very much of the next three weeks, in which my body fought against its two powerful invaders. Antibiotics had yet to come into use, so my "resistance" was on its own, fighting a rearguard action through which I mostly slept or lay over the side of the bed to cough up the "rust-colored sputum" that indicated I was still very sick. When I would awaken, Mom would be there in the chair by my bedside. If she was sleeping on the cot that had been brought in, my first cough would bring her to me. Illness seemed to materialize her, blow away her dreaminess, make her tirelessly attentive and efficient—never more so than during that month. Seeing the love in her eyes when I would awaken and find her at my bedside or catch her gazing at me as we listened to soap operas together, I felt as my father must have when she nursed him through his serious pneumonia. With nothing to prove to anyone and no game to get to, I let the illness gentle me, put me, as it were, in her hands when the weakness and distress weren't doing so on their own. I remember her gently threading a bent glass straw into my riven and all but sealed mouth, through which I sipped the malteds and eggnogs she would shake up and then hold for me in a glass jar. I remember the exquisite chill and tingling sweet odor of the alcohol she sponged over my body to bring down the fever at night. Even the dreaded enemas she gave me had a gentle touch to them, and she handled my bedpan with as little aversion as if it were an infant's diaper.

I remember the daily visits of portly, gentle Dr. Gittelman, his face growing intense as he listened to my chest. During the first week he would also come back in the evening, and I remember a barely audible discussion about the risk of rheumatic fever in moving me to the hospital. I remember my father bringing home a small new Emerson radio to replace the old one Mom sometimes had to hold in her hands to reduce the static. He would come up to my room when he got home from The Shop and sit by the bed and tell me about the pneumonia he had had, how he had pulled through, how I would too. He had gotten over being angry about my going to Field Day, and I could tell my condition was very serious by his gentleness and look of concern. During the terrible night of "the crisis" when my sickness rose up like a great dark wave and dragged me under and carried me out to sea so that I kept screaming "the undertow, the undertow" in my delirium, he was the one who stayed with me and held me.

By the next morning the fever had broken and I woke up to find my mother beaming at me with tears in her eyes. "I was so worried," she said and said, her relieved face like sunshine and dew. The heavy squeezing hand had lifted from my chest. Soon the lining began to return to the roof of my mouth, and I was able to go to the bathroom and then walk a bit.

When I finally was allowed to get out of bed for good, I was twenty pounds lighter, a husky kid who had turned into a scarecrow. Much of my lung tissue was scarred, its drainage impaired, my wind permanently diminished. The black wing that had hovered over me had left me with a more sensitive and anxious sense of my physical being. It wasn't just my impaired breathing and worsened chronic cough, for I soon learned to pace myself and to inhale more deeply, and by fall was playing JV soccer at junior high. The sense of diminishment had more to do with a skinnier body that remained so and that I no longer threw recklessly into tackles or belly slides or fistfights. Instead of feeling rugged, I felt fragile.

There was a subtle emotional component to this change For that month I was given the two things I most needed—a caring father and an effective mother, for lack of which I had been growing up as a semi-orphan, much as my father had, and, like him, I was hardening my spirit accordingly. During my illness, I discovered that he cared about me, which was, emotionally speaking, stunning news. Meanwhile my mother was transformed during my illness into a strong woman whose devotion to me was no longer a burden but a blessing, day after day, night after night. A little of that quality care went a long way, and when each relationship returned to what it had been, the month of having been fully parented left me more sensitive and depressed.

PART THREE

BREAKAGE

AND

SALVAGE

1 WHEN I WAS about ten, Dad began taking me regularly to The Shop on Saturday mornings. He needed someone in the place so that Bill Jordan, his inside man and driver, could make deliveries and do small glazing jobs and he himself could "run up" to the bank before it closed or "run out" to Linden, Rahway, Garwood, or Hillside to check on the storefront jobs he had underway or figure some new ones in the course of his whirlwind day. On Saturdays, his two "union men" didn't work; nor did "the girl"—whoever she was at the time, they came and went, three or four a year, as though each were locked in a race with Dad to see who would become fed up first. At which point Mom would step into the breach again until he more or less fired her too by getting the next new girl.

Mostly I would sit in the little "office" up front. It looked more like a storage room jammed with two desks, a battered filing cabinet with a drawer usually pulled open, and samples of structural glass, of picture frames, of glass block strewn around, along with rolled-up blueprints, stacks of invoice paper, a waist-high collection of Brindley Mixture tobacco cans, a couple of framed price lists for window glass, and a drafting board that was buried under old catalogs, phone books, ledgers, back issues of *Time*, the *Elks* magazine, and one put out by the Glass Dealers Association of New Jersey. Bored spitless during those endless Saturday afternoons, I would wait for the phone to ring or once in a while sell a picture frame or a piece of window glass that didn't have to be cut to size.

Most of the time I read the pulp sports magazines I bought secondhand for a nickel, four or five at a time, and from November to April tried to get warm. The office had a grille on the floor through which rose a thin, barely warmed current of air from the basement. When my father wasn't there I'd put the chair over the grille and sit there in my mackinaw, watching my breath, and pretend to be smoking a cigarette.

Or I would poke around. The surface and drawers of the girl's desk were relatively empty, except for the ledgers in my mother's graceful hand. But my father's desk was a trove for curiosity and speculation. Old pipes, into which I'd put a pinch or two of Brindley's Mixture, or a forgotten cigar: I'd take one or the other into the back and test my threshold of nausea. Also a welter of business letters, receipts, estimates, invoices, business cards, traffic court summonses, canceled checks, memos, hotel brochures, the desk of a man on the run, fleeing from order. The top of his desk was covered by several layers of delivered mail envelopes which he used to take down messages and orders. The active ones were jammed on a couple of spindles, but sometimes they weren't, had disappeared into the welter of the other envelopes like a coin in the sand, and he'd stand there with the phone in one hand and his other rummaging around while he glared at the rotten world that never gave him any time to get properly organized.

One Saturday morning we left for The Shop in the tail wind of a particularly furious storm against my mother.

"You treat me like dirt," she said at the end, with tears and shudders as she ran from the room.

"You know how you make me feel?" he shouted after her. "I'll tell you how you make me feel. You make me feel like going down into the cellar with some rat poison and never having to see your stupid face again."

As he drove even faster than usual through the quiet Saturday streets, his hands clenched on the wheel, his face clenched on his anger, I was frightened, for the first time, for him instead of by him. Rat poison? He'd threatened many times to walk away and let the business crash behind him, but he'd never threatened anything like taking rat poison. I thought of him writhing around on the floor of the cellar in the coal dust and ashes with horrible things happening inside his stomach.

Trying to get away from this horror show, I cast about for something I could say that would get him talking and alter his mood. I had become adept at that, with both of my parents. Usually business did that for him. I asked him if he was bidding on any big jobs. "What difference does it make?" he snapped. "I'm aggravated to death no matter which way I turn. I work myself to death. For what? Can you tell me that?"

"I guess it's for us," I said. "You're working to give us a better life."

"That's what they tell me," he said bitterly. "Does anyone lift a finger to give me a better life? Or even a moment of consideration?"

"We try," I said. "Mom takes care of the house, comes to The Shop when you need her. Now I'm coming to The Shop too. We try to help. We know how hard you work. You work harder than any father I know of." Which was true.

"No one knows," he said. After a time, he said, "There's no companionship between your mother and me. You're old enough to understand that."

I did. But there was nothing I could say, because it was his fault. Aunt Leah had recently said to him, "Why don't you take Rose out some night for a movie and an ice cream soda. It won't break you." And he'd said, "I can't even take her to a soda fountain without her slurping the bottom of the glass with her straw."

"She's got you children and her piano," he said now. "That's all she cares about anyway."

I wanted to say "You've got your business," but didn't. I didn't know what to say. I'd never been out on this thin ice with him before.

"My father used to say, 'Alone is like a stone.' That's how I feel. Like him. As alone and aggravated to death as he was." He stared straight ahead, as though facing a truth so overwhelming that he had forgotten I was there.

His remark hung in the air between us. I remembered something Mom had told me that Poppa Solotaroff had said to her, "that if it wasn't for two Russian writers he'd be dead from loneliness by now." It was like being let in on a Solotaroff family secret.

When we got to The Shop, he went into the office, but instead of going through the mail he had picked up at the post office, he just sat at his desk, still wearing his overcoat and hat. Then he said, "Go find something to do. Sweep up the shop." There was no door to the office, and so when I walked into the window glass racks across from it where the broom was usually kept, I could see him still sitting there. Then he took off his hat and glasses and carefully laid his glasses on the desk as though it were a ritual of some kind, then lowered his face into his hands, and began to weep. And weep. And weep.

I had never seen a man break down before, and my father was the last man on earth I would have expected to see doing so. It was like some astonishing act of nature, like the rain coming to the Serengeti Plain, turning all that dry, harsh, bitter soil of anger into a green

savanna of sorrow. What got to me most was the careful way he had
taken his glasses off and placed them precisely, just so, an unusual
gesture in itself for this impatient man I'd always known. As he continued to weep it didn't make him unmanly or less a grown-up in my
eyes, it made him, for the first time, more understandable and more
related to me. I was seeing the secret softness under his hard, hard
shell. He wasn't only domineering and oblivious and not to be trust-
ed, he was also unhappy, and unhappiness went a long way with me.
It was what I was most at home with and understood.

Around this time, Dad joined the Union County Hiking Club, perhaps as a way of feeling less alone. He was brought into the club by
his lawyer, Max Tieger, who had a son my age, and sometimes Artie
and I tramped along in the rear of the pack of twenty-five or so adults,
making sarcastic remarks about one or another of them or about the
idiocy and boredom of hiking.

On the hikes, Dad turned into a different person. With his navy-
blue waterproof parka, checked woolen shirt, twill pants, hiking
boots, and quick tan, he looked like he'd stepped out of an ad in
Field & Stream. Instead of impatient and charging, he was relaxed
and poised; instead of morose, he was affable; instead of outspoken,
he was almost reserved. Unlike the inept buffoon on the softball
field, he seemed to fit right in with these polite, strenuous hikers, and
soon he became one of the leaders.

He was also nicer to me, particularly on the hikes that he scouted
the Sunday before he had to lead one. The sixteen miles or so of a
hiking trail were marked by its particular blaze of paint every hundred yards or so, but in unfamiliar and heavily wooded and hilly areas
it was easy to go astray, and so he would sometimes go ahead and
leave me at the last marker to mind the trail as I did The Shop. Often
the camaraderie of effort and task would settle between us. He'd say
friendly things like "How're you doing, Teedle?" or "Let's keep going
for another half hour and then we'll stop for lunch," or "Do you
think this hike is too tough for some of the older members?"

His behavior was different from our earlier better times. On the
scouting hikes we'd actually talk about subjects, not exactly man to
man or father to son, since he had no curiosity about my life, but more

like a teacher and his eager student, whom he would draw out and explain things to, rather than just roughly set him straight. I knew that he got some of his ideas from *Time*, because by then I was reading it from cover to cover while I sat around at The Shop or waited for him on his long stops to *kibitz* on the way home, but he had his own quick way of seeing and putting things. He liked to say, "I'm a very acquisitive person," and he did have a talent for talking on a wide range of subjects. He also liked having the "inside" information and point of view. He told me that Roosevelt was a great political salesman and showman, but that the real brains behind the administration were Harold Ickes and Henry Morgenthau and the other members of his "Brain Trust," that Roosevelt would have been nothing special as a speaker without his speech writer, Sam Rosenman. He asked me who I thought was the most powerful man in New Jersey. I guessed Governor Hoffman. "Allow me to correct you," he said. "It's a fellow in Jersey City named Frank Hague who has most of your state senators and assemblymen and even the judges in his hip pocket. Now how does he do that?"

I'd heard, of course, about Frank Hague. "He's got a machine," I said.

"And what's a machine?"

"A sort of political gang?"

"No. Longy Zwillman over in Newark has a gang. Frank Hague has a machine. What's the difference between them?"

"A gang steals and a machine takes?"

"That's pretty smart, Teedle," he said, "except that Hague also steals and Zwillman also takes a cut of this and that, slot machines, union dues, what-have-you. What does a political machine manufacture? What's its main source of power and influence?"

"Money? Bribes? Graft?"

"Votes. Hague is not only a Democrat. He's very democratic. He sees to it that you continue to have a vote even if you're sick or dead." He went on to tell me how politics worked in New Jersey—the networks of power, influence, and graft that built the highways, brought in big business, elected and appointed the officials. He knew a lot about them, some of the Elizabeth ones at first hand. It was an education in how the real world worked.

If he was in a particularly good mood he would even take me into his confidence about his plans for developing the business—how the big money wasn't in storefront work but in becoming a major glass distributor. I learned that he had turned down an opportunity to become a distributor in Mobile, Alabama, where you didn't "have to eat your heart out to make a buck," but the market was too limited and he couldn't "get" the slow way people did business there. He had recently moved his business a few doors down on Elizabeth Avenue because he needed the additional space. He was "very extended" these days because of the mortgage and because he was buying as much glass as he could get credit for; he said that America was certain to enter the war in the next year, and he wanted to be ready for the shortages that would soon come in plate, window, construction, and auto glass. "A year or two from now," he said, "if someone needs a windshield for a '39 Plymouth, I plan to be the only place in Union County where he can get it."

Sometimes he would include me in his long-term plans and prospects. His biggest disadvantage, he said, was his lack of education. He said he understood the glass business from top to bottom but lacked the organizational skills to get to the top that a good education provided. "If you keep your nose clean," he would say to me, "you're going to have the kind of education other people dream about." He asked me if I'd heard of the Wharton School of Finance. I hadn't. But, captured by my father's positive regard, I would have gone along with him if he had plans to send me to the University of Mars.

My other favorite feature of "scouting" hikes was lunch. Dad would have specially shopped for it on Saturday night, and before we set out in the early morning, he would make our sandwiches himself. There would be pastrami or rolled beef or sometimes even sturgeon on onion rye, a container of potato salad or coleslaw, dill pickles that he would halve with his hiking knife, two luscious Bartlett pears or navel oranges or fancy apples. Usually we stopped by a stream and our beverage would be its water, pure and cold enough to make our teeth ache as we passed it back and forth in the maroon cup of the thermos.

One time we were scouting a hike in late October in the Orange Mountains up around Dover. The weather was particularly fine, the trail winding up through the warmth of the glades and the coolness of the timberland, and the sun-splashed reds and yellows of the foliage were more glorious to look down on the higher we went. We didn't stop at our usual lunchtime because Dad wanted to make it to the top, where he said there was a picnic area and a special treat waiting for us. When we got there he told me to gather some wood to replace what we'd use in the fireplace, and by the time I got back he had fixed our plates and had two porterhouse steaks broiling on the grill. It was the first time we had cooked outdoors together. When the steaks were done, he halved and slit a long loaf of bread, my first French bread, and tucked chunks of the incredibly thick yet tender steak and slices of beefsteak tomatoes into them, the mingled juices and textures turning the crusty bread even softer and more savory. "This is really something," I said, imitating his expression for peak moments.

"Glad you like it," he said. "But you haven't eaten anything until you've tasted fresh-killed venison cooked on a spit." He began telling me of a hike he had made twenty years ago in the Sierras. "Your father was a pretty good woodsman back then," he said. "I never knew about the real country, growing up in Yonkers and around Elizabeth, so when I got to California I couldn't believe it. I'm talking about the redwood forests and the ocean around Big Sur, and the High Sierras up north. I felt like a different person. To tell you the truth, I probably wouldn't have come back east if it hadn't been that my father needed me. Anyway, I was hiking with this medical student from Berkeley who really knew his way around in the woods and liked to hunt with a bow and arrow. So late one afternoon he picks up the tracks of a deer . . ." The story went on in full detail, as his stories generally did, but now it was a charmed time, the bond between us making the sandwich even more delicious, the water from the brook as heady to me as wine. When I saw him so sharing, so relaxed and hardy in his blue parka, so carried away by the story, he seemed like the different person he'd been in California and a real father after all.

2 THE NEW YORK Yankees were my team because of Gehrig and because they, like him, seemed a paragon of power, classiness, and consistency. In their distinctive pinstripe uniforms they lorded it over the other teams, winning the American League

pennant almost every year and often the World Series in four straight games. Like most children of ten or eleven I was eager for the world but conscious of being insignificant and ignorant in its eyes. Being a Yankee fan gave me a conquering tribe to belong to and much new information and lore to command—baseball being preeminent in both, its present teeming with player statistics and news, its past with records and legends.

Alexander Hamilton, my junior high school, took in its students from the main residential areas of the city that lay west of Broad Street. The other three junior high schools, which I'd travel to when our teams played them, were in the still impoverished Italian and Slavic industrial neighborhoods and slums that spread outward from Bayway and the Port. Over the next year as the Elizabeth beyond my neighborhood became more visible, American society loomed as a place of paths and pitfalls, in which I was beginning to see and plan my way, though still attached to the leading strings of my imagination.

So, at least, it seems from my baseball perspective at the time. Without Gehrig, the Yankees were now like the big corporations in and around Elizabeth, such as Standard Oil, Texaco, American Typefounders, Singer Sewing Machines, Merck, General Aniline, Phelps Dodge. The Yankees were owned by Jacob Ruppert, whose huge brewery in nearby Newark produced, aptly, "the king of beers." With their consistent domination of the American League the Yankees were not so much a team as a dynasty, part of the high and mighty Gentile empire that not even the Depression could thwart and whose success had no relation to my situation. Out of the corner of my eye I had been watching the rise of the Brooklyn Dodgers, and during their 1941 World Series with the Yankees, I turned, game by game, into a Dodger fan.

The Dodgers were upstarts. Through most of the 1930s they were known for their ineptness and eccentricity. Their star outfielder, Babe Herman, had been hit on the head by a fly ball; their best pitcher, Burleigh Grimes, was notorious for his illegal spitball. Willard Mullen, the king of the sports cartoonists, caricatured the Dodgers as a Depression tramp with holes in his shoes, stubble on his chin, a cigar butt in his mouth, and they became known as "Dem Bums." But under their enterprising new general manager, Larry MacPhail, they suddenly became contenders—third place in 1939, second in 1940, the pennant in 1941.

Known still as "Dem Bums," their players had ragtag names like Cookie Lavagetto, Pee Wee Reese, and Kirby Higbee. Their center fielder, Pistol Pete Reiser, in his reckless pursuit of deep fly balls, was always crashing into the outfield wall. Instead of the magisterial long ball that the Yankee strategy deployed, the Dodgers singled and doubled, stole, sacrificed, squeezed in their runs. Their manager, Leo Durocher, a high-strung, conniving loudmouth, was known as "the Lip." Their management was smart and innovative: the first to broadcast its games, one of the first to play night games.

In sum, the Dodgers were the Jews of baseball. Moreover, many of the city's Jews lived in Brooklyn, including aunt Leah and her husband Mickey. Even its stadium, Ebbets Field, had a Yiddish lilt to its name and was small and *haimish*, unlike majestic Yankee Stadium and the spacious, aristocratic Polo Grounds, the home of our main rival, the New York Giants. Arrogant from their winning tradition—their manager, Bill Terry, had once asked the reporters if the Dodgers were still in the league. Seeing the world in 1941, even more than I had before in Gentile Elmora, as a place where Jews struggled against ignominy and worse, where they hustled, tried harder, looked for an edge that enabled them to keep their heads up and to get ahead, I took to the Dodgers as my team.

The bond was cemented for good in the fourth game of the 1941 World Series, which the Dodgers lost in the ninth inning when their catcher, Mickey Owen, failed to hold on to a called third strike which allowed the Yankees to score the tying run and go on to win the game and eventually the Series. The passed ball by the sure-handed Owen, one of the great defensive catchers, gave a heartbreaking, ironic outcome to the team's gallant climb to the top. The Yankees provided only victory, the Dodgers added tragedy. What more could a young Jewish fan with an inchoate literary temperament ask for?

The Dodgers were also Uncle Mickey's team. He and Aunt Leah lived within walking distance of Ebbets Field, and now that I was old enough to travel to the city by myself I would take the railroad to Pennsylvania Station and then the long subway ride on the Flatbush line deep into Brooklyn to their pretty redbrick apartment house with Colonial trim on Lefferts Avenue. In some ways it was like going back to the early happiness and security of Cream Ridge, for Aunt Leah, the spunkiest and funniest of my mother's sisters, had married a handsome and prodigiously sweet-natured tenor, Mickey Landau, who was content to clerk in his brothers' huge cigar store on Wall Street while he trained his voice for the operatic stage

When I went to a night game—a thrill in itself—with Mickey, I sat in the grandstand rather than in the bleachers. We would go high up in the unreserved seats, sacrificing immediacy for perspective. Fielding practice was the beginning of the real thing, the diamond cleared after batting practice, the starting players—Lavagetto, Reese, Herman, Camilli—taking their respective positions, gracefully moving into the sharply hit grounders, letting out their rifle arms. Then came the double plays—rangy Cookie Lavagetto and his swift but exactly aimed, timed throw waist-high to second base, where solid Billy Herman caught, pivoted, and released the ball in one fluent motion; or Pee Wee Reese darting toward second base, catching Herman's toss and throwing to first at the same instant his foot crossed the inside of the bag; no other sport had so much style.

I loved going to games with gentle, debonair, witty Mickey. He was not a particularly partisan or even a knowledgeable fan; a glance or two at the sports section of the *World Telegram* was enough for him, while I read Dan Daniel and Murray Schumacher with the rapt attention of a boy shepherd in the Galilee reading the books of Samuel and Kings. I think Mickey got as much of a kick out of watching me as he did from the game itself. "This kid has come all the way from Elizabeth, New Jersey," he'd say to the people around us. "That's why he looks like he's in heaven." Or he'd say, "If you have any questions about the game, past or present, Teddy will be glad to answer them." He was the most amiable of men, and because of his years behind the counter in his brothers' tobacco store he could talk to anyone. And so after a few innings I'd find myself the pet of a circle of friendly adults, sharing a look of elation at a sudden home run, of dejection when a promising rally fizzled out, of nervous tension when the rallies came and the game was on the line—racial, ethnic, age differences dissolving in the easygoing communion of baseball fandom and the pleasant surprise of having a Dodger team that was "still up there."

Also there was Mickey's generosity. Though he was known in the family as a man who worked hard for peanuts, the unaccountable victim of his wealthy brothers' exploitiveness, he handled money in a princely way. Frugal Aunt Leah would want to put up some sandwiches and fruit to take to the game, but he'd say, "No ma'am, Teddy and I are going out on the town." "How about some ice cream," he'd ask only an inning or two after he'd bought me a hot dog. "You look like you could use some nourishment after all that excitement." He didn't ply me with a lot of stuff, just anticipated my desires, ministered to the occasion. It was a lesson in graciousness.

Those two-or three-day sojourns with Leah and Mickey Landau were also graced by their relationship. A husband arriving home every evening as sunny as he had left in he morning, after a nonstop day behind the counter and a long subway ride in the rush hour, to a wife who was as delighted to see him as he was her—it was, to say the least, a whole other view of marriage. His job was going nowhere, his career as a tenor mostly likewise, but he wore his situation in life like a new suit of clothes, his satisfactions rooted deep in his nature, his sense of humor always on tap. Freshly bathed and made up, Leah would quickly put an ample meal on the table and settle back to listen to his droll account of his day with the Wall Street big shots and small fry, adding her own quips and sallies. They were a cross between two newlyweds who couldn't get over their luck and a comedy team taking the night off.

After dinner and washing up, there would be a favorite radio program or two, followed by casino or Chinese checkers or a jigsaw puzzle. Sometimes Mickey would sing to us one or two of the arias he was working on with his teacher, and then announce he was taking favorites. Mine was "Danny Boy," which he sang with a slight Irish lilt, a piercing tenderness, a thrilling leap and landing on the high note toward the end. I could still hear the song an hour later, feeling like Danny Boy himself as I lay happily on the couch they would fix up for me in the living room.

During the day Leah would be busy with one or another of the clerical jobs she did at home. She was a genius at managing money, always able to snip off a bit of the shoestring they lived on in those years and put it away. She was hoping for children; also she was Gil's banker of last resort, the one he'd turn to when Belle, the family one, was fed up with meeting his margin calls. Jack, Gil, Belle, Leah, even scholarly Fan—they all played the market right through the Depression. "It's the Weiss form of *davening*," Mickey would say. They had wry names for their stocks—"Cancer Oil"; "American Cyanide."

Often I would go off with Mickey's sister's son, Irving Ringler, a couple of years older than I, a fast-running, streetwise kid from Borough Park. Georgie Landau, the son of the cigar store mogul, had gone to Staunton Military Academy, and Leah still had two of his uniforms. Irving and I would clamp ourselves into the heavy worsted gray tunic, hitch up the trousers with the black stripe running down the legs, and tramp around the neighborhood. The uniforms gave a little touch of glamour to my Brooklyn visits, a token of the Landau money that had evaded Mickey and vice versa. Play-acting with Irving as two rich kids home from military academy made me that much more aware of Mickey and Leah's money-isn't-everything enjoyment of life. As he liked to say, "John D. Rockefeller would have given a million dollars for my stomach." Going from our home to theirs was like going from the Depression to prosperity.

3   ALMOST EVERY AUGUST, right through the Depression, our family went to Belmar, New Jersey, for the whole month. What made this possible was the *kuchalayn*, the summer boardinghouse with kitchen privileges, which though it may not have been invented by the post-immigrant Jews came naturally to us, a kind of upscale vestige of ghetto life; the descendants of the huddled masses crammed into places with names like Schine's Villa, the Oceanvue, or the Bonniebern (which was not a misspelling of a Scottish brook but an amalgam of the owners' names). They offered a family vacation at bargain-basement rates. We had our own room, and in the "nicer" ones our own icebox in the communal kitchen. Not sharing an icebox was

one of the few issues on which Mom put her foot down ("It always leads to a fight"), and since my father liked being with a "better class of people" he went along with the additional expense.

For Mom, Sandy, Bob, and me, August in Belmar was family R&R from the battle zone under Dad's command. With enough money for the week and no one putting her down, Mom's natural charm emerged. Sometimes when I came back to the beach blanket from the water there would be some man or a supervisor of the lifeguards talking to her. "He's just trying out his line," she would say, though she clearly liked the attention. She also became a valued presence among the other women in the house, the "so interesting" and "so pleasant" Rose who got along with everyone and was glad to take your small child if you had to shop, watch your chicken while you took a phone call from your husband back in Jersey City, or listen to your problems.

The three of us children drew closer to her and to each other. She still left us alone a good deal, first Sandy and me, and then Bobby too by the time he was four or so, while she shopped in the morning, schmoozed with one or two of the women she became friends with, communed with the piano if there was one, which there usually was, an old upright being a standard item of middle-class Jewish furniture even in a *kuchalayn*.

By nine-thirty the three of us were off to the beach, a block away, for another day of swimming and basking and being free. I loved to come back from riding the waves and cover my body in hot sand and think, "still twenty-five more days." Around one o'clock Mom would arrive at our blanket toting a big brown paper bag crammed with sandwiches, hard-boiled eggs, carrot sticks, cherry tomatoes, a big jar of iced lemonade, and three Dugan's honey-glazed donuts, an extravagance she wouldn't have dared in Elizabeth.

Though each summer I would find a group to play ball with late afternoons and hit the boardwalk with after supper, I spent my beach time with Sandy and Bobby. In Belmar, as in Elizabeth, we were a kind of junior family of our own, shaped by the influences coming down on us from above but also sheltering ourselves from them by our bond. In Belmar we were happier together, as we were inside ourselves. I was the big brother, an authority on sand castles and running bases, and how long to wait after breakfast before they could go in the water and how far in each of them could go given the tide. In the afternoon, Mom would stay on after lunch and I'd be free to hang out elsewhere, but if I stayed at the beach, I'd keep any eye on Sandy and Bobby, since she often didn't. One time I was heading out to ride the big waves and saw a little kid facedown in the surf, being pulled toward them. I reached down and grabbed him by the arm as he went by. It was my five-year-old brother—so caught up in his own water game that he didn't realize yet he was heading out to sea.

By the time he was four or five, Bobby was the big project of my family life, my chance to play Uncle Gil, who came into my life at about the same age. He'd called me Butch McDevitt, I called Bobby Butch, gave him boxing, catching, and tackling lessons, taught him to be proud to be a Jew. He was a sturdy, handsome, witty little boy,

with a straight nose and a precocious mathematical and verbal ability, so there was a lot of vicarious gain to my side of the relationship.

With Sandra too, I was the good shepherd at the beach. Often I
wasn't that at home. There the family modeling tended to assert
itself, and little Benny would come forth in my bad moods to oppress
her with merciless teasing. She was a shy high-strung girl who, like
Mom, was easy to rattle. Then I would turn "nice," sometimes in a
burst of conscience but more often to keep her off-balance and under
my control and to stop her from running to Mom. That in itself did-
n't much faze me, since Mom's disapproval was mostly a weak and
wounded "You're not my son when you behave like that," more material for the little theater of nastiness I was passing on.

On the other hand there was a lot of affection between us. Sandy
was a very pretty girl whose photograph had been displayed in the
Thomas Studio on Broad Street, and I was as proud of that as I was of
her musical gift. She had perfect pitch, and much was made of her
ability not only to identify any note or chord on the keyboard but also
to remember any melody and then transpose it into a different key.
To Mom, this meant that her own thwarted musical career would be
fulfilled by her exceptional daughter, whom she began at an early
age to groom and to tout at any opportunity.

Our daily idyll at the beach, the sweet dinnertimes when we'd dig
into the chicken or meat or bluefish and eat bread of our own
accord—this would come to an end on Saturday evening when Dad
arrived. A cot would be brought into our room for me, and the space
that had been tight but livable—Mom and Sandy sharing one bed,
Bobby and I the other—seemed to contract to half its size. It wasn't
just the cot, it was what it betokened.

After the pneumonia I woke up coughing all the more because of
the pitted plumbing in my lungs. When I did it one Saturday night in
Belmar, I heard Mom moaning, then Dad's harsh whisper telling me
to get a drink of water and shut up. Almost twelve by then, I could
put one and one together (we boys referred to the Friday-evening
train that brought some of our fathers from Newark and Elizabeth as
the Hard-on Express), but when I got back into bed again, I was still
shocked by what I'd heard. Though my sexual curiosity had grown
ravenous that summer from hanging around the dance arcade on the

boardwalk, watching the lifeguards and other college guys jitterbug-
ging and cheek-to-cheeking and going under the boardwalk with the
older girls and younger women, the last thing I wanted was to satisfy
it in this way, and I tried very hard to go back to sleep. Which of
course meant that I could no more fall asleep than I could disappear.

"You asleep yet?" came from across the room.

I had a tragic choice — the conflict of two dreads. I could pretend I
was asleep and then suffer what I would hear or I could tell the truth
and perhaps bring his rage down on me. "I'm trying," I said.

"He's trying . . ." Dad muttered to his gods.

"Ben, he can't help it," said Mom to hers.

The next week my carefree beach life began to be invaded by
another one in which I sat in a dark corner of my mind, counting the
days until Saturday and thinking of possible reprieves and escapes.
Once in a while my father would decide he needed "a real rest" or
"some stimulating conversation" and go to a resort called
Tammamint Lodge in Pennsylvania for the weekend. I also thought
about ways to tell my mother what was going on in me. But how
could I tell her that I was upset by the thought that Dad was going to
do it to her on Saturday night? I was so paralyzed by embarrassment I
couldn't even tell one or another of the guys I was running with that
summer to get it off my chest and try to get some advice.

After dinner on Saturday night the men would sit around on the
porch talking about business conditions, or the situation in Europe
now that France had fallen and the invasion of England could come
at any time, or the question on everyone's mind by then, how to help
the German and now the French Jews. Dad, as usual, was holding
forth, the man with the lowdown. His "company" voice floated to me
as I sat on the porch steps in a countdown to the hour I would spend
with my eyes jammed shut and a finger pressed into each ear. That is
how I figured I would get through it unless I managed to fall asleep
before they came upstairs, which was unlikely. Meanwhile his domination of the conversation went on and on, whether it was about rising interest rates or Roosevelt's Lend-Lease tactic, or why he couldn't
help the Jews because Congress had tied his hands by shutting off the
German immigration quota.

When I couldn't take his voice anymore, I called up to my mother, who was sitting with the women, and said that I was going for a walk. "I want you back and in bed by ten o'clock," Dad called after me. Somewhere between rage and tears I headed for the boardwalk. Usually I'd hang out with the guys at the penny arcade, but hearing the comforting crash of the waves I kept on going.

The ocean was a big presence to me that summer. I'd become adept at body-surfing and had elected myself a member of a secret society called "the Riders of the Sea." Infatuated with waves, I'd even pat one when I caught the first tug of its mounting and swam with it, feeling as close to it as a cowboy to his horse before it launched me down its crest and held and propelled me in its cap, my face down, my arms curved like an arrowhead as it took me as far as it could.

The tide was up and there wasn't much of a surf; the ocean was in one of its peaceful moods, more like a mother than a mighty father or a playful friend. I thought that if I swam out to the last rope and then from the left pole to the right one and back ten times it might make me tired enough to sleep. Also I wanted the cool, clean feeling of the water to take away the anxious, dirty feeling that was tormenting me. So I pulled off my shirt and socks and sneakers and did my running dive into the water.

After I'd swum the laps across the roped-in area I sat on the last rope and let each big soft swell coming in swing me. I was calm by now, and as the night expanded around me, my mind filled with the spell that the sea induced when I gave myself up to its hugeness and timelessness and rhythm, its imaging of the profound mysteries of the world, of the universe, of my existence itself, such a tiny speck in all of that visible cosmos. I thought of the line of accidents beginning with my parents coming together to make me and their parents finding each other and making them, all the way back to Adam and Eve or whoever the first couple was. All those bezillion accidents that had had to happen for me to exist, and to be me instead of some dead or terrified kid in Germany or France or a starving Chinese boy or one of the billions of people that had lived before me or for that matter a seagull on the beach, since the same things, blind chance and screwing had created it too. I tried to console myself with the thought that if my parents hadn't met each other and screwed, I wouldn't have my sister and brother, whom I loved more than anything else in the world. So what was there to be so upset about?

But I got upset all over again thinking about being in our room two hours from now, faced with the terrible choice all over again. I thought of staying on the beach all night and saying I'd fallen asleep by accident, but Mom would start getting terrified that I'd drowned and Dad would take me upstairs and give me the strap or worse.

So it was time to talk to God, which I still did every year or so, when I was deeply perplexed about something in my life. I didn't pray anymore at bedtime, which seemed childish, and prayer at school seemed Christian — "Our Father who art in heaven," in which I changed "art" to "are" to make it seem less so. By now, God was like a higher, vaster version of Lou Gehrig, the ultimate Someone who watched over me and brought out the Weiss boy part to talk to. Humming the tune of the song "Someone to Watch Over Me," swaying up and down in His ocean and looking up at the sky, which was His face and all the stars His eyes, one of which was fixed on me, I asked Him what I should do. He told me to go home and take two aspirin, which Mom did when she was very upset.

But that didn't work either.

4   AT HAMILTON JUNIOR High School the two ends of Elmora came together, and I found myself among a lot of Jewish kids. It was like dropping the missing ingredients into the soup: the part of me that had been fishy now belonged in the spicy ethnic stew that we served to and sometimes flung at each other. Few of us spoke Yiddish, the language in which our parents muttered and whispered their secrets, but we had all been raised in homes in which the immigrant culture that Yiddish expressed led a lingering life and shaped our common ambitions and aversions, our Yinglish wisecracks and jokes.

In the Shelley Avenue school the fact that I had one of the high IQs and did well in class had not set my ego tingling. I was so much involved with my performance as an athlete that getting high marks was mostly something I took for granted: Jewish kids were supposed to be smart, and so, being Jewish, I was. It was like being tall, a nice feature that I didn't have to pay any attention to. At Hamilton all that changed decisively. I was too light for football, so-so in soccer, flashy but inconsistent in basketball, my main game now. If I missed my first few shots or turned the ball over or was beat by the boy I was guarding in a class intramural game, the sneerer in my head went to work, making me try to make an exceptional shot or pass to shut him up. Also I didn't have the wind anymore to go all-out in sustained running games like soccer and basketball and so tended to hang around up front on defense, catching my breath and positioning myself to score, which added to my reputation as "hungry." Meanwhile Ned Sprague continued to excel, a school hero in the making. He hung out now with the older jocks he played with and the pretty, sassy girls they chased, both groups out of my league.

In the league I mainly played in now—the Jewish one—the high scoring was in English, math, social studies, and science. All of us were in the X or college track. In the past the top students had been in the X1 class, the second rank in X2, and so forth, but that had been done away with, and the ranking was now kept in the minds of the students themselves, which made the competition all the more fierce and incessant. The cult word among the Jewish seventh-graders was an aggressive "Wudjaget?" which rose from desk to desk when a test or report was returned and in the halls at crunch time when the report cards for the marking period were handed out.

Marks were what we were about as a group, and since they were numerical, grade averages were as determinate of one's standing and prospects as batting and earned run averages were for minor league baseball players. For we were competing not only for status but for a chance at the big time, the major league of opportunity known as the Ivy League, for which only a few of us would be chosen because of the quotas we already knew about.

Most of us had our school picked out and the career that would follow from it, choices that expressed ambition and fantasy but were adjusted to achievement and ability and monitored by the group's assent or derision. The "brains," those with a 95 average, could get away with touting their choice as Harvard or Yale, or, if they were especially outstanding in math and science, MIT. The students around 90 slated themselves for Columbia and Cornell; below that your only hope was Penn, which, like Columbia and Cornell, was also a little easier for Jews to get into. Princeton, Brown, and Dartmouth didn't figure in at all, being in our narrowed eyes too Gentile to even think about, and the latter two were for drinkers and playboys.

I was hanging on in the second group and chose Cornell because I had decided to become a civil engineer, which it was known for producing. This was a strange career choice for someone who was all thumbs in shop courses and literally clueless in mechanical drawing. I chose it because I thought my father would approve; civil engineering was as close as college got to storefronts and industrial glazing. The maps of the continents I drew and colored painstakingly in the sixth grade turned into clumsily drawn bridges in the seventh. My ambition was also inspired by the views of the George Washington Bridge from the roof garden of the Franklin Towers, off Riverside Drive, where my aunts Belle and Fan now lived.

What I liked to do in school and was best at was writing poems and book reports, but I no more would have thought of going to college to become a writer than I would have to become a caddy. Our obsession with the best colleges was fueled by the anxiety and thwarted ambition we had grown up with. Most of us came from families that had bought heavily into the Jewish American dream—if you worked day and night, lived frugally, and used your head, you would get somewhere, even become somebody. So it had proved out: from the Lower East Side and "the Port" to the middle class and Elmora in one generation. Then the Depression had suddenly swept most or all of the winnings off the board. The fault was not America's or capitalism's. How could it be?—democracy and the New Deal, not Judaism, were our real religion, President Roosevelt our God. No, the fault was our parents' own, as they told us themselves; they, like our uncles and aunts, hadn't persevered enough, been foresighted enough, or lucky enough to get an education in one of the professions. It was not the doctor or dentist or lawyer who had gone bankrupt or lost his job. We could see for ourselves. Their sons were the ones who had their own room and went to summer camp.

It was as though a special draft law had been passed for us. All

Jewish males twelve or older are required to report five days a week to the professional class of the future and receive basic training in college preparatory courses and intensely competitive tests and assignments in order to be considered for a place in a topflight college, followed by one in a leading medical, dental, law, or other prestigious professional school. We mustered in our corduroy pants and sleeveless sweaters at the desks at the front of the classroom, the better to be seen and called on by the teacher. However cool and sarcastic we might be otherwise, in class we waved our hands like mad American versions of the yeshiva student who comes rushing out of the study house yelling "Jews! Jews! I've got the answer! Give me a question."

By the eighth grade, the most vaunted among us was a large, stout, uncoordinated boy named Irwin Taubman who always wore a suit and conducted himself with the towering confidence of one of the "Quiz Kids," our favorite radio show. Like the other "biggest brains" who stood aloft on the 95-average rung, Irwin was an ambidextrous student, as good with numbers and formulas as with words, Latin conjugations, and facts. But whereas Harold Vhugen and Paul Weltcheck were otherwise pretty much like the rest of us—ball players, comedians, girl watchers—Irwin had already risen above such "callow" (a word I learned from him) behavior. He behaved as though he were ready to bypass the remaining five years of adolescence and go directly to Harvard. What he liked to do was to lord. Lording was his sport, a power performance meant to weaken, force mistakes, and overcome.

We would be sitting in the lunch room after history class and he might say, "I agree with the Fugitive Slave Law."

"That's because you're a prize bullshit artist," one of us might say, often me, because I hated his "superiority complex" with the passion bred by my father's.

"Reason from the reasonable versus contempt from the contemptible. Would you mind addressing my position? Why are you against it?"

"Because I'm against slavery. Because once a slave reaches free territory he has as much right to stay there as if he'd come there in the first place. Because you have to be a prize *putz* like you to think otherwise."

He'd then ask if I was against the Constitution and proceed to inform us that slaves were recognized by the founding fathers to be private property.

"Sure, the Southern ones."

"Most of the chief ones were Southern, but that's not the point. Madison and Jefferson and all the other heroes of democracy agreed that where slavery is legal, slaves are property. I'm sure even you can see why a man had a right to his stolen property, for that's what an escaped slave was."

"Yeah. He stole himself. What bullshit."

"Not bullshit. Law. The law of the land. When you've read Catherine Drinker Bowen's *Miracle at Philadelphia* come back and talk to me."

Over the next four years Irwin and I maintained a wary, often disdainful relationship susceptible at odd moments to a fugitive rapport, as though within each of us was a kindred spirit that now and then slipped out to meet the other's. Usually this occurred when we found ourselves walking home from school and began to talk about books we liked. Irwin tipped me off to Sinclair Lewis's *Arrowsmith*, and though it didn't make me want to join him on the next frontier of medical research, it sent me racing through *Main Street*, *Babbitt*, and *Elmer Gantry*, which I told him he had to read for its horniness.

But in between the nice times were long stretches of rough ones. He was contemptuous of my performances as a class clown and disrupter, but what really got his goat was when I did unexpectedly well. Out of the blue I made the second-highest score on the eighth-grade Latin achievement test. Latin was a serious subject: the basis of the language of the two favorite professions. "*You* second," he sneered. "Wudjaget?" I coolly replied, knowing he wasn't first.

Otherwise, during the three years at Hamilton, I remained in the second rank, and not securely, since I was so-so in math and science, and the *bête noire* of at least one of my teachers each semester. My game again was mischief-making, my high scoring after school was now in hours spent in detention, my fame in the disruptive wisecrack, the question or response that got the teacher's goat. By the eighth grade I had the principal's attention to the extent that in the midst of the assembly of six hundred students he spotted me passing on the latest dirty joke while he was lecturing us. He sent me to his office to wait and tremble until he arrived to call my father for the second time that school year, and we were only in November.

Out of school I was also on a tear. Buddy Rischin was my new Bruce Brown, an older boy who broke me into smoking with the cigarettes he took from his father's grocery store and into shoplifting at Levy Brothers, the main department store on Broad Street. Buddy was the only Jewish boy of my generation who regularly played hooky from school. No matter how demoralized, how much in trouble, I might be at Hamilton, I could no more have stayed away than my father could have from the The Shop. School was where they kept your future, and the idea of playing hooky, much less dropping out of school, was as alien as majoring in shop. But Buddy had little use for high school, because it interfered with his education.

The English he was learning to use resourcefully was on a cue ball. His teacher and role model as a pool shark was Ace Levine, who hung out with the other Jewish sports at the tables and bowling alley of the YMHA. Ace was said to be "connected with" Sheik Haber, our leading gangster. One of his associates had recently been murdered in the barbershop of the Elizabeth Carteret Hotel, so Sheik and his "rough customers," as Dad called them, had plenty of scary glamour for us boys who made a folk hero out of Longy Zwillman, northern New Jersey's Godfather, and macho boxers such as Al "Bummy" Davis in order to counter the Jewish stereotypes. When Buddy wasn't learning from Ace and his colleagues how to run the table in straight pool or leave an opponent with nothing in eight-ball, he set pins at the Y's bowling alley to pay for his tuition.

I liked hanging out with Buddy and didn't like it. What mainly bound me to him was the long rush of hot, nervous energy that would come over me when we did one of our "jobs." Along with stealing from the department stores, we would sometimes meet after supper with one or two other boys my age from the neighborhood with a taste for delinquency. We'd hang out for a while smoking or shooting baskets in the dark. Then as we were leaving the playground each of us would pick up a stone. I would have the same hot flush of scariness and excitement that I had when I boosted a wallet or a fountain pen or a knife for my high-top boots, a feeling that was right next door to the feeling that I'd begun to summon in the bathroom or in bed. Awash in it, I'd join the others in making a perfect throw in unison from the outfield to home plate, which in this case was from the wooded lot across the street to three or four of the Shelley Avenue school's windows, which I loved to hear smash, not because they were the school's but because they were glass.

In the eighth grade, I entered and was held fast in a comprehensive spell of theft, window-breaking, and masturbating. I no longer needed to be with Buddy to perform the first two; they were now as much a solo act as the third one was, all limbs of the same irresistible sneaky urge that had grown up almost overnight in the middle of my being like the tree in Eden, complete with the snake's voice.

Some of my friends had been beating their meat for a year or more before I tried it myself. Though I was about to become a man in the Jewish chronology, I was nowhere near that in the adolescent one: the only thing that seemed to be growing down there was a few threads of hair. In the showers at gym, at the YMHA steam bath and pool where you went naked, I'd become a furtive, obsessive measurer of genital heft and hider of my own peanut. Now and then I'd see a fat boy who was even worse off than I was, and there were slightly built boys who were still in my boat, though even some of them could surprise you. Most of the other Jewish boys, who weren't supposed to be "hung," were better off than I was. Around water, I got even smaller. Turned away as much as I could manage in the shower room and keeping my hands as low as possible I became the fastest kid in gym class (probably in Union County) in showering and drying off. Full of penis envy (Freud told the lesser half of that story), still skinny and easily winded, still timid about tackling a hard runner or driving to the basket, I felt like a team being pushed back toward its own goaline.

The footage produced by my newfound horniness and directed by my quickened imagination starred Ginny Engel, who had the most mobile ass and delicious-looking thighs and wore the shortest skirt of any girl in the eighth grade. What the other girls giggled about, Ginny seemed already to know; it was in her eyes, the rolling eyes of a girl to whom the very air around her was breathing propositions. As well as a tune of the day that we revised and sang just for her:

> Did you ever see a wet dream walking,
> Well, I did.

At home, though, or at The Shop when I was left alone in the office, she would be there just for me, my very own wet daydream, who would get me going by breathing in my ear, "Oh you're my rough customer. My big rough customer . . ." "Oh, Ginny," I would say back, "Make the earth move, make the earth move."

On the Wednesday before Thanksgiving, a messenger came into print shop with a note from the principal. I was told to get my coat from my locker and report to his office. When I entered it a policeman was standing there. As he gave me a cold once-over, the principal said, "You've really come a cropper this time."

"Put on your coat, Theodore," the policeman said. "There's some-one at the police station that wants to talk to you."

I remember the ride to the station and entering the forbidding squat brick building on Scott Place as being awake in a nightmare, the unthinkably awful actually happening. To my knowledge only grown-up criminals like Sheik Haber were taken to this place, except for an older boy in Elmora who had accidentally killed his best friend a year before with a .22 when they were shooting at a target in his basement. Now suddenly I was in that dark company, not just of the rough customers but of the genuinely guilty. It didn't matter that I had no idea which of my offenses had led to this. I was here mainly because I was me, because the suffering my father had prophesied had begun. If I had been told that I was being taken directly to the state reform school in Rahway, I wouldn't have felt that much more cast out of the life I had been leading up to fifteen minutes ago.

I was taken to a room with two desks and a long, bare green metal table. Two men were sitting at desks, each wearing a white shirt and tie and a shoulder holster with a gun in it. One of them, a big, hand-some man with an iron look turned to me and said curtly, "Sit down at that table, Theodore." I knew who he was, Sergeant Frank Ward, the father of the fighting Ward brothers. When after a few minutes he came to the table and began questioning me, it was as though God himself were speaking out of his tight-lipped mouth.

"I want you to tell me what you know about the windows that have been broken in the Shelley Avenue school."

So it was only the windows and not the wallet, key case, fountain pens, and pocket knife.

"I broke some of them," I said. "I'm really sorry I did."

He nodded, unmoved by my confession or contrition. " I know that you did," he said. "How many?"

"Maybe seven or eight."

"By yourself?"

I nodded.

"And who broke the other fifteen or sixteen?"

My mind reeled all over again. I didn't know what to say, paralyzed by awe of him on one side, the boyhood code on the other.

Sergeant Ward told me that he didn't have all day. That I had a very simple choice. I could tell him who else was responsible or he could call my father and tell him to come down to the station and pay for replacing twenty-three broken windows. Later on, we could see what the juvenile judge thought was appropriate punishment.

I had two bad choices to process in very little time. Guys like me didn't squeal; on the other hand, only a fool would take the rap for all the windows. I also had to weigh the beating I would get from my father for six windows against the berserk one for all twenty-three and compare the latter with the beating I would get from Buddy with the other two stone throwers holding my arms like they did in the Mob. Then there was the code of taking my punishment like a man versus the idea that if it weren't for Buddy, I wouldn't be here.

"You're in a mess," Sergeant Ward said. "The best thing you can do, Theodore, is tell me the truth."

His slightly warmer tone did it. The voice of the father of the Ward brothers reached into my conscience and turned on its faucet full force. Or almost full force. I gave him the other three names. I stopped short of telling him about the thefts, though if he had asked me I would have told him about them and probably the jerking off too. When I finished, he called my father and told him to come there and get me. I must have waited an hour or more in cold, shamed misery before he arrived, which wasn't unusual. Waiting for him was as much a fact of my life as his losing his temper and flying at me, which I expected to happen when he got me at home that night. But it didn't. Since he did a lot of glazing for the city, he had already worked out an arrangement to replace all of the windows at cost to cover my share of the damage, which I was to repay by reporting every day after school to The Shop, which effectively meant that I couldn't go out for the JV basketball team. That hurt more than the four or five lashes with his belt to pay for the embarrassment I had caused him with his contacts at City Hall.

The next day, Thanksgiving, he upped the ante of retribution by leaving me at home "to think it over," while the family went to New York for Thanksgiving dinner at my aunts' apartment in the Franklin Towers. "Right now," he said, "you don't belong in this family. And if you want to go on living here, you'd better turn over a new leaf. I'm tired of feeding and clothing someone who is growing up to be a no-good bum."

He needn't have worried. My brief career as a juvenile delinquent had ended in Sergent Frank Ward's office. By the next day I had turned over a new leaf by burying in Union Woods the wallet, key case, and fountain pens I'd stolen, and, with a tug of regret, I even removed the stolen knife from my high-top boot and threw it into the hole. By the time I returned home and tuned in a football game, I felt much better. Still, I was stabbed every few minutes by the thought that Buddy Rischin would be coming after me, which nagged on for another three days and nights until I decided to face the music and go to the Y on Sunday. He was there setting pins, but when he spotted me he was the one who looked away, giving me the answer to the question it hadn't occurred to me to ask.

5   IN JULY OF 1941, my parents' marriage blew up again, and this time it didn't come back together in a few days. I don't remember the circumstances, but they were sufficiently dire or perhaps just sufficiently cumulative for Mom's sisters Belle and Fan to intervene

and persuade her to pack her bags and ours and come to stay with them in New York.

Though now in their late forties, Fan and Belle were still known as "the Girls" because they were single. At the same time they were deferred to as the officers of the Weiss family who had kept it afloat during the Depression—Belle the intrepid captain and Fan her thoughtful first mate. So it had been all the way back to Cream Ridge and the winter hotel in Lakewood, where, in each case, Belle had led the family from the country boarding house into the hotel business, Fan following close behind, more retiring but efficiently creating order. Belle got the financing, organized the expansion, ran the kitchen; Fan was the office person and also wrote the brochures and ads. When they lost everything in the Depression, Fan had brought the family to New York, supporting her sisters and mother on her teacher's salary, until Belle came up with the idea of creating a New York office for resort hotels, which was soon a going concern.

Belle would have been plain were her pop eyes not lit and set dancing by a bouncy, clever spirit. She looked a lot like Eddie Cantor, the singer and comedian, and, like him, came on as cute and remained to command. She hadn't finished high school and wasn't that much of a reader, but she was one of nature's sophisticates, and her clipped, cigarette-hoarsened voice on the phone made the Lake Tarleton Club in Pike, New Hampshire, and the Lord Tarleton in Miami Beach seem as sporty and swanky as a week in St. Moritz.

I remember only two phone numbers from my youth—Elizabeth 2-4772, The Shop, and Trafalgar 4-1249, my aunts' apartment. The first is freighted with boredom and dreariness; the second radiates the good life, Upper West Side version. On the twelfth floor of the Franklin Towers off Riverside Drive, the apartment was the one touch of class in our life. It had only three rooms—the Girls' bedroom, a living/dining area, and small back room that housed files, office supplies, and brochures for the hotel and at night became my uncle Gil's room and mine the time we came to live there. But the rooms, with their dark Tudor woodwork, were so tastefully furnished and efficiently organized and so aloft in the New York sky that they seemed deluxe to us. Even the little alcove that served as a kitchen took on distinction by being called a "serving pantry," as though it came equipped with a butler.

Since the summer playground league was in full swing, I didn't want to leave to go to New York. For several days, with Bobby and Sandy in tow, I moped around Riverside Park, as empty and dead in the July heat as Grant's Tomb. But dull as the days were, the evenings were a revelation. After supper we would go up to the roof garden of the Franklin Towers, where a number of the other residents would gather to relax, talk, and enjoy the breeze coming off the Hudson River. There would be three or four different groups, each with its own discussion, each of them friendly to us as Fan and Belle's sister, nephews, and niece. After an evening or two, the "Weiss kids," as we were called, became something of a hit, Bobby especially because of his gift for arithmetic. Some of the men would delight in giving him a series of numbers to add and subtract in his head, and in his precocious five-year-old way, he would then take them through his system of combining and shedding to arrive at the answer. Sandy's knowledge of music would also be made to shine, and mine of geography, which I had a passion for at the time, poring over and drawing maps of countries and continents, as though it had come with my father's genes.

But the lift of the experience came precisely from its being Life Without Father, that is, in a milieu in which he had no place, in which Mom's values prevailed. She, Sandy, and Bob were staying in the apartment in the building of my aunts' close friends Charley and Bess Previn, who were away for the summer. He was the conductor of the Radio City Music Hall orchestra, the uncle of a musical prodigy my age named André, and the apartment, from its grand piano to its awards and framed photographs and letters, breathed the musical life. And thrilling as living there was to her, it was but one part of the Franklin Towers' ambiance of Upper West Side "refinement."

She had often used the term in a wistful way, as though it were the name of a beautiful foreign city from which she was a refugee. Certainly it seemed as distant from our life in Elizabeth as Paris or Vienna, as unlikely to come into it as my father was to behave like Mr. Sprague. With a boy's stake in coarseness as well as a touch of Dad's disdain, I'd made her use of "refined" into a joking matter, like her crush on the actor Walter Pidgeon as a "fine, wholesome, manly chap." But at the Franklin Towers, all that changed. Mom would come back to the roof after putting Sandy and Bobby to bed and join me in Fan's group, the two of us relishing everything we heard, as close as Mickey and I were at a Dodgers' game.

The roof garden was Fan's element. Her quiet voice, which was matter-of-fact when she answered one of the Lake Tarleton reservation phones, became intense when she discussed books and plays, American politics, or the war in Europe with the other residents. Some of the conversation was over my head, but she had a way of filling me in and drawing Mom and me into the discussion. The talk was so clear and expressive that I quickly picked up on issues that I hadn't understood, like American isolationism, or hadn't known about, like State Department anti-Semitism, the Popular Front in Hollywood, whether Eugene O'Neill or Clifford Odets was the better playwright, and the interpretations of Rubinstein and other pianists versus Paderewski's, who had just died. The last topic gave Mom a chance to put her two cents in. I could tell from the way she spoke that she felt awkward in this company, but by the end of the first week she had lost a lot of her shyness and none of her thrill.

Even the talk about sports was different. One of the men was a baseball fan and told me stories about players in his day, like Hal Chance and Ty Cobb and Ross Young, who were legends in mine. It wasn't the usual man-to-boy baseball talk, the adult reminiscing while the boy sat there like a microphone. Bill Edmonds, a twinkling, sandy-haired man, had just the right touch in drawing me out, as though conversation itself were a finesse sport like tennis or golf. The fact that he was a businessman and a Gentile made the experience all the more remarkable. In the roof garden of the Franklin Towers, people seemed to be New Yorkers before they were anything else. There was an elderly couple who spoke English in a foreign but delicate way, my first "refugees," who were interested in, of all things, my junior high school education. Like Mr. Edmonds, like most of the others, they took me seriously, actually listened.

It wasn't only the attention and the new information that both stimulated and sobered me but even more the style and fluency of the language it came in, the well-chosen words of cultivated minds. I began to see what "refined" really was and that I could become it. It became to me the realm of Jewish quality that was beyond money—a whole new perspective. I don't imagine there was much financial distress on the roof of the Franklin Towers or that I failed to understand that money didn't grow on trees for these people. What I was picking up, for the first time, was the civilized life that money was merely the means to: it bought you a ticket to the concert but did nothing for your appreciation and understanding of the music and its performance. Until then, I had gotten my idea of refinement mostly from the movies—that you had to be handsome, rich, or English, preferably all three, like Cary Grant or Ronald Colman. But on the roof of the Franklin Towers I began to sense the potential for refinement in myself. I already felt a little that way—a kind of buoyant, softspoken clarity, as though my mind, like my body each evening, had taken a shower and gotten dressed in nice clothes. It was as physical as that: being refined meant the dirty, homely Jew-beaked image I had of myself was replaced by a clean, cultured, Jewishly attractive one.

All of which, I think, was mainly connected to being with Aunt Fan. Perhaps because she had been homely herself as a child, she looked at me in a different way than did my mother, who had been the family beauty. If I basked in the regard of sophisticated adults, it was as Fan's nephew, since this was so much her milieu. But beyond that, it was her countenance that was shining upon me and would continue to do so, does so as I write these words.

Her hair was unruly, like mine, but otherwise she was a modestly modish New York woman. She taught high school English at the Crown Heights Yeshiva in Brooklyn, where she produced a mimeographed "literary magazine" of her students' prose and poems and directed their performances of contemporary plays. She had a gift for placing the right book at the right time in a young reader's hands. In my case, the one that summer was Ring Lardner's *Round Up*, a collection of his stories, most of them about maverick baseball players and other eccentric or crazed Americans from the heartland, many of them from Michigan no less. I could see that John R. Tunis wasn't a patch, as Midwesterners said, on Ring Lardner. *Iron Duke* and *The Kid from Tomkinsville* were like going to the movies, because you knew it was made up even when it held you, but *Round Up* was like taking a train through the Middle West and listening to all the passengers telling you or each other their life stories in their own way of talking. I told her that, and she repeated the part about Lardner that evening. Bill Edmonds said that Ring Lardner was Mark Twain brought up to date, which seemed just right to me.

I must have read all of the stories in *Round Up* five times each in the next few years. I couldn't get enough of Alibi Ike, the demon outfielder who lies as compulsively about his hits as he does about his errors and anything in between, and is always being strung along. "Boys," the manager says to the others in the dugout after Ike has explained why he homered instead of sacrificing, "Ike's learned how to hit Marquard's curve. Pretend a fast one's coming and then try to miss it." Or Hurry Cane, the lovelorn "rube" who unwittingly takes his team to the "World Serious" with a fastball that "made it seem like Walter Johnson had never pitched nothing but toy balloons." Or the demented all-hit, no-field "roomie" who on road trips runs the bath through the night and shaves in the middle of it, terrifyingly waving his straight razor while he bellows "Silver Threads Among the Gold."

Lardner's sardonic baseball stories were the perfect next step beyond the ethos of pluck and hard work of the Tunis series and the impersonal matter-of-factness of the sports pages. They came from the part of the baseball psyche inhabited by Dizzy and Daffy Dean and Al Schacht ("The Clown Prince of Baseball") and appealed to my emerging adolescent's discovery of the ridiculous.

Other stories provided my imagination with its first taste of literary blood—the speaker telling you one thing and the story another, as Lardner did in the boys-will-be-boys brutality of "Haircut." Or the small-town mentality of "The Golden Honeymoon" turning the yuks and clichés of programs like *Fibber McGee and Molly* into home truths. Or the mounting items of phoniness and treachery in "A Day with Conrad Green" that add up to a portrait of a hypocritical shit, a much more complete one in a few pages than that of Uriah Heep. From the gas company in Niles, Michigan, to the offices and mansions of show biz, from the country club golf course to the boxing arena, Ring Lardner had everybody's number.

During the period we lived in the Franklin Towers, Aunt Fan displaced Gil as the most significant Weiss in my life. I still idolized him, but he had little time for me or the family anymore. After moving back to New York from Elizabeth he had taken up with a theater producer, Gustav Bloom, and his stunning daughter, Betty. Though

Gil was driving a laundry truck for the same company that employed his brother Jack, you wouldn't know it from seeing him evenings in his fancy Manhattan clothes or listening to him talking about his contacts with showmen like Billy Rose. His sisters were divided about the new course his career had taken. Fan thought he should stick to acting, at which he was having some success with a small theater company in New York. Belle, who was more swayed by the glamorous life, said that becoming a producer was just right for Gil because he had always been so good at organizing things at the hotel and could "charm the birds from the trees"—that is, businessmen into becoming backers.

But their main concern now was us. Mom told me that they wanted her to move to New York for good, that instead of holding the marriage together for the sake of the children, she had to break it up for just that reason, that Dad was an even worse father than he was a husband. Their plan was to help her find a job as a bookkeeper, which would be easy to do because of the new military draft, and an apartment nearby. She communed with me in her uncertain way about staying in New York. I was used to being taken into her confidence, I felt more at home there than anywhere else in our relationship. But I had stood in my own shoes there; now I was being asked to step into Dad's, to be the man of the house instead of a twelve-year-old boy watching the organized softball season slip away, and with it my life as I'd known it. Also the the idea of us without Dad was like Elmora seceding from Elizabeth.

After about ten days, Dad showed up at the apartment one evening and announced he had come to "bring my wife and children home where they belong," as though Belle and Fan had kidnapped us. An hour or two of Dad's sweet talk followed, all that was needed to reattach his lasso to Mom's heart. By the time Sandy, Bobby, and I got back from the roof garden where we had been sent, our suitcases were packed.

Dad's "improvement" lasted through most of the summer. He even rented two rooms in an old hotel in Belmar that was doing wartime service as a boardinghouse, so my Saturday-night worries were over. The first night back in Elizabeth he took Mom shopping at Fishman's, a swanky women's store, and bought her a handsome

coat with a full-length skunk trim. She proudly wore the coat that fall
to Rosh Hashanah services at the Temple, Elizabeth's fashionable
synagogue, which she began to attend on her own. But she soon discovered that in wet weather the animal seemed to come alive again
and cast an odor.

6 THOUGH INTENSELY AWARE of being Jewish, I knew next to
nothing about Judaism. My mother had bundled much of her
strict Orthodox upbringing with the rest of her unhappy Cream
Ridge experience; my father regarded his heritage as the Zionist nonsense that his father had "*schlepped* after." So I didn't have to go to
Hebrew school and spent Sunday mornings in our neighborhood,
where the only Jewish artifact was a little blue-and-white collection
box for Palestine at Sam Felber's candy store, a weird Jewish version
of the March of Dimes.

When I went to Hamilton Junior High I began to hang out with
my classmates during Rosh Hashanah and Yom Kippur outside the
Murray Street shul. Enjoying the time off from school, we lightly
horsed around in our good clothes, our only observance being to pass
around the vial of smelling salts that was supposed to help us fast
until we went home for lunch. I had zero interest in the significance
of either holiday and seldom went inside the shul to watch and listen.
In the early 1940s, Judaism had not yet entered its suburban
American revival, and the Murray Street schul reminded me of the
old men, the family relics, I would sometimes see in the back of a
Jewish candy store or tailor shop, poring over a religious book—
ignored, barely alive, beside the point. The shul's yellowish prayer
shawls, its prayer books with their broken spines, its shabby altar
cloth, the faded velvet Torah mantle—it all seemed like the last of
the luggage that had been brought over from the Old World.

About halfway through my thirteenth year, Mom's friends at
Hadassah and Aunt Fan began to lean on her about having me bar
mitzvahed, which woke her up to the realization that her father

would turn over in his grave if I wasn't. She approached Dad, but he wasn't interested. "Your family wants him bar mitzvahed? Good, let them pay for it." She had to go to Aunt Belle for my tuition.

At Young Israel, I was put in the older class because of my age. Not knowing even the Hebrew alphabet when I started, I would have been at a serious disadvantage if learning, instead of mischief-making, had been our principal activity. Our teacher, a refugee, spoke only enough English to be ridiculed. When the class got completely out of hand he would send for the director, Rabbi Halberstadter, who taught the younger class. Rabbi was a muscular, still youngish man, who was said to have been a big-time soccer fullback in Palestine, and he brought peace with a sword. He entered the suddenly quiet room, slowly rolled his shirt sleeve over his right bicep, and asked who was looking for trouble.

On Sunday morning Rabbi would bring both classes together for religious instruction, which would culminate in a story from the Bible. He had a gift for locating these stories in an imaginative place that straddled Biblical times and ours, so that his Jacob in Haran was also a greenhorn who through diligence and cunning triumphs in his new land. His son Joseph was also the first Jewish intellectual, whose visionary power, organizing ability, and eloquence enabled him, like Theodore Herzl, to rescue his people.

After a month or so, Rabbi came into class one afternoon and took me with him to his study. It was a small bare room filled with books, two chairs, a table, and him. "Sit down, Theodore," he said, his tone the verbal version of rolling up his sleeve.

I didn't set him straight about calling me Ted. Theodore was his name too, and it had a different aura as such, nothing sissy about it. Besides, he was clearly all male business. It wasn't like talking to a teacher, even a principal. It was like talking to Mr. Nolan, the JV basketball coach, who didn't like my game.

"When are you bar mitzvah?" he asked in his rumbling baritone edged with Germanic steel.

"October," I said.

"What year?"

"This year."

"At the rate you are learning, you will be ready, perhaps, when you are twenty-one. You are still too ignorant for even tutoring. Also Mr. Neiderlander says you give him more trouble than anyone."

He let that sink in and then told me that he was putting me in his own afternoon class. He could have hit me with his bulging arm and I wouldn't have been more rocked. His class was the little kids' class. I told him I would feel like a total jerk in it.

He looked straight into me. "No," he said. "You are now the total jerk. An ignoramus who thinks he's a comedian. You will remain neither in my class."

I could have walked out then and there, but I didn't. Instead I followed him to his class, both admiring and fearing him for the breadth and roll of those shoulders. I followed him because what else could I do? He talked and moved like a coach.

After two sessions with the little kids and lots of practice with Mom at home, I was pronouncing the words accurately, and soon I was writing them in script, even constructing simple sentences about *yeleds* and *yaldahs*. Rabbi allowed me to return to the other class, where I did enough work and kept quiet enough to keep from being demoted again. The older class was mostly a kind of holding pen for boys in the peculiar terminal stage of Jewish education called the bar mitzvah, in which the traditional rite of passage that made us a member of the congregation generally marked our passage out of Judaism until we married and had children of our own, if then.

In June, four months before my thirteenth birthday, I began to report to Rabbi's apartment once a week to prepare my *haftorah*, the portion of the Torah I had to learn to chant on the day of my bar mitzvah. I thought I would still just be going through the motions of learning, running the last long lap of the slow race against boredom until the day when I would star for an hour in the synagogue and then at a party where I would collect lots of money. But in the bookish peacefulness of his apartment, Rabbi Halberstadter made me a genuine pupil. He was different from the disciplinarian of the poky little school and even from the dramatic Sunday-morning storyteller. He patiently corrected my faulty pronunciation and guided my faltering chant with a rich baritone that gave the rather singsong pitches and cantillation of the accompaniment some flair, made it more pleasurable and even at times lovely to learn.

When I told him that my Solotaroff grandparents had been part of the First Aliyah, I became interesting to him, rather than just another American pagan who didn't begin to realize what it meant to be a Jew. And when I told him about the Solotaroff property in Hadera and said that my grandfather had been one of the original colonists and my grandmother the nurse there, it was like telling a Texan that my ancestors had been at the Alamo. "You have good Jewish blood, Theodore," he said. "Don't waste it." He helped me to understand the text I was *davening*, a very eloquent one from the prophet Isaiah. He also inspired the customary little speech I gave, mine being about Jewish manliness, kindness mixed with strength. By then I had incorporated him into the expanding list of Jewish males (somewhere between Sid Luckman, now of the mighty Chicago Bears, and Albert Einstein) that I carried in my head to remind me why I was proud to be a Jew and also that there were all kinds of us.

The big Saturday came. To my classmates' surprise, I delivered my *haftorah* flawlessly and gave my speech without giggling. Rabbi embraced me with an enthusiastic bear hug, as though I had just scored a goal for Judaism. Afterward, as was the custom, my family supplied the *kiddush*—herring on crackers and wine for the congregants of the shul, Milky Ways for my classmates. That evening there was a party at our house, the high point of our social life during this time. Lou Holtz, my father's best friend, and his wife, Molly, played violin duets, Aunt Sophie played one of her prodigious pieces, Sandy one of her sensitive ones. Mickey sang several arias, and then he and Gil went into a deadpan comedy routine of a clumsy doctor and a nervous patient. At the end Gil thanked Dad for the lavish spread of food and liquor. "You know, I've always thought of Ben as a man with short arms and deep pockets, but . . ." Dad was furious.

I collected close to sixty dollars, a teenage fortune in 1941. With most of it, I planned to buy the Columbia bicycle with balloon tires. The next morning, in one of his foul moods, Dad put the arm on the money. "It will go for paying me back for that party of yours and my expenses at the shul."

There was no further explanation, nor did I argue with him. Still working with the givens, I went upstairs, got forty-two dollars, mostly in the checks I couldn't deposit myself, and hid the rest. He took the checks and cash, shoved the wad in his pocket without counting it. When I told Mom, she said that he had been very offended by Gil's joke, but that was no excuse for taking my bar mitzvah money. "I hope you didn't give him all of it."

"Of course not," I said. I bought a good bike from a friend with the money left over. She told Dad that it was a special gift from Belle and Fan. I told myself that his behavior wasn't the Jews' fault.

During the week or so we lived at the Franklin Towers, Aunt Fan had read to me an item in the *New York Times* reporting a sermon delivered the previous Sunday at St. Patrick's Cathedral. Speaking about the chaotic condition of America, the bishop said that it was caused by too much of Shylock's practices and too little of Christ's. He asked his parishioners if they were going to let the modern Samsons pull the Church down over their heads.

Fan asked me if I knew what he was talking about. I said that it wasn't as bad as what Father Coughlin and Gerald L. K. Smith said about us. Fan said it was worse, because it was coming from a Catholic bishop and its venom was more subtle and dangerous. She showed me how the poison was skillfully injected without mentioning the word "Jew," using the Bible and Shakespeare to deliver it. The Irish Catholics were the worst, she said, because they hated England and they blamed Jews for wanting to get America into the war on England's side. That's what the reference to Samson was about.

This was troubling information. Like many American boys I had a crush on the Irish, the most prominent and romantic of the minority groups. Popular culture was awash in Irish sentiment, a kind of ongoing St. Patrick's Day celebrated in politics and sports as well as in Hollywood and Tin Pan Alley. The Irish political machine was to politics what the Italian Syndicate, as it was called then, was to organized crime: a glamorous corruption. In New York there was Tammany Hall, waiting in the wings of the La Guardia administration to take over again, which it would soon do. In New Jersey there was the Hague machine, in Boston the Curley, in Chicago the Kelly—the bandit chiefs of the democratic process. In Elizabeth we had James Brophy, who was mayor through most of my boyhood and adolescence, though he was said to be honest.

In football, of course, there were "the Fighting Irish" of Notre Dame, with its vast "subway alumni." In my imagination South Bend, Indiana, was the Camelot of college football, whose king, Knute Rockne, had seized the Excalibur of the forward pass from the stone of the rule book and made it into the brilliant weapon that defeated much-favored Army and then everyone else. It didn't much matter that the progenitor of the Fighting Irish was himself of Norwegian stock, as his Lancelot figure, the forward passer Gus Dorais, was of French, or that many of the legendary heroes that followed, such as George Gipp and two of the Four Horsemen, were not Irish either. In my mind, as in everyone else's, the words "Notre Dame" were colored kelly green and gold.

In boxing, Irish fighters were automatically the "crowd favorite," as though they possessed more courage and "class" by belonging to the most virile and colorful of the white ethnic groups. That they were at best contenders by this time, the champs coming from the lower, hotter levels of the melting pot—Negroes, Italians, and Slavs—made the Irish boxer even more a figure of romance. The whitest of the white hopes to unseat Joe Louis was handsome Billy Conn, who had outpointed the Brown Bomber until he cockily tried to slug with him. The manner of his defeat made him all the more America's favorite boxer, the Jimmy Cagney of the ring.

Being still an ardent Joe Louis fan, I hadn't rooted for Conn, but I had my own romance with Irishness. Part of this was fostered by the movies of the day. In the Great American Superego projected by Hollywood, the Irish were the DAs and the cops; the Italians were the robbers; the Jews were the Mob advisers, the expert safecrackers, the defense lawyers; and the Wasps were the judges. Even the Irish criminals, as played by Jimmy Cagney and others, remained sympathetic rogues in the starry eyes of the Hollywood studios.

It was grand to be Catholic as well as Irish, thanks to a succession of able priests, who were both firm and understanding: Spencer Tracy as Father Flanagan in *Boys Town*, and Pat O'Brien, as the priest in *The Fighting 69th* and *Angels With Dirty Faces*, and later Barry Fitzgerald and Bing Crosby in *Going My Way*. But that is only the tip of this iceberg of memory, for film after film would have one manly actor or another in a Roman collar, stationed halfway between society and God, a salt-of-the-earth figure of compassion and rectitude, helping the crooked to go straight, the bereaved to regain their faith, the defeated to remember that tomorrow is a whole new ball game.

All of this was generic. My crush on the St. Genevieve guys was specific and long-standing. One Saturday evening that July, seven or eight of them, including the three vaunted Ward brothers, turned up at the school playground and got a softball game going. It was sort of like the summer league again, and again I was put in the outfield as one of the younger and weaker players. But I made a couple of nice catches and threw out a runner at third, and the positive image of myself took over, which I was then calling "rangy."

Until that evening I had been just another one of the playground kids hanging around on the fringe of the St. Genevieve crowd, a secret fan of their athletic skills, parochial prep school culture, Irish Catholic ways. George Tiernan, whom I knew best, since he lived across from the school, was on the track team at Seton Hall in South Orange. Howie Newhart pitched for the junior varsity at St. Benedict's in Newark. Miles Gilson, the "brain" in the group, went to Xavier in New York. Jim and Jack Ward, the twins, had gone to my junior high, where they were star ends on the football team and forwards on the basketball team. Next year their brother Shrimp would go there and become the dominant athlete, because he was even tougher than the twins. (He would later be an All-American lineman at Maryland.) The others traveled to prep schools an hour or more from Elizabeth and had to handle hours of homework in Latin and Ethics and something called Rhetoric as well as much tougher versions of the math, science, and history that were taught in the public schools. It all seemed very strict and yet bracing, a Marine boot camp for the mind.

Over the last summer or two I had become friendly with George Tiernan, a quiet, solid teenager, two years older than I. We had listened at his house to the All-Star game, which Ted Williams had won with a home run in the ninth, a great climax to a game that was particularly memorable because it had taken me into my first Catholic home. George lived with his aunt, because his mother had died. She was an elderly woman whose face was covered in faded freckles, and her presence seemed as stiff and dry as a carton of old curtains. For refreshments she gave us a box of Vermont maple sugar to share. I had never tasted it before, and its too-sweet, crumbly texture in my mouth also seemed part of this austere atmosphere where a mother had died. This, too, was somehow Catholic, death being easily associated in my fervent curiosity with the severe clothes and faces of real-life priests who gave people last rites all the time, and the even more perturbing black-and-white habits and the bare, pallid faces of nuns that made them seem like God's witches.

Normally after an evening game like this one the St. Genevieve guys went off together and I went home by myself. But tonight George asked me if I wanted to come along. They were going to Felber's for a soda, then they all had to go to confession, but after that they would hang out somewhere. There was a welcome in the others' faces as well, at least some of them, including Jim Ward's, the nicest of the Ward brothers. He had always called me Ted instead of Solly or Sol as the others did, one or two of them with a mock-Yiddish "Sz." But tonight they were all calling me Ted or Sol without a smirk in it, dealing me into the conversation, as I elatedly straggled along with them up Shelley Avenue, as though a new person, a confident, rangy athlete and full American, was being born inside of me.

A half hour later I was sitting by myself on the front steps of Miles Gilson's nice house across the street from St. Genevieve's, where they had left me while they went inside for confession. Tommy Hopkins and Jim Curry, who were my age, were serving as altar boys at mass the next day, but they all had to confess their sins, as George Tiernan had explained to me, so that they could do penance for them and receive Holy Communion at mass. On the way over, there had been a lot of casual talk about the priests and even jokes and teasing about serving and confession and so forth, but these practices of their religion invested it with a moral and spiritual aura in my mind and made its rules loom with a compelling power. Here were the best athletes and the toughest fighters in my end of Elmora, who for all of their horsing around about it took their religion seriously and respected its obligations.

As I sat there in the quiet darkness, gazing through the spiked iron fence at the handsome gray stone church, the words "serve" and "confession," "penance" and "Holy Communion" and "high mass," entered and rose in my mind like solemn, thrilling music. It was like the moment in a movie when some unlikely person steps forward and sings "Ave Maria" beautifully, and a great hush of reverence descends on all of the characters, even if they are in prison. I had no idea what a mass was or why people believed that a little wafer and a sip of wine could contain the body and blood of Jesus Christ, but the idea of getting your sins off your chest by saying a few prayers that cleaned up your conscience seemed like a wonderful gift from your religion, particularly for someone like myself who kept doing things he was ashamed of.

As I sat there pondering the trade-off between going to confession and having to go to a school for eight years where the priests cuffed your ear and the nuns rapped your knuckles hard with a ruler, a figure came out of the church, and as he passed through the gate of the spiked fence, I saw that he was a priest. Nervously, I watched him cross the street and turn and walk toward the Gilson house as though my presence in this Catholic neighborhood had been reported to him. I looked away as he drew near, but he stopped and began peering at me.

"Good evening, my son," he said. "Are you staying with the Gilsons?"

I was seized by confusion. I didn't know how to address him. Half of me wanted to call him Father and half of me didn't. I managed to shake my head.

"Cat got your tongue?" he asked, his eyes crinkling. He was a small, slender, elderly man, with a brisk, businesslike manner rather than a stern one.

"I'm just waiting here," I said. "I'm a friend of George Tiernan's. He and Miles and the others are at confession and Miles said I could wait here for them."

"I don't think I've seen you before. Do you live in the neighborhood?"

"No . . ." I said, my mind again tripping and falling flat over the Father word. But I wanted to say something that would show him respect, that would use my good manners, so that he wouldn't think that I was some dumb Italian or Greek kid from the Port, or one of the Jewish louts who shot pool at the YMHA, which were the ways I saw myself in his eyes. So I said, "No, sir. I'm from the Shelley

Avenue neighborhood, near where George lives. We were all playing softball together."

"I see," he said. "Just cooling off." He continued looking at me. "You're not Catholic, are you?"

I shook my head.

"I thought for a moment you might be. You look Italian. What's your name?"

I told him. I had to say it twice and then spell it for him to get it. Then I said, "It's Jewish."

"It sounds Russian," he said in his brisk way. "Is your nationality Russian?"

"No, it's American. My parents were both born here."

"I was wondering about your extraction. Of course we're all Americans now," he said. "And we all worship the same God, don't we?"

I nodded, not wanting him to know that I didn't worship God in the way he meant. I was afraid he would ask me why I wasn't home or at temple on my Sabbath, though by now it was already over.

After he went on, I thought about what it would be like to be Catholic, to have someone like him in my life who was in charge of the part of me that wanted to behave better and whom I could call Father. I said the word aloud several times, trying it out. "Yes, Father." "No, Father." Then I said, "Father, I have sinned." It seemed the best thing of all about being Catholic.

But also, as I realized, the thing that made being Catholic most remote from me. My taking bar mitzvah lessons had nothing to do with worshiping God in the way that George and Miles and the others were doing right now. I liked and respected Rabbi Halberstadter, but he was not someone I could go to and say, "Rabbi, I have sinned. I have jerked off every night this week and twice today at The Shop," or "I have teased my sister until she cried," or "I have broken three windows in the Shelley Avenue school and can't stop." Learning my *haftorah* from him had nothing to do with my conscience or with the feelings that made me pray on the beach in Belmar.

Once I started thinking about Rabbi Halberstadter I came in touch again with what prevented me from calling the priest Father, what made the word as I breathed it now both a self-mockery and a betrayal. I looked across the street again at St. Genevieve's, but what I saw now was not the graceful portals and arches but the black iron fence in front of it with its grim spikes on which it was said a boy climbing over them was once so badly injured that he'd almost lost his leg from blood poisoning. While the building receded again into the remoteness of its doctrines and practices, the fence came forbiddingly forward as a barrier not only to it but to the different person I had felt like with the St. Genevieve boys. Now there was just me again; a few good catches didn't change anything, didn't make me belong with the St. Genevieve guys. I got to my feet and hurried away before they came out of confession.

7 BILL JORDAN WAS a small, bandy-legged Englishman in his late fifties, with merry blue eyes, leathery skin, a few discolored teeth, and an imperturbable disposition. There was usually a Chesterfield dangling from his mouth and a gravelly cough in his chest. He'd say, "'Twasn't the cough that took him off / 'Twas the coffin they took him off'n."

Bill worked for my father six days a week, from eight to six, riding a bus for an hour to and from Irvington, where he lived with his wife and two sons—Bill Jr., an apprentice electrician at Westinghouse, and Bobby, a high school student who also "contributed" by working after school and Saturdays in a machine shop. I hung on Bill's every word about his sons, as though they were characters in a moving and edifying novel. That Bill Jr. didn't mind being called that spoke to me of family happiness and solidarity and what a father-son relationship could be. So did Bill's warm accounts of their Thanksgiving and Christmas dinners, birthday celebrations, Sunday outings, and other occasions of family joy and harmony. Then Bill Jr. enlisted in the Navy and in six months was in the thick of it on a cruiser in the Pacific, which personalized the war for me more than anything else did.

Bill was also remarkable because he got along so well with my father, his good nature impervious to the sarcasm and anger that were turned on him more than the others because he was around more and was nonunion. But no matter how short or even abusive Dad was with him, Bill never lost his dignity. "You have to understand your dad," he'd say to me. "He's got a nasty streak he can't control. You can't take it personally, any more than you would a little boy's temper." In a good mood, Dad would say, "Bill's like a father to me. There's nothing he wouldn't do if I asked him."

On Saturday afternoons I helped Bill in the warehouse and shop in back or on the delivery truck. It was an old GMC with a raised bed covered by an old mattress. Between the mattress and a couple of filthy quilts a desktop or a large wall mirror or a window would ride, as Bill said, "like a bloody beggar in a doss-house." Along with keeping me entertained, Bill made me feel useful. Dad was always saying, "You don't know how to apply yourself." But under Bill's patient guidance (he could have taught a monkey to cut glass or point and putty a window), I learned how to work. Dad liked to say, "If it's worth doing, it's worth doing well." But if I got the soundtrack of that from him, I didn't get the picture. His working motto was really "Time is money," and he reinforced mental quickness, drive, and impatience in me rather than painstakingness. That was inculcated during the five years or so I hung around Bill Jordan and learned how to handle glass.

The Shop was a pungent place. There was the fresh, country smell of straw when you unpacked the long cases of rough or polished wire glass that had come all the way from Mississippi. There was the cold, damp aroma of the linseed oil puddled on the surface when you opened a can of putty, and the heady smell of the oil that you dipped your glass cutter into to protect its diamond edge. There was the wet sand odor of the Carborundum that you used to smooth and bevel the edges of plate glass and to drill holes in it. Fifty years ago, an automobile windshield or door window often had to be cut to size; a thin coil of red-hot wire was positioned along the cut to melt the laminate between the two sheets, which would give off a baked-apple smell. But the odor that remains most keenly evocative for me, stationed permanently at the juncture of my olfactory nerve and my long-term memory, is that of ammonia, the fluid glaziers use to revive and clean the surface of used glass.

I need only a whiff of those biting fumes and I am back again at The Shop—anytime from my twelfth to eighteenth year—standing on a box so that I can lean farther out over the big cutting table on which there is a slab of plate glass that I am cleaning and polishing with a bottle of ammonia and wad of newspaper, my eyes tearing, my nostrils smarting, but my mind engrossed by the task of doing a good job without getting cut by the jagged edge of the break or the razor edges of the sides that can slice right through my rubber gloves.

In the glass business, a broken storefront window or "lite" is generally not a complete loss. It is removed carefully from its molding, lifted out and set down, then cut on one or more sides of the break, both to prevent the break from extending, possibly maiming the men handling it, and to preserve the usable remnant. This is called "salvage," and its value is deducted from the price that the insurance company pays for the replacement, but it is usually worth twice that deduction.

Dad was so intent on maximizing salvage that he could keep two or three men standing around on a replacement job for half an hour at union wages until he got there and inspected the possibilities. Also he was the one who did the cutting. He could look at a sixteen-by twenty-foot lite with two breaks in it and know almost immediately how to cut it to create the largest possible piece or pieces of salvage. He would take off his overcoat or suit jacket and, climbing a ladder, begin cutting at the top, sustaining the incision all the way to the break and then continuing it to the bottom, the line as steady as though he were cutting along one of the big L Squares we used for table cutting. Then he would tap the cut and the massive glass would part cleanly all the way down.

On Saturday afternoon, when things slowed down and the huge carpet-covered cutting table was free, Bill Jordan and I would go into the floor-to-ceiling rack that held the salvage and select the pieces to fill next week's orders. Using thick rubber pads that curved in the hand, we'd shift the lites of salvage to the other side of the rack until we got to the ones that would do. Then he and I would walk the first one out to the cutting table, rest it on wooden blocks to protect the edge, and with a "one-two-three, lift," hoist its top up and onto the table and slide it forward.

I'd set to work with my ammonia bottle and a razor blade to remove the display paint and any other "crap" on the lite; then, turning my head as much as I could from the ammonia fumes, I'd go over the surface with a wad of newspaper, polishing the lite until I could see my reflection in it. My job was to make it look like new, so that, cut to size, it could go back on the big side-panel Ford as a new plate glass "return," or side window, or, if it was too small for that, as the top of a desk or of a couple of coffee or vanity tables, whose edges Bill and I would smooth and polish and sometimes bevel on the big grindstone to a lovely sea green.

My most onerous and yet satisfying task at The Shop, cleaning and polishing salvage and turning it into something useful and sometimes lovely, seems now like a head start, for someone who was going to make his living from the well-written word.

The other thing I came to do well at The Shop was type. There were still stretches of a month or three when Dad didn't have a girl in the office. Along with reporting there after school to relieve my mother, and on Saturdays for my own day of servitude, I sometimes would have to go with him on Sunday afternoons to type up the bids and covering letters and other correspondence he'd dictate to me as well as the bills he was sending out. He would hand me a bunch of scribbled invoices from the spindle on his desk or from the cigar box in which the big orders were kept, and I would turn them into neat, businesslike bills. It was my one mental skill that found favor with him, and it gave me confidence. I had more anxiety cutting a piece of window glass to size when he was around than I did typing bills or bids in which hundreds and sometimes thousands of dollars were involved. That I could do something well that he couldn't do at all, and that was important to his business, gave me at last a bit of ground to stand on in our relationship.

My new role made him a bit more appreciative and a lot more critical of me. I realized how right Mom was when she'd say to him, "You're only happy when you're finding fault." I could type nine bills flawlessly but it was the barely detectable erasure on the tenth that he would let me know about. "Do this one over. It's a mess."

But that kind of disapproval didn't take the heart out of me anymore. It was the nine flawless ones that mattered to me. "If it's worth doing, it's worth doing well," as he said. Also I was now giving him my Sunday afternoons when I could have been hitting my set shot and making plays in the league at the Y. So instead of getting depressed, I'd get angry when he criticized my typing and hold on to my share of the cold silences. On the way home, he might say, "What're *you* so sullen about?"

"You're always finding fault with me. I make one lousy erasure and you're jumping all over me."

"I'm not finding fault," he might reply. "I'm trying to stay in business. When you send out a bid, you're putting your whole operation on display."

"It wasn't a bid, Dad. It was just a bill for twelve boxes of window glass."

"Is that so, just twelve boxes of window glass. Just enough profit to pay one of my men for the day. There's no such thing as 'just twelve boxes.' Twelve boxes or two hundred boxes. Business is business. But of course having an understanding of how business works is beneath you. You with your head in the clouds."

"That's what I mean. You can't even explain yourself without criticizing me." Or I might just shrug and let the silence resume. As Mom said, he was oblivious of people's feelings.

The irony was that at the belated age of fourteen, I was beginning to take a reluctant interest in his business. He'd moved to a new location up the street and The Shop was a big place now, with three converted and connected stores in front—the showroom, office, and window glass shop—and a new warehouse and plate glass shop out back. The new office soon was a two-tier version of the old one— cold, dirty, and cluttered. Behind the girl's desk that was up two steps from the rest of the office at the back, I typed my way into the workings of the Standard Plate Glass Co.—where the glass came from and where it went, the prices and discounts, the materials and labor, the overhead, receivables, and notes, the stalling, maneuvering, and finagling.

I was also typing my way into Dad's head for business, which I began to comprehend and admire. I watched him as he swung his main operation from plate glass replacements and storefronts, dormant in the early years of the war, to industrial glazing, which was taking off because of the defense plants springing up or expanding in the New Jersey industrial belt whose buckle was Elizabeth.

It was a terrific opportunity and a terrific headache, because the demand for the rough and polished wire glass that formed the walls and the skylights of the plants was so intense and the supply was rationed by a handful of manufacturers. But Dad always seemed to come up with a way of slipping around the line of glazing contractors clamoring for delivery. He would use one of his few friendly competitors, a small outfit in Roselle, to order a full allotment of wire glass it didn't need and then have his check and his truck there the next day to take the shipment. He would locate a small manufacturer, and buy his way into its good graces by furnishing the transportation himself. He'd then sell what he couldn't use of the carload at a premium price to the trade, and use the proceeds to pay off the note he'd taken out to finance it. "There's always an angle," he'd say, "if you know where to look." Sometimes, though, it was just pure drive. He would learn that a distributor in New York had a dozen crates of odd sizes, take them off his hands, and then he, Bill Jordan, and I would spend the weekend cutting a thousand pieces of wire glass to the size and shape he needed. "Everyone says there's a glass shortage," he'd say, "but somehow Ben Solotaroff always seems to have what he needs."

So it was that I received my basic training in relentlessness and opportunism, in thinking around the competition, in talking rough or smooth, in doing whatever it takes to be ready on Monday morning. Twenty years later when I was given a Sunday book review section and then a paperback magazine to run, I didn't need any lessons in imposing myself, working all hours, seeing the openings, playing the angles. One side of me talked to the writers and colleagues; the other one, still in close psychological touch with my father, talked to management, to production, sales, advertising, and promotion people, to wholesalers and retailers. Like Sam Toperoff, whose memoir of his youth revolves around working in his father's candy store in Brooklyn, I had, in this respect, "all the advantages."

Now and then Dad would talk of my coming into the business as what he was working for. We'd be the major wholesaler in the area.

Even with a war on, he had me typing letters to get the inside track with glass manufacturers in France and Belgium who turned out tints and designs of decorative glass that were not available here. When the time came, he could do a lot of business with them, particularly if he had someone who spoke French and knew how to handle himself abroad. But even as I nodded and tried to look interested, I knew by now that none of this was for me—not the glass business, not Elizabeth, certainly not working with him. I hated this Shop that had already kept me from my rightful life, and hated even more the diminished, squelched sense of myself I often still had when I was around him. At such times I felt like a filial version of my mother; just as when she irritated or depressed me, I so readily turned into a filial version of my bitter father.

8   ABOUT A YEAR before I became Dad's typist, I was riding home from the Y in the darkness of a wintry Sunday late afternoon when I learned from the only other passenger that Japan had just bombed Pearl Harbor and destroyed most of our Pacific Fleet. I remember gazing into the empty bus for the next fifteen minutes, as though it were a vehicle taking me and the rest of America to "the great rendezvous with destiny" that had finally begun.

The next three hours were a kind of countdown to Walter Winchell's *Jergens Journal* when the momentousness of the day and the urgency of the task that lay ahead would be confirmed. Winchell came on at nine o'clock, right after Fred Allen's show. For the past two years—with the first staccato tapping of his signature telegraph transmitter, followed by the rapid-fire volley of "Good evening Mr. and Mrs. America and all the ships at sea, let's go to press. Flash! . . ."—we had been bounced out of the Sunday-night fun and back into the daily drama of living on the brink of a second world war. In us, as in twenty million other Americans, Winchell provoked a state of urgent attentiveness. Even Dad inclined his head toward the large Atwater Kent so as not to miss a word.

This gossip columnist turned news melodramatist by now had a grip on the public ear and on Jewish minds and hearts that was second only to President Roosevelt's. Part of his power came from the medium itself, which wired the imagination as well as the eardrum to it, so that we seemed like one of the ships at sea receiving our navigation instructions in these dark times from the command center at WJZ New York. Walter Winchell was one of us—like Jack Benny, Al Jolson, Eddie Cantor, and other media celebrities—but beyond that he was our unofficial ambassador to the White House in behalf of the imperiled Jews of Europe and, given Hitler's lightning conquest of Europe, ourselves.

Not that Winchell spoke out as a Jew. Far from it. I'd assumed he was Irish from his name, his brash voice, his rivalry with Ed Sullivan as the voice of Broadway, until Dad set me straight, telling me that Winchell was not only a Jew but the son of a cantor. But more important than any acknowledgment of his background was his role as our spokesman against the bigots and the isolationists. His broadcasts were full of strong statements like "All good nations hate force, yet every good American would not hesitate to defend his country from attack by international bandits." That's what we Jews were—not a threatened minority begging for special protection for our brethren overseas, but good Americans ready to fight for our freedom.

Winchell was also our spokesman precisely because he stood for the American part of our identity and threw only a vague shadow on the Jewish part. The great project that virtually every one of my friends at Hamilton shared was to become ever more American to ourselves as well as to the world. Jews and post-immigrants we already were—the postulates of our identity—whereas Americans was what we were constantly trying to prove we were. (In the eighth grade I spelled my last name with only one *f* at the end, so that it wouldn't be as long and hence as foreign.) Now the war would help us to be recognized as true Americans. That was its primary meaning; the plight of European Jewry was secondary, often a dim secondary.

With the symbiotic relation of American Jews to Israel or the demonstrations in behalf of Soviet Jewry fresh in mind, it has been hard for younger Jews to understand our relative obliviousness to the Holocaust that was just getting underway. Did I know about the ship crammed to the gunwales with desperate refugees that was turned back from New York Harbor? Dimly. "It's a shame," we said, hardly taking the phrase to heart, much less to conscience. In our hearts we were still partially refugees ourselves, lucky to belong to families that had had the foresight to leave Europe when the going was good. Neither the Weisses nor the Solotaroffs, as far as we knew, had any relatives left there, which conceivably would have made the plight of Europe's Jews more immediate and pressing. Without this prod to thinking otherwise, our family, like most others, docilely put our trust in President Roosevelt, assured that he was doing the most and best that he could for us.

America's entrance into the war ushered in the most positive and thrilling phase of the American century. Never before or after was it possible for almost everyone to be harmoniously a patriot, a nationalist, a liberal, a militarist, a capitalist, a populist, a Soviet sympathizer, and a moralist. We civilians enjoyed the solidarity, drama, and conviction of a righteous people in a just war with none of the risks, hardships, destruction, and death (except for military casualties) that the civilians of other countries engaged in it had to endure. Nor any of the mass anxiety and terror once we won the first Pacific sea battles, invaded North Africa, and turned the U.S. into virtually a three-thousand-mile-long military base and war plant.

Though we were now part of the "home front," there were no real burdens to speak of. Gas was rationed, but as a contractor for the city, Dad got plenty of fuel for his trucks and his car. Food was rationed, but I don't remember it affecting our diet. Otherwise we drew curtains over our windows at night to counter the remotest of possibilities that German bombers would reach Elizabeth or its submarines would navigate by the lamplight from Belmar. My main contribution to the war effort was selling war stamps in the hallway at school, stamps which one could save up for a war bond. All in all, it was like being enjoined to remember that "loose lips sink ships," when about the only information I had to impart was that my uncle Gil, a public relations officer, was stationed in England and my uncle Mickey was singing with a USO group in Europe and Asia.

I don't remember for a moment fearing that America would lose the war. We were righteous, we were undefeated—God's terrible swift sword against the indisputably evil Axis powers. By 1943 there was also a social component to my faith that developed through the rest of the war, not unlike my shift from the Yankees to the Dodgers. Uncle Sam, the patrician Yankee with his top hat, goatee, and rolled-up sleeves, gave way to plebeian GI Joe as the personification of the American cause. We armed our troops not only with more and better weapons but also with the higher and stauncher morale of a democracy. As the war went on, I eagerly watched the society take on more of the equality we read about in citizenship class. Industrialists and defense workers, male and female, of all complexions and creeds, were united, just as our armed forces were, by an empowered egalitarianism doing battle against the forces of regimented oppression. Just as so much was made of the heel-clicking, goose-stepping, and "Heil Hitler" saluting of the cold robotlike Nazis and of the treachery and rapacity leading on the crazed hordes of Japanese, so the American fighting man came to be seen as a war-heightened version of not only the boy next door but of the good man from the other side of the tracks—brave, resolute but decent, armed with chocolate bars as well as ammo.

So it was that the war years extended and amplified the faith in the common man that I'd been growing up with during the 1930s. Just as Tom Joad, Mr. Deeds, the hero of *Sullivan's Travels*, even the Dead End Kids were thrust at me by the Hollywood of the Depression as both victims of society and the vanguard of a populist renewal of it, so the culture of World War II tended to find the chief exemplars of our fighting spirit in the ranks. There was less of the traditional general and admiral worship, of the romantic spotlight playing upon the young officers. The heroes of the movies were more often the Sergeant Yorks and the Audie Murphys, and most often the democratic unit—the infantry squad, the bomber crew, the ship's company—almost always composed of the requisite cross section, including, occasionally, an Hispanic or Negro. Going to the war movies, listening to the radio plays of Norman Corwin and Arch Obler, reading the dispatches of Ernie Pyle, poring over the cartoons of Bill Mauldin and Dave Breger, each presenting the war from the viewpoint of GI Joe or "the little guy"—all of this produced a great crest of patriotic liberalism that I and most of my generation rode into the postwar era. At the same time, the egalitarian triumph began to relax some of the Jewish outsiderness and defensiveness I'd been carrying around in my head. "All races and religions," I crooned along with Frank Sinatra. "That's America to me."

9 LITTLE OF THE wartime profit at the Standard Plate Glass Co. flowed to our house on Shelley Avenue. There was a slight easing of the household money shortage, but the most notable change was that Dad went away more on weekends to get the "little rest and relaxation" he needed to keep going and couldn't get at home. His Sunday mornings at the Y or hikes with the club were replaced by weekends at nearby resorts in spring and summer and ski trips in winter to Vermont and even to the Laurentian Mountains in Canada. Skiing required a whole new wardrobe for him—a fleece-lined parka, special waterproof pants and doeskin mittens, turtleneck shirts in several colors, a sweater from prewar Norway with reindeer across the front, silk inner socks and thick wool outer ones, and a pair of stylish low boots with leather laces and grooves in the heels that were worn only to ski in. He had never done any household tasks, but now as we watched him meticulously wax his skis, "made from the finest ash," and adjust the cable bindings, it was as though we were suddenly living with an aristocratic sportsman.

His skiing brought him into a new circle of people, "people who know how to live," as he put it. One of them was "quite a gal" named Flo Chanin. There didn't appear to be a Mr. Chanin, or maybe he didn't ski. Flo made the arrangements for the ski train and the lodge, and a couple of times when she called The Shop, I answered the phone. She had a quick husky voice like Aunt Belle's, so I imagined she was one of those worldly women who talked a man's language and drank Scotch.

What Mom made of these expensive new goings-on was not evident to us. She seemed to regard Dad's weekends as she did his taking the cream from the milk bottle for his coffee—prerogatives that were beyond her questions, much less demands. She would say to her sisters

or her friend Rae Bloch, "I don't stand in Ben's way," in the same matter-of-fact way one might talk about the *Twentieth Century Limited.*

She herself was branching out a bit. She had met Rae in the neighborhood. An energetic, companionable woman, Rae had brought
Mom into Hadassah, the Jewish women's organization, where she
had found an avocation in selling concert and opera tickets for the
series and benefits it sponsored at the Mosque Theater. Also Rae had
led Mom into her social circle, which played mah-jongg at one
another's house and went to services at Temple B'nai Israel, on
Friday nights. Mom went once or twice and loved it but felt awkward
because her friends were there with their husbands and she was
always alone. She asked me if I would mind going with her. Friday
was the big basketball night in Elizabeth—the high school varsity,
which I fell in love with that year, would often be playing at home.
But I went with her once or twice when the team was away, and then,
in the spring, I began to go with her regularly.

With its spacious sanctuary painted in white and gold, its red plush
seats, stained-glass window, soft lighting and fresh-looking prayer
books, the Temple was the class act of Judaism in Elizabeth. Its rabbi
was called Dr. Malamed; he had a goatee and pince-nez and was said
to be a man of learning. The service was translated into English on
facing pages, so we could join in and get into the Shabbos spirit of
peacefulness and thoughtfulness. Neither Mom nor I had been
exposed to modern Judaism before, and the service was a far cry from
the dry, interminable ones that her father had inflicted on his family
and that I had brushed up against at the Murray Street shul.

What we liked most of all was the talks toward the end. I remember one series in particular that was given by a member of the congregation, a lawyer named Harry Weltchek, the elegant father and
uncle of two of my friends. Its title was something like "Judaism at
the Dawn of Ethics." He talked about how the early Jews were a
primitive people who slowly gave up their barbaric ways by making
a covenant with God, binding them to more righteous, just, and
humane behavior, in the form of the Ten Commandments and the
other laws. I remember his showing that there was plenty of brutal,
deceitful behavior by the Jews of the Bible, but that it would be
punished by the retribution system of the covenant, so that Jacob's

stealing the birthright of his brother from his blind father led to his exile and his years of having to work for Laban because Laban played a similar trick on him by substituting Leah for Rachel in the dark. In another of the talks he showed how the story of Abraham and Isaac was about the giving up of human sacrifice by the early Jews and replacing it with animals and then how the killing of animals was controlled and redeemed by the laws and rituals of slaughtering and *kashering* meat. He made us imagine what the Temple in Jerusalem must have been like, with the young bulls and flawless heifers being dragged to the altar and held there bellowing and screaming in their thrashing and death throes, the altar reeking with the blood and wastes. That was why there was so much stress laid on the sanctity of the enterprise, the painstaking rituals by which the choice parts were reserved as a "sweet odor" for the Lord. In other words, he made us see the Biblical Jews realistically, not as a nation of wise and holy men but as a people of its time struggling toward the light and laws cast by its faith in one God and its faith in His faith in them.

"This is fascinating," Mom would exclaim, or else sigh or grunt approvingly. People would turn around and look at her, but she didn't notice, avidly taking in the ideas as the nourishment of which she'd been deprived for the past fifteen years in Elizabeth. It made me proud of her as well as embarrassed, for I could feel some of her excitement stirring in me at this provocative, convincing way of viewing our religion.

After the service we would walk up to Broad Street, where we caught the Number 30 bus back to Elmora. As we walked, Mom would often take my arm, escort-style. My embarrassment at her remarks and little grunts of approval would melt away and I would turn the gentle, thoughtful side of myself to her as we walked through the deserted business district in the sweet spring air.

"Harry Weltchek is such a fine wholesome manly chap," she might say.

I would agree, both of us probably wishing the same thing.

"It's thrilling to listen to someone with a fine mind who is so well-spoken."

Her words lingered in this new mood between us, and made me

resolve, as I had at the Franklin Towers, to read more, study harder, so that someday I too would have a fine mind and refined vocabulary. It was listening to Harry Weltchek that gave me the idea of becoming a lawyer.

"That's what it all comes down to," she might say then, with one of her typical mental sidesteps.

"What does, Mom?"

"Being Jewish. Wanting to be a better person. That's what it means to be Jewish. It all comes down to that. Higher aspirations. We inherit higher aspirations going all the way back to the time we sacrificed animals. My father became a *shochet*, you know, a ritual slaughterer, though he only killed chickens because he couldn't stand shedding more blood than that. He was really a scholar and became a *shochet* so that his family could at least have chicken in Cream Ridge. We were so isolated in the early years."

"I still don't see why saying a prayer before you cut the chicken's throat makes you a better person."

"It has to do with killing, with shedding blood. Of controlling the animal impulse, and transforming the bloodlust. That's why Jews don't like to hunt. Even the ones who are assimilated, who don't keep kosher anymore. It probably goes back to our being carnivores. It's part of the development of mankind, in which Jews have played a very important role. We're the people of life. That's why we say *L'chayim*, to life, when we make a toast. We don't worship a dead person on a cross. We leave that to the Gentiles."

These little flares of vehemence about the Gentiles in her other-wise mild and pliant nature let me see her in a new, fuller way, as the girl she had been in Cream Ridge, one of the Weiss children who would be asked where their horns were. Even more so did her enthusiasm about the talks. Like the time I was almost in the Maskers play, our Friday nights lit her mind, lightened her spirit, took away the years of being squelched, brought out the questing mind she had developed by herself or with her sister Fan during those early years. It was as though the Mom I took for granted and sometimes derided had turned into someone more like an inquisi-tive older sister. I began to enjoy our Fridays nights almost as much as she did.

This bond between us continued to grow, that is, when I wasn't skulking and fuming, taking out the dissatisfactions of my darkening adolescence on her. Then I would spring back in the other direction as her knight in white armor. My chief way became doing the supper dishes, the suddenly meticulous me wading into the greasy mess of pots and dishes and utensils in the sink, the peelings and leavings and ingredients on the counter, spillage on the floor, wrack and ruin at the stove—which I would then, item by item, space by space, put to spic-and-span rights. The more mess, the greater my satisfaction. This learning to take pains was like the glass cleaning and typing I did for my father, though calmer, dreamier, a time when I often had my most interesting thoughts and hopeful daydreams.

One day I came home from school to find my mother singing,

> "Somebody's coming to our house,
> Somebody's coming to stay . . ."

I had heard her sing the song twice before, and with one look at her, I knew it was happening again. Her smile was already expectant.

Ours was not a household in which important decisions were made in a calm, circumspect fashion. Family communication was like a radio tuned between two stations, one coming in loudly, the other weakly and intermittently, with static in the background. The next few days were particularly fraught with bad transmission. An evening or so after Mom announced her news, and a few minutes after Dad had had his say and stormed out of the house, she came to Bobby's and my room, where I was trying to do my homework, sat down on my bed, and began to weep.

I put my arm around her and touched her temples and hair, which usually calmed her.

"I don't know what to do," she said finally. "He says he'll move out if I have another child."

"He can't stop you from having a baby. That's one thing he can't do."

"He says I have to have an abortion."

I thought of the joke song the guys sang to the tune of "My Devotion":

> My abortion
> Was painful and cost me
> A fortune

That's all I knew about it. That and something awful about back alleys and coat hangers.

"Maybe you should talk to Belle and Fan," I said.

"I talked to Belle. She thinks I should too." The thought made her break down again.

It didn't make sense. "So Dad won't move out?"

"She thinks if I have another child I'll be stuck here for life. But I'm not *stuck here*. This is my home."

"Well, I think you should have it. And if Dad moves out we'll get a lawyer, maybe Harry Weltchek, to make him support us." Suddenly the idea of not having to live with him became possible and, once possible, desirable. Every day would be like the weekends when he was away, only we would now have more of his money. I knew about alimony from a story of Ring Lardner's. I didn't want to have to take care of Sandy and Bob in New York, but being the man of the house on Shelley Avenue was a different story. Also having a new kid brother, which I was sure the baby would be, was a thrilling prospect.

"I don't see why Dad cares so much," I said. "He's hardly around here anyway."

"So you think I should carry the baby." She pulled me to her, held me, then pushed me back and gave me a long, loving look. "Everyone tells me I'm crazy. Even Rae says it's too much. But what else do I have to show for my life but you children." The weeping began again. But then she stopped, pulled herself together, and a smile lit her wet eyes. "I don't know what I would do without you," she said, putting her arms around me again. "You're my *mensch*."

That night the browbeating began again, my father's voice thudding through the walls. "I'm finally getting on my feet. . . ." "You can't handle the three you've got now. . . ." "Consider your feelings? What about considering my feelings for a change?. . . ." "All right.

Let's wind it up then. You can live in New York with your sisters, there's always room for four or five more at Belle's, and you can have as many children as you want with anyone you want."

The next day, though, he changed his tune completely. When I got home from school, he had already called Mom from The Shop, apologized for flying off the handle, said he was so busy he couldn't think straight, that it was her welfare not his that he was concerned about, that he'd talked to Dr. Gittelman, who was very concerned about her carrying a baby because of a possible rheumatic condition. He arrived home that evening with a Whitman Sampler box of chocolates and his sweetest talk and manners at the dinner table. He stayed home that evening, listened to *The Lux Radio Theater* with us, then sent Sandy and me off to bed, their low murmurous talk drifting upstairs along with the silky strains of Carmen Dragonette, as I lay there tossing and worrying, hours from sleep.

By the next evening it was all settled for the following afternoon. In the morning, Dad asked me to leave early with him so that he could drop me off at Hamilton on his way to The Shop. I got into the car, wondering what form his soft-soap routine would take with me. He didn't waste any time. "There are things a boy your age shouldn't have to know about," he said. "What are you, fourteen yet?"

I said I was. Six months ago. Then I said, "Since I do know, I want to be sure she'll be in good hands."

"Of course she will," he snapped. "What're you talking about? He's a regular women's doctor who does these things only for medical reasons."

"Good," I said, with a note of sarcasm meant to convey that I knew this "thing" was happening because he didn't want "another mouth to feed."

"I was starting to say I know how you feel," he said. "Your mother has told me you've been encouraging her to have another child." His voice modulated quickly back to the gentle and understanding tone—the tone I yearned to hear from him but also the one I distrusted the most because it was his other way of getting what he wanted.

"It's a problem of calcium," he explained. "And other things. They don't know much about arthritis, but she could be really bad off if she carried another child in her condition."

Perhaps he was sincere. He had been nice to her and to us when she was in the Elizabeth General Hospital the year before for a few days after her knee suddenly blew up with arthritis. But I didn't trust him. I thought he didn't know himself when he was being sincere or just manipulative.

Anyway, I took his behavior as an opportunity. "She thinks she got the arthritis at The Shop. The office has never been properly heated." The new place didn't even have a furnace, only a coal stove in the office part.

"I'm going to change things to make it easier for her," he said. "She won't be going to The Shop anymore. It's too cold for her there, too drafty. I'm going to make sure I have proper help there from now on. I'm looking for a reliable man to handle the office, so I won't need you after school either when I'm stuck."

As he went on in this vein, I didn't know what to think or feel. He was not only making the right promises but making them to me as though we were equal partners in ensuring Mom's welfare. Also he was giving me the freedom all of my friends had. I so much wanted to believe him that I began to.

As I was getting out of the car, he said, still in his nice voice, "I want you to go home directly after school. I want you to reassure your sister and brother that everything is fine, they have nothing to worry about. We'll be back by five at the latest."

I'd never been in this position before, that is, standing in a quiet middle ground between Mom and Dad. Either I was consoling her for his behavior or wishing that she'd stand up to him. But now there seemed to be a whole new stage emerging, a real possibility of a sensible and considerate family in which Dad had acknowledged I had a role to play. This carried me through the school day and blunted the thrust of what was going to happen that afternoon.

I took the bus home instead of walking, and it was there, sitting by myself, that suddenly a terrible thought blindsided me. At this very moment, my baby brother was about to be or already had been murdered. It wasn't just an egg inside my helpless mother that was being poked dead and washed away; it was someone I would have loved and big-brothered—a baby I would have held held in my arms and fed a bottle to, a toddler I would have swung up in the air and then thrust toward me like a dive bomber, as I'd done so much with Bobby; a little kid I would have taught to catch and throw, tackle and ride a bike. Now none of that would happen. Instead this little creature was being killed, executed.

Hot tears welled in my eyes as the bus made its way along Magee Avenue, the driver and the other passengers oblivious to what was happening at this very moment and unable to do anything about it if they knew. If we were Catholic, I could have called up a priest and he would have stepped in and stopped it. I remembered what Harry Weltchek at the Temple had said about the Jews and killing, why they made such a big deal out of the way they slaughtered animals, then salted and washed the meat so they wouldn't be eating the animal's blood, which was holy. That was just an animal. What about a human being? What about *L' Chaim*, "To Life"? With even greater sickness of heart I remembered about Abraham and Isaac. Was there really any difference between them and my mother being taken to wherever the abortion doctor was? And suppose God were to speak to them at the last minute? Would Dad listen to Him? Fat chance. He'd tell Mom sarcastically that she was hearing things, that she was in one of her "trances" again.

Meanwhile, the bus had made its big loop around Magee Avenue and was picking up passengers for the downtown run. I had ridden past my stop five minutes ago. Lurching to my feet, I pulled the stop cord. After I got off, I ran all the way home to my surviving sister and brother.

We were playing three-handed War at the dining-room table when Dad brought Mom home. He took her directly upstairs to lie down. After he went back to The Shop, we went up to her room. She looked very weak but calm. "Well, it's over," she said. But we could still smell the ether he had given her.

10 ONCE PUBERTY AT last set in and I began to sprout body hair and a few precious inches of penile tissue, I found myself with half a dozen cavities every time I went to the dentist. In New York, Aunt Belle was developing a close friendship with Dr.

Adrian Simons, who practiced dentistry in a brownstone off Columbus Avenue, and in the course of the next year I became one of his steady patients.

Uncle Adrian, as we began to call him, was supremely refined. His name originally was Abe, but he hadn't let that or his humble immigrant background or even the practice of dentistry stand in the way of his life's work, which was to fashion himself as a man of taste, charm, and ideas. He was a soft, heavyset fellow with jowls, basset eyes, a pursed mouth, and a well-barbered head of hair, and his distinguishing feature was his low, slow, rich voice that punctiliously ironed the mangled *o's* and *r's* of New Yawk speech into folded, fluffy English. A product of City College whom you would have taken for at least Columbia, Uncle Adrian was a superb raconteur whose life as an Upper West Side boulevardier seemed to furnish him with stories at every turn. He also told subtle Jewish jokes, the first I'd ever heard.

He had plenty of opportunities to amuse and instruct. His patients all appeared to belong to the special New York social class, the one of "fascinating people," that spanned and transcended the other three. Adrian's wide circle tended to fall into two groups. One was young actors, dancers, musicians, painters, and playwrights; the other was men and women who read *PM*, the liberal tabloid ("the only major newspaper in New York you can half trust," according to Mel Sarnoff, Adrian's closet friend), and magazines I had never heard of such as *New Masses*. The older group included a professional bridge player who wore spats, a psychologist who had been trained by Alfred Adler, and his wife, who painted in the nude.

On any Saturday afternoon, there would be four or five people sitting in the dining area between Adrian's office and the kitchen, chatting over coffee while they waited to have their cavities filled and their smiles brightened. It was half a dental practice, half a salon that Belle presided over, dispensing delicious refreshments and conviviality, deftly keeping the conversation circulating until Adrian finished with a patient. Then the two of them would join the circle. Sometimes he would become so immersed in one of his stories or ideas that Belle would have to remind him that someone had been waiting two hours.

Dentistry was only one of the helping hands he extended to the world. And it didn't appear to be the one he took most seriously. If I had an early appointment I might arrive to find him still in his dressing gown, having a late breakfast with Belle, and he wouldn't bother to change into his white jacket when he began working on me. He worked slowly, trying to be as gentle as possible (we were still in the era of painful dentistry), and somewhat distractedly, often taking phone calls from people who needed to talk to him and then telling me about the person and often the problem or news he or she had told him. It was as though he could stand to work on my cavities as long as he had something more significant to talk about.

Our conversations were mostly one-way, since my mouth would be otherwise occupied, but now and then I'd get out a response through the cotton and suction hook. "That's a very insightful question, Teddy," he'd say. Or "That's an interesting observation." Often, either at the beginning or the end of a session, he would ask me about, or I would bring up, the situation at home.

It was a little better for Mom since the abortion and a lot worse for me. The man Dad had hired for the office had lasted only a few months. Now that I was going to Jefferson High, which was only a few blocks from The Shop, I had to report there after school to relieve the new girl—actually an older woman with a family who left at three. The thought of being stuck there for the rest of high school weighed heavily on me. I'd stay in the back of the office space, out of sight of my classmates going by—horsing around, leading their normal adolescent lives, even the Italian and Polish kids who lived in the Port. It particularly killed me that some of them were on their way to the Midtown Community Center or other gyms and courts to sharpen their basketball skills for JV tryouts, which I wouldn't even be able to go to. Adrian suggested that I ask my mother to intervene. I told him that was hopeless, that my father hated my interest in sports, that if Mom asked him to find someone else, he'd just say, "Okay, you don't want him here. You come."

The leopard's spots were fully in view again. He had just bought himself new skis but had torn into Mom because she had given Sandy two dollars to buy socks instead of shopping for them herself. Sandy had told him she was ashamed to have him for a father, which had stopped him in his tracks. "Why can't Mom do that?" I asked Adrian. Why does she let him walk all over her and us?"

He told me that Mom was a fine but depressed woman with great potential who would benefit enormously from seeing Bob Hitz, the psychologist. That was one of the reasons why she needed to move to New York. He said that our situation in Elizabeth was hopeless because my father had "serious emotional deficits" and "an impoverished ego." This was strange news, since I thought of him as being overly emotional because of his temper and very egotistical because of his selfishness. But as I began to understand Adrian's terms, it was interesting as well as helpful to listen to someone speak of Dad objectively; no one ever had. Adrian helped me to see why the marriage brought out the worst in both of them (as he put it, they were "ideally unsuited" for each other). He said they both needed help but that Mom needed it more because the harm that had been done to her by the marriage made it impossible for her to change it or to leave it, which Dad might already be doing. I was very much impressed by this formulation because of its enlightenment and because he had shared such complex, grown-up information with me. I felt that he was counting on me to help Fan and Belle to get Mom to leave Dad.

Mom and I had become another of Adrian's projects ("Adrian is doing so much for Teddy," I overheard Aunt Belle say). In my ongoing and often losing battle to think better of myself he was a godsend. Like the people on the roof at the Franklin Towers, only more so, he enabled me to see myself as more intelligent and less homely than I did when I was in Elizabeth. Also knowing that he would be there if and when we moved to New York made it seem less like the four of us trying to swim across the Hudson River.

From our discussions between the drilling and the filling I also began to understand more of the conversations I overheard in the dining area about figures such Trotsky and Kamenev, Bukharin and Kirov, Kolchak and Denikin. Adrian explained to me how the United States had been involved in sending money and munitions to the White Russian army. When I asked him why this country would want to overthrow a revolution that was so far away, he stopped drilling for ten delicious minutes to explain the capitalist conspiracy to me, which included not only the history books I'd read in school but even the *New York Times*, which was Aunt Fan's bible.

This was very heady stuff to a fifteen-year-old whose political views began and ended with veneration of President Roosevelt and his "Brain Trust." Adrian said that I wouldn't understand the true nature of American society until I'd read Charles Beard and Karl Marx. He loaned me his copy of the Beards' *Basic History of the United States* and a book of Marx's writings. When I mentioned to Aunt Fan Adrian's view of "the necessity and the necessary course" of the Russian Revolution, she scoffed and told me about the murder of the peasants and the Moscow show trials, the nonaggression pact with Germany, and the execution of Trotsky. She said that Mel Sarnoff was a Stalinist and Adrian was a fellow traveler. For her part, Fan put a book into my hands—a Russian one called *The Seven Who Were Hanged*.

I was too patriotic to agree with much of the Beards' history and I didn't try to tackle Marx until I entered my own fellow-traveler phase a few years later, but Leonid Andreyev's short novel was a whole new story. That Andreyev showed the young revolutionaries to be foolish, vain, and pathetic was the least of it. In its unusual leather cover, which added to its exotic appeal, it stirred roots in me that I didn't know I had. Until then the fiction I had read, from Dick and Jane to *For Whom the Bell Tolls*, was always entirely or mainly about "Them," the Gentiles, the few Jewish characters being outsiders—bad guys like Shylock and Fagin and Meyer Wolfsheim, or pushy ones like Sammy Glick and Robert Cohn. But with Andreyev's story of a band of young Russian anarchists thrown into jail with peasants and thieves, I began to relate to a literature that was about "Us." Not that it and Andreyev's other stories were about Jews as such; yet they spoke to me as though they were, as though Jews and Russians were branches of the same family. Names like Sergei Golovin and Tanya Kovalchuk weren't strange to someone named Solotaroff; nor was the dark, soulful music of their lives, made up of yearning, strife, and melancholy, just like Mom's and mine.

Aunt Fan and I spent a whole hour talking about Andreyev's novel. When I told her about how different it was from the fiction I was used to and yet how much closer to it I felt, she said that it had awakened my Russian background as well as my Jewish one. She asked me why *The Seven Who Were Hanged* was different from, say, *A Tale of Two Cities*, which was also about revolutionaries. I said something like Andreyev's book was more like psychology and Dickens's was more like history. As I was stumbling around in the fog of trying to explain myself, she said, "What I think you've understood and are trying to say is that Andreyev writes about people from the inside out and Dickens from the outside in." She explained that what made Andreyev seem Jewish was that Russian Jews for centuries were cut off from the world around them and so lived mostly within themselves, like the five anarchists, the peasant, and the Tartar thief who is called "the Gypsy." I said that the Gypsy reminded me a little of the Solotaroffs, because of his obliviousness and his wild mood swings. Fan also showed me how the prison where the anarchists and the others are kept becomes a metaphor for czarist Russian society as a whole—savage, idealistic, brilliant, and stupid people alike cooped up in and then killed by a corrupt system. She wanted me to read the book after listening to Adrian's talk about the Russian Revolution because it was a good antidote to his romanticism about the revolution. The five young anarchists would as likely have been killed fifty years later in the Stalinist purges of the 1930s.

It was thrilling to listen to her, to see how much meaning there was in this short novel if you knew how to look. I had never seen or heard the word "metaphor" employed the way she used it. I loved being with her, the two of us talking about matters I never had discussed with anyone else.

Her new apartment was the other destination of my Saturday journeys to New York. She and Belle were no longer "the Girls"—her life had changed even more dramatically than her sister's. After a sudden, almost secret romance, Fan had married the most unlikely guy. Bert Mann was a big, shambling, gaudy, vociferous hustler from Tin Pan Alley who made his living as a song plugger. Bert's horn-rimmed glasses gave him a studious look, but his talk was mostly show business palaver. The family was shocked by the marriage of the quiet, studious, dignified Fan and the brash, nightclubbing Bert, who trailed after the Walter Winchells and Johnny Mercers and Guy Lombardos of the world.

Yet the marriage seemed to click. Fan found a spacious apartment on West End Avenue, a few blocks from the Franklin Towers, gave up teaching and commuting to Brooklyn, and devoted herself to making a handsome home and writing radio plays. Bert, in turn, took to Fan's serious ways and let go of much of his business-related dissipations. Inspired by this change, he wrote a song of his own that reflected it.

> I don't want to set the world on fire,
> I just want to start a flame in your heart . . .

Putting all of his energy and savvy behind it, he plugged it right onto *Your Hit Parade*, the Saturday-night pop music show that played the top ten tunes that America was singing and dancing to. It was our first family connection to fame, and on Saturday night each of the Weiss households would gather at the radio at nine o'clock and wait with the tense expectancy of presidential election night for the MC to announce, "And number eight this week is the catchy little ballad 'I Don't Want to Set the World on Fire.' " The song continued its steady ascent, and lo and behold there came the night when it was number one.

My Saturday trips sometimes ended at Fan's apartment. For my fifteenth birthday, she took me to my first Broadway show, *Junior Miss*, which dazzled me. Literally—the curtain rose on a living room and an actor answering the phone, the father of the family, bathed in a light that seemed like a concentrated version of the bright lights of Broadway. Then he proceeded to light a cigarette, the first time I had ever seen anyone smoke in a theater. I remember these two details more than the play itself, mostly a high-Gentile version of the fashionable, secure, fun-filled teenage life I wasn't leading.

Afterward Fan took me to a milk bar in Times Square where three or four men served up malteds and wisecracks for ten cents, which seemed more like New York to me than the Fifth Avenue comedy I had been watching. That was New York too, of course, but it was more like the Elmora Country Club, which was where sophistication lodged in Elizabeth. With Uncle Adrian or Aunt Fan I glimpsed a more democratically sophisticated New York that was beckoning to me from the root of the Franklin Towers like a beacon from my future.

"You didn't like the play very much, did you?" asked Fan as I sipped though my second malted, She seemed more amused than disappointed. "It's a big hit, but I should have known better. Why didn't you like it?"

I didn't know what to say. I didn't want to say it was boring, because it wasn't. It was funny and vivid and full of surprises. But it was all about kids whose life was made up of dates and formal dances and getting the car and having parents who were charming. I said that it reminded me of the rich kids in Elizabeth who went to Pingry and Vail-Deane, who didn't have to think about the future because it would be handed to them on a silver platter. They were getting a better education than I was but it seemed to matter less to them.

"You're becoming a thoughtful young man," Fan said.

"I feel more like my true self in New York," I said.

"What do you mean by that?" It was a serious question, like most of her questions. In trying to answer it, I told her about the Weiss boy and Little Benny, the first time I had ever told anyone.

She kept looking at me and now and then shook her head as I spoke, as though she could hardly believe what she was hearing. When I finished she put her hands on my shoulders and looked me straight in the eyes. "I want you to promise me something. I want you to promise me that no matter what, the Weiss boy will get a good education. And that if you need help, which you probably will, you'll come to me."

I promised, my mind flying on the realization that I could now go to college without having to ask my father or else pay my own way through the Newark branch of Rutgers. I knew that Uncle Bert had made a lot of money with his song and also Aunt Fan and their apartment looked like he had. It wasn't expensive or fancy, just that the new furniture and drapes and a modern floor lamp that curved over you and the thick towels in the bathroom and the leather couch in Uncle Bert's study on which I slept over, under a warm kind of light quilt called a comforter, made everything nicer and brighter and more comfortable in the Manhattan way that I was beginning to take to.

11 BUT AT JEFFERSON High, my decline as a student and athlete continued. Mom relieved me at The Shop so that I could try out for the JV team, but at the second practice I screwed up a fast-break drill, throwing a lead pass to a forward instead of a short one to the center. The coach jumped on me—"Were you in the toilet when I was showing what I wanted?"—and cut me at the end of practice, which was particularly upsetting because I prided myself on playing smart.

In most of my classes I was less smart too, and in plane geometry barely managed to pass. Even gym class, where I had always been in my element, was now agony and defeat, for it was designed to prepare us for military service—a two-mile run three mornings a week, which I had to gut out, my lungs flaming by the second lap, followed by an obstacle course which, already exhausted, I could barely complete, finishing with the rest of "the feebs."

As my self-confidence sank further, I once again raised the level of my smart-aleck behavior. Its particular domain was biology class, taught by a very stout, earnest, mild, and slow-witted man, a bull's-eye at ten feet for my tormenting questions and stunts. One day, another student and I were reflecting light from the mirrors on our microscopes into his eyes, and when he caught me he came down the aisle like an enraged bear, pulled me from my seat, and dragged me out of the room, a triumph of provocation and attention-getting that left me feeling even more dismal, since I had managed to change this pitiable man into my father.

The one bright spot for me at Jefferson was that I had been chosen to pledge for the Jewish fraternity, Pi Upsilon Phi. Because all the male high school students in Elizabeth went to Jefferson, we Jews were now a distinct minority in a student body made up largely of guys from the industrial bottom and sides of the city who took the shop and commercial courses. So we tended to hang that much more tightly and competitively together, and it was a big deal to be singled out to pledge for the Pups, as the fraternity was known.

One of the other pledges was Irwin Taubman. He was still large and stout for his age and no less imperious, still seeming to be leading a different adolescence from the rest of us. He had continued to high-hat me as a second-rate student and a first-class jerk, while I would sneer at his big-shot ways. Yet, as with other kings and clowns, there was still the underlying responsiveness between us that now and then would resurface.

After one meeting we found ourselves walking home together. Alan Gordon, the fraternity president, had talked to us that evening about the strong bond that we should feel toward each other, one that superseded whatever our feelings had been before. A fraternity wasn't just a social club but had a higher purpose that went back to the Greek idea of fraternalism, of a band of young men who helped each other to develop the male virtues of self-discipline and loyalty.

I said that I didn't see how running errands in the lunchroom or getting my ass paddled for forgetting a handkerchief was going to give me feelings of brotherly love.

"They're trying to retrain you," Irwin said in his authoritative way. "You don't have any self-control to speak of."

"You sound like a school report card," I said. "Self-control."

"Well, you don't. That's why you get paddled twice as much as anyone else. I'd like to see you get in, but you're already on thin ice."

"How do you know?

"I know. Trust me. If you really want to get in, you're going to have to mend your ways."

"Okay, big shot. What do I have to do?"

"It's what you have to stop doing. When you got Herbie Poch a piece of pie in the cafeteria, why did you have to bow when you gave it to him?"

"Was that so bad?

"It was doubly bad. It was both silly and sarcastic. The way you often are."

"Thanks a lot."

"I'm trying to be helpful. I'm trying to be fraternal. It's not easy, believe me."

I resented his superior tone but was touched that he was trying to wise me up, to be brotherly.

"So you think I'm screwing up?"

"I don't think it. I know it."

"How do you know it? You're just a pledge yourself."

"There you go again. You don't like the message, so you give the messenger a kick in the ass." Then he said, "I'll tell you something else I know. You remember the essay we had to write when we first started pledging?"

"You mean that dumb one about what happened to Farmer Brown's fart in the Blizzard of '88?"

"I happen to know that they thought yours and mine were by far the best ones."

I was floored—both by the information and by his telling me. Maybe he was sincere. Maybe he was even trying to make friends.

The possibility brought a powerful feeling of gratitude with it. Not only did he care about my getting into the fraternity but by telling me about the essay he was acknowledging my ability that he had so much threatened. Like Adrian and Fan, he was telling me that I could become somebody instead of sinking further into mediocrity.

As we walked from the business district into the night silence of Elmora, we got to talking about colleges. Irwin said that I would have to bring up my grades even more if I wanted to go to a good college because if the war was over by the time we applied, as he thought it would be, we would have that much more competition. I said I thought I would do better next year when I didn't have geometry. He said that I couldn't wait until next year, that the grades I got now were part of the record they sent to the colleges. Even though I wasn't doing well in geometry I could be getting much higher grades to make up for it. "With your verbal ability, you should be getting 95s in English and Latin and history. You have the highest IQ in your homeroom, you know."

"How do you know *that* ? You're not even in my homeroom."

"I have my sources. You're the worst underachiever in our whole group. You're worse than Arty Tieger." Arty spent most of his school time drawing sarcastic caricatures and cartoons.

"Arty's just a jerk," I said, treacherously, riding high on the information Irwin had been giving me, already preparing a place for myself among the high achievers.

Irwin stopped dead in his tracks. "That's another aspect of your inferiority complex," he said quietly. "You're always so critical of everyone. I know what you say behind my back. How can anyone afford to be friends with you?"

I came back to earth with a crash. Was it true? Was I always talking behind people's backs? Hadn't I just belittled Arty, one of my few kindred spirits? What was most troubling was Irwin's sincerity. I hadn't thought that I did, but now I could see that it was so. I was a chip off the old block. Mom would often say to Dad, as a final weeping retort, "Nothing I do ever pleases you. You're not happy unless you're belittling me."

The pledge period lasted through the fall. Irwin and I were less hostile, but the intimacy of the walk home didn't return. He seemed to be waiting to see if I was going to improve. I did try harder for a while, carefully writing an essay on why revenge is best when eaten cold, as borne out by "The Cask of Amontillado," which got a high grade. But otherwise I still struggled with geometry and now and then added to my tawdry laurels for the sly disruption, the bold wisecrack, in class.

After the first of the year, the pledges began to be initiated. Each week, two would appear in school in a white shirt with a red bow tied under the collar and have to go through the day without talking to anyone. Irwin was in the first pair selected. With each week of watching the next preferred pair go through the pledge drill, I became more angry and anxious. Surely that ass-kisser or that blowhard or that schmuck wouldn't be chosen before me—but he was. Who wanted to be in such a fraternity? But each week I drove my mother crazy with my anxiety about her handling the mail until I had seen it because the initiation notice was sure to be there.

I turned out to be the last one taken, number nine, the right fielder of the pledges. By now no one paid much attention to the Jews in the pansy ties who couldn't talk, and my stint went along uneventfully. I tried to watch my step, to keep a poker face as well as a silent mouth, but the wiseguy in me, the tester of limits, the resentful odd man in, found little covert ways to get into the act—a surreptitious nod here, a shrug there, a signal or two elsewhere of grabbing my tongue, shaking my head, and cutting my throat.

When I got to biology class that afternoon there was a note folded on my desk. It said that I could take off the ribbon and talk all I wanted, that I was being blackballed. As it happened, Irwin sat at the work table behind mine. Dumbfounded as well as wretched, I turned and looked at him. His big, suave face coldly looked back and then turned away; the stone look of the older fraternity brothers when the paddling punishment was being dished out. He was one of them now. I was never to find out if he had gotten me blackballed, but it didn't make much difference; the disdain in his eyes had virtually the same meaning.

The disappointment and humiliation hurt for days and then weeks, and, in the way certain blows lock like rocks into the dam in the heart, was deposited permanently. I had a choice between hating Irwin or one of the others for being so chickenshit and hating myself for screwing around enough to give whoever it was the opportunity to get me. Often I took both choices and spent much time playing *J'accuse* with myself—cracking the accusation at Them and then rushing to the other side of the question to crack it back against Me. But none of it changed the fact that I'd screwed up again, had added a further failure to my string of them. As when I was banned from the playground for two weeks, my Elizabeth personality seemed like another version of my nose, and the sense of myself as basically a loser who would know what it meant to suffer grew stronger and more persistent. It cast a pall over the possibility of starting over in Manhattan. How could I become the man of the house in New York when I couldn't even get through a day of initiation at school?

Meanwhile, I tried to hold on to the other, positive image of myself that I was receiving from Adrian and Fan as well as from Mom with her high, even extravagant view of me, vested in my "sensitivity" and "understanding" and "feeling for the finer things." Whatever I was at Jeff or in The Shop, at home with her I was George Willard, the young journalist hero of *Winesburg, Ohio*, whose stricken, lonely, high-minded mother lives for him and believes in him. A passage in the story "Mother" particularly spoke to me. Ella Willard determines to protect George from his father's baleful influence, to draw upon "the secret bond that existed between them . . . . 'He is not a dull clod, all words and smartness. Within him there is a secret something that is striving to grow. It is the thing I let be killed in myself.' "

Also I had too much of the Weiss and Solotaroff energy to mope for very long, and, like my father, I did most of my brooding on the go. Nailed to the back of my mind was the motto of Kid Galahad — Down but Not Out. I worked on my basketball at the Y that winter and also got into a boxing class there taught by Georgie Ward, a former ranking lightweight, to restore my confidence and courage. He taught me to jab from the shoulder instead of the elbow, to punch in combinations, to move inside a punch instead of back. "You got fast hands," he said, "but you need to develop more moxie."

Also a rival Jewish fraternity, Mu Sigma, had come into the picture. It was less together than the Pups and devoted mostly to having parties, but I was delighted to be chosen to pledge. This time I kept my nose clean, pledged and was initiated without incident, and best of all, had a big game at bat when we played the Pups in softball.

My main way of dealing with my bum situation at home and in school and of training for the future was earning money. It was the one thing I did that Dad seemed to respect, that could even stop him from dragooning me into The Shop. The spring I was fourteen I worked in a fruit and vegetable market after school and on Saturdays, and retrieved foul balls in the semipro league at Warinanco Park on Sundays, for which another I got the two-dollar deposit the home team paid for the bases.

One Sunday morning that summer, Tommy Hopkins and another boy from St. Genevieve's took me with them to the Suburban Country Club in Union. After hitchhiking there, we joined a group of thirty or so, men as well as boys, sitting on a rise that faced the caddy shack. For the next hour I took in the caddy talk and the abusive humor of Frank, the caddy master, and watched the "regulars" saddle up two bags and head for the clubhouse. Then suddenly

Frank was scowling and crooking his finger at me. He lifted two bags at me across the half door of the shack. They were both pro-sized leather bags. I dragged them around to the side of the shack where he couldn't watch me and struggled to get one on each shoulder as I had seen some of the other caddies do rather than hoist both onto one shoulder. But I could barely get one of them to stay on, and while I was trying to lift up the other, the first upended and all the clubs fell out. As I was putting them back in the bag, I felt a very strong hand on my neck. "You ever caddied before, Jerkoff?"

I shook my head—as much as the caddy master's grip would let me.

"Why didn't you tell me when I gave you a double? You want me to lose my fucking job?"

For the next two hours I watched the door open and all the other caddies be chosen. Tommy Hopkins told me to hang around, that Frank might let me go out in the afternoon with a women's four-some. But Frank continued to look through me for the rest of the day.

I came back on Tuesday, then Wednesday, then Thursday, hoping that he would run out of caddies and give me a second chance. With a lot of time on my hands, I soaked in the ambience. Everything about the Suburban Country Club intrigued me: the lush fairways and taut greens, the players' sporty outfits and golf gear, the big English-style clubhouse that seemed all the more opulent because caddies weren't allowed in it. Even the names of the clubs fascinated me: the brassie and spoon, midirons and wedges, the mashie niblick.

Finally, on Thursday morning Frank sent me out to shag balls for a member who was practicing his drives. That afternoon there was a Kiwanis outing, and he put a cloth bag on my shoulder and swung it around so that it hung properly across my back. "Maybe you can handle this," he said. "If you lose a single ball out there you're through."

Once on the course I did fine. I had a good eye for the flight of the ball, and after a few weeks a workable sense of the game. I learned the members' swings and other idiosyncrasies that often predicted the direction of the shot, and with whom and when to put in my two cents about a shot or a club selection. A couple of the members even began to ask for me. By the end of the summer I was carrying doubles and making eight dollars a day. I loved the green, spacious, ambient world of the golf course, its blend of the natural and the groomed, of distance and precision. I'd found a well-paying job that exercised my body, made me feel competent, and would keep me solvent through spring and fall of the next three years.

I was happily caddying five or six days a week the following summer (Dad had a full-time girl again) when, out of the blue, I got even luckier. My mother's best friend in her Lakewood days, Fay Goldstein, owned a small hotel, the Carleton, in the Jewish heart of Belmar, and when one of its two bellhops was drafted in the middle of the season, Mom managed to get me taken on.

At fifteen I was two or three years younger than the rest of the staff. The waiters and bus boys were almost all college students who were waiting for their draft numbers to be called or their ROTC appointment to come through. In the help's quarter, I would lie on my cot and listen to their endless speculations about the waitresses and some of the younger wives, as well as their play-by-play accounts of making out on a date or with a pickup on the boardwalk. The tongues and tits, thighs and pussies they regaled each other with seemed like a vision of the promised land that I would only glimpse from afar until my nose was fixed.

I was growing rapidly now, nearing six feet, and my nose had grown too. Its twisted bridge had erupted into a massive, hooked schnozzola. Each angle I turned my face to in the mirror made the ugly hunk of cartilage look worse than the last—an inferiority complex all by itself. Like some teenage character of Gogol's, I became haunted by it, as though it were a deformed creature who accompanied me, stepping right in front whenever there were girls around. It mattered so enormously, and then, one evening, it stopped mattering at all.

Her name was Honey Abrams—a bosomy, black-haired, laughing, flirtatious girl whose tawny skin and sweet face matched her nickname. I avidly watched her sunbathing on the beach with the waiters and busboys from the Carleton, dancing cheek to cheek with them or other guys at the Fifth Street Pavilion, walking the boardwalk with a friend, both of them with the animated sidelong glances of girls waiting to be picked up. She looked eighteen, a fine, ripe peach, much too high on the tree for me to reach. Then Howie Stampfer, one of the waiters, told me that Honey had asked him about me, had said that I was cute.

"Yeah, like a kid brother," I said.

"Why do you say that?"

"She must be eighteen."

"What're you talking about? She's probably younger than you are."

She was—by a few months. But she was dealing with someone who thought necking was putting your arm around a girl's neck and getting a date with a pretty one akin to making a royal flush at Pokerino. Egged on by the older guys, I finally managed to ask her out, and then couldn't get over how she said, "I'd love to." For the next few days, I kept fingering and opening the phrase in my mind like the Scout knife I'd stolen two years before.

We went to Asbury Park, the Coney Island of the area, but my memory of the date doesn't begin until the ride home on a double-decker bus. Still feeling like her kid brother, I managed to inch my arm around the seat and brushed her shoulder. "Don't be shy," Honey said, pulling my arm around her shoulder and nestling her forehead in the crook of my neck. I touched her hair, she touched my face. Blissed out by her soft skin, her perfume, her caressing fingers, I hardly moved a limb, a muscle, until she sat up straight again. Giving me an appraising look, she said, "You have a great face when you smile. You're a lot cuter than you think you are." It was as though she had performed the nose job then and there.

As I walked her home on the boardwalk, our hands met and clasped. With this new show of her affection, this even more public pairing, I began to walk slowly on air. The sea breeze, the crash and hush of the waves, our fingers intertwined, our heads touching—the stars fell on Belmar.

On the steps of her aunt's cottage, I reached for her other hand. We stood there in a daze. At least I did. Honey was so attuned to the dating moment that she may have just been adjusting to my punchiness. I was trying to decide my next move. Should I push this incredible development in my life by trying to kiss her on our first date? Also she would feel the erection I was toting (along with the rest of me, even it felt more substantial). I settled for squeezing both her hands and asking to see her again. She laughed, pulled me close, erection and all, and kissed me softly, lingeringly, on the mouth.

The next four weeks passed in a long glide of elation. With one remark, Honey had turned me into a normal male teenager, with one kiss into a winner. Ten minutes after the evening shift ended, I would be hitting the boardwalk, my hair slicked down with Kreml, wearing my black-and-gold Mu Sigma cardigan as though it were a varsity letter sweater, my trouser cuffs fashionably double-rolled over the white- and-black saddle shoes I had bought with my first week's tips. Honey would be waiting, perched on the low wall that ran around the Fifth Street Dance Pavilion. Often some guy would be talking to her, but that only added another triumph to my string, for I was the guy she would hurry over to hug, kiss, and pull onto the dance floor.

She taught me to fox-trot, to break and promenade, to dip, to Charleston, and jitterbug. On our favorite bench at the lagoon, she taught me to French kiss and to make her nipples hard. I could now come back to the help's shack at the Carleton in the small hours, boast to Howie and the others of making a girl pant, complain mightily of blue balls. Having mastered the agenda of puppy love and summer romance, Honey led me through all of its details. We had our song, "A Door Will Open," our favorite band, Tommy Dorsey, our favorite couple to date with, even our favorite color and article of the other's clothing.

Labor Day night, on our final date, we stayed up until two in the morning at the lagoon, drinking draft after draft of the other's saliva and sweet sorrow. She gave me a heavy silver-plated ID bracelet, and I gave her a delicate ankle chain, our names on both. I took off her bobby sock, attached the chain, and kissed her ankle. Then, to give me something even more serious to remember her by—the lyric of one of the other songs of the season—she slipped her bra off and let my hand write the first entry in my annals of ecstasy.

Once we'd started going steady, Honey's flirtiness seemed to drop away as my shyness did. She not only looked but was precociously nubile. The only child of a happy home, she saw her future as a continuation of the life she led in New Brunswick. I would go to Rutgers there, she would help to support me until I was a lawyer, and then we would live with our two children in the house she was already designing and furnishing. I wondered about the rush but went along with her scenario. All of this new happiness and self-confidence, plus sex and a professional education—all I would have to do was show up.

On the last Sunday afternoon of the season a small fly flew into the ointment . She brought her parents over to the Carleton to meet me. They were nice people who seemed to approve of me, but they weren't the urbane couple I had been led to expect. Murray and Bess Abrams came from the big bottom drawer of the Jewish middle class. The tip-off for me was Mr. Abrams's shirt—a cheap yellow rayon sport shirt with a stain just above his paunch. The stain was like a speck in my vision of the future. Back in Elizabeth again, I tried and tried but couldn't wink it away. It evoked the other end of Elmora, and I was headed for Riverside Drive.

So instead of the ID bracelet and her bosom, the spot on Honey's father's shirt proved to be what I most remembered her by. I found myself evading her invitations to visit New Brunswick, and the relationship fell apart at the reunion of our group in November. Acting on my mother's view that I "shouldn't waste a girl's time," I had just written to her that we were too young and New Brunswick too far from Elizabeth for us to go steady. At the reunion she said she had been realizing that too. I said that she still meant a lot to me, that I'd always be grateful to her. She gave me a hard, ten-years-older look and said, "You sure have a funny way of showing it." There seemed to be several other conversations going on in the same vein in the room, a living room in East Orange. We danced carefully with each other. Even the songs of that summer we had swooned or jitterbugged to at the Pavilion had a dated feel to them now. We kissed goodbye on the cheek, saying we would stay in touch, knowing from the chill in the evening air, endings everywhere, that we wouldn't. This, too, made me feel normal again.

12 BACK AT JEFFERSON High and at The Shop, it was as though the summer hadn't happened. One of the Elmora guys said to me, "I hear you had a beautiful girlfriend this summer in Belmar. What'd you do, drug her?" He informed me, in case I didn't know it, I was already developing a bald spot to go with the rest of my disastrous appearance. I told him that his mother was tearing my hair out in her passion ("the dozens" had come to Jefferson), but his

remarks clanged in my head and returned me to my old self. And then, early in November, life dealt me a whole new hand.

The owner of our house on Shelley Avenue put it on the market for a very modest sum—about eight times the yearly rental of $720. But it was too expensive for Dad, and before we knew it he had found a house for us in Roselle Park for half the price of the Shelley Avenue one and "with three beautiful fruit trees," he told us, in the backyard. He'd had to move fast to snap up this bargain, and the house was all but bought by the time we saw it.

Roselle Park, which bordered on Elizabeth, was an older plain-Jane borough with a large Italian neighborhood and very few Jews. Our house was at the gritty edge of the town, not across the tracks but virtually on them. After the cherry, apple, and pear trees and an old shed in back came the tracks of the Jersey Central, still in its heyday as a freight carrier. In front was East Westfield Avenue, the main traffic route from Elizabeth into the western suburbs. The house itself was a gaunt weather-beaten affair, hunched over a spindly portico; one could easily imagine the three spinster sisters who had owned it shutting themselves up in it for life. It had a primitive hot-air system like the one in the earlier Shop, a morbid pea-green paint scheme, and fixtures and features that seemed to go back to the dawn of household electricity and indoor plumbing. It made our house on Shelley Avenue seem palatial.

When Mom first saw its grim location and interior she almost wept in disbelief and chagrin. Her taste, determination, and timing of Dad's good moods had managed to triumph over her meager resources and she'd made the Shelley Avenue house pretty enough that she could invite her group from Hadassah and her family without embarrassment. She said the only people she could invite into "this dump," were the hoboes from the railroad. Dad said that she was seeing it undecorated and unfurnished. He'd already arranged for a decorator he did business with to come in. With her own colors and wallpaper and furniture—he might even spring for some new drapes and curtains—she wouldn't recognize it. But when we moved in at the end of the month, the decorator still hadn't been able to get around to it, and the few new downstairs pieces and the rosewood bedroom set Mom had been so proud of on Shelley Avenue faded into the general gloom.

There were, though, at least for me, important trade-offs. I no longer had to go to The Shop after school. Moreover, Roselle Park High was a small, easygoing school, it was coed, it had many fewer basketball players than Jefferson, and, as I quickly discovered, many fewer students who were smarter or more ambitious than I was. When I reported to my third-year Latin class, there were only two other students, both girls. It was rather like a high school version of the Shelley Avenue school: a simpler, more homogeneous place in which sports were king—the football team had just won the state championship in its group—and the main interests otherwise were cars and the opposite sex. The sense of a fresh start and heightened opportunities was reinforced by the relief at being sprung from the Jewish pecking order at Jefferson and the race to the Ivy League and beyond in which I was fated to trail badly. There were only three other Jews in the junior class at RPHS : Belle Notkin, one of my fellow Latin students; affable Sol Bunin, whose prowess was on the basketball court and baseball diamond; and Audrey Singer, a dark, slender transfer student with a subtle wit, who still lived on Shelley Avenue in Elizabeth and with whom I hoped to find other things in common.

The interest in me as a newcomer was immediately enhanced by my letting it be known that I was a crack basketball player who had made the junior varsity at Jefferson but had then been felled by appendicitis. It was a carryover from my summer "line" in Belmar, where I'd gotten away with it. But the odds of doing so in Roselle Park were about as short as the distance from the Elizabeth side of Westfield Avenue to the Roselle Park one. Also my need to be immediately noticed put heavy pressure on my short-breath, high-strung game. At the first practice I played with the varsity, at the third with the JVs; by the second game of the season I was riding the bench of a pretty inept JV team.

I soon learned that being the only boy in advanced Latin had its downside at RPHS. It more or less went hand in hand with my fizzled status as a player and turned me, at least in the eyes of the Brothers, the jock contingent and school heroes, into a "freak"—the term that in those better-natured days did double duty for "nerd" and "asshole." To this was soon attached the word "Jewish" and its synonyms. Because simple, hearty Sol Bunin was so likable as well as important, a starting forward on the varsity, Belle Notkin so respected for having an IQ that was off the charts, and Audrey Singer so beguiling, there wasn't much anti-Semitism in the air; but what there was began to collect around me. Wearing my Mu Sigma sweater, as I occasionally did, I came out of Latin class one afternoon to find Herm Herring, the class hero, disdainfully asking me what the sweater meant, while one of the two other Brothers who were with him cracked, "It must be a Heeb letter sweater—you get it in Elizabeth for being pushy."

"Nah," said the other Brother, "you get it for studying Latin with girls."

As it happened, the class that most engaged me was Latin. Both Belle and Nancy Higgins were a mile ahead of me when I arrived, having been much more rigorously taught by Mrs. Winquist than I had been at Jefferson. Also they were doing Virgil instead of Cicero, and so I had to catch up in the *Aeneid* and learn Latin prosody as well as strengthen my grasp of its grammar and vocabulary if I wasn't to be the boy dunce. During the Christmas vacation I huddled over the coal stove at The Shop in my RPHS warmup sweater and force-fed my mind Latin, writing down the meaning and paradigm of every noun or verb I failed to recognize. By the time we reached Book IV in mid-January, I was up to class speed, ready for Dido and Aeneas.

For the rest of the school year, I had the intellectual time of my life. Winnie Winquist was both a crack teacher and a hoot. "I don't see, Nancy, how you can miss all of the lust. It's not just Venus's doing. Here is Aeneas striding around every day like Joe Dimaggio in a little tunic. What's a young widow to feel?" In order to master the prosody, Winnie had me write simple little poems in Latin, opening the door to a magical new mode of expressiveness, an apprentice mason being given the chance to sculpt. As the three of us got to know each other and Virgil intricately, the charm of higher learning descended upon us as well as a companionship freed from the dizzy boy-girl concerns of adolescence, particularly for three fringe beings like ourselves. The intense, studious Belle kept us on our toes; the warm, sensible Nancy steadied us; I provided most of the laughs; the stylish and droll Winnie, a gray Rosalind Russell, became our model of the sophistication possible even in Roselle Park. It was my first experience of belonging to a cultural elite that was my own age, of turning my precarious, oddball side to advantage, of being the same person in New Jersey that I was in Manhattan. Also Latin became a new close connection between Mom and me: She could still follow some of the *Aeneid,* and I remember us trying to understand the periphrastic syntax as we sat in the dining room on a cold night in that chilly old house, which brought back to mind her sessions with Fan by the big kitchen stove in Cream Ridge.

Meanwhile the basketball season progressed and, after my initial tailspin, so did I. Tommy Mead, a very quick and savvy forward, and Red Langstaff, a tall, strong center—the seventh and eighth players on the essentially six-man varsity team—began to play in the JV games, I began hitting shots and making smart passes in practice and then in games, and I became the penetrating guard. By the middle of the season the three of us had teamed up, the team handily won four games in a row, and we were giving the varsity a competitive scrimmage.

Toward the end of January came the big night—our regular season game against mighty Jefferson, which this year was played in Elizabeth. It was a Friday-night game, and the gym was already packed when we came out on court for the JV preliminary—by far the biggest crowd at any of our games. As we went through our layup drill in that intense brightness and noise I was so high that I felt like I was playing for a powerhouse. During shooting practice some of the guys I'd known at Jeff were waving or wisecracking at me, but I handled that with a studied obliviousness, the focused sharpshooter finding his range. Their presence made all the more real the momentousness of the moment, my returning as a starter to the school that had cut me, and my playing in the gym where I had rooted for the Jeff varsity teams of the last two years. As I coolly lofted my set shots, flipped my leaping one-handers off the dribble, I was sinking two out of three. I was "on," and for the game of my life so far. I could hardly wait for this fantasy that had strangely come true to begin.

When we took our places for the center jump I saw that the Jeff players were wearing the red-and-black uniforms of the previous varsity— that my heroes—Pauly Krasauskas, the stalwart defender and rebounder, and Weasel Wilson, with his lightning-quick moves and movie-star looks, and deadly Eddie Tkac—had worn. Suddenly I felt flimsy to myself, unstrung. On the center jump, the ball came loose and was batted toward me. I tipped it ahead, found myself in an open court with a clear line to the basket—and was called for walking. A moment later I went up for a long rebound and tried to shoot the ball while still in the air. It was a nice shot that might have gotten me off, but it rolled around the rim and out. I stood there, the thought stabbing my mind that I wasn't going to be "on" now that it counted. I lost a second or two brooding. By the time I got back to the other end of the court, someone was making a layup in my area of our zone defense.

The confidence I had built up in the previous three weeks bled away. I played in a state of near panic—doing very little with the ball as well as being passive on defense. The score steadily mounted against us, and by the time I was taken out it was 14 to 2.

And that proved to be that. My substitute played an awkward but steady game and our team slowly fought its way back in the second quarter, while I sat on the bench and stewed. The paralyzing anxiety was gone; it was comeback time for Kid Galahad, but my renewed determination and poise had no place to go. Mr. Shaw, the coach, was not a fan of mine, and though he had let me play my way out of the pit I'd initially dug for myself, he now had nothing to say to me, and I was no longer a starter when the second half began. Tommy and Red brought our team even, and the game went down to the wire. Fuming and stewing, I hardly paid attention to their comeback. Several of my former classmates were sitting behind our bench, and I began to exchange looks with them, making visible my incomprehension of and rage at the coach who knew how much this game mattered to me, who could see how overwrought I'd been, who owed the starter I'd become a second chance, who had abruptly decided to persecute me with his heedlessness, who was probably paying me back for lying about having made the team we were playing.

Those moments before, during, and after the debacle are as vivid to me fifty years later as they were in the week following. The blows you don't get over are not necessarily the most severe ones; they're the ones that land in just the place where you have already taken the most punishment, whose pain is too familiar to confront and remedy. For the rest of the season I remained a sub, playing anxiously in games, dispiritedly in practice, a sense of Coach Shaw's disapproval or indifference accompanying me up and down the court. Every night I worked on a fantasy of making that first shot in midair at the Jeff game, and going on—basket by basket, assist by assist—to lead the team close to victory until I was knocked unconscious in the final minute and had to be carried off the court, the sellout crowd hushed in its esteem and sympathy.

13 WITHOUT ANY FRIENDS in Roselle Park, without a home that she could invite her few Elizabeth friends into, Mom did the best thing she could for her shaken and demoralized condition. She decided to look for a job of her own, and quickly found one in the accounting department of a local war plant.

In high heels and a pretty dress, her face and mind still animated by a day of contacts with coworkers at ATF, she would arrive home with the couple of pounds of meat or a chicken for which, ration book in hand, she had waited for an hour or more. Her more strenuous life pleased her. "I'm not Rosie the Riveter," she'd joke. "I'm Rosie the bookkeeper, but I'm doing my part." Or she'd say, "It's so good to get out of the house, particularly this one." Or "I haven't been out in the world for too long unless you count The Shop, which I don't. I've finally taken myself off the Ben Solotaroff dole." Humming the melody of one of the pieces she played, she would cook our dinner, then entertain us at the table with incidents and observations from work. While Sandy and I did the dishes together, she settled down with a good book, more contented than I'd ever seen her.

Our family life was changing too. Dad was around less in Roselle Park, adding two or three dinners a week for which he was "too busy to come home" to the two or three weekends a month he "needed to get away." So, though the house remained dreary—"the decorator" turning into another of Dad's promises we laughed about—there was less of his reign in the air and more of Mom's new independence. It was like raising the shade and the window of a shut-in room. We still saw the highway in front, the railroad in back, but we could see there was a world beyond them and breathe more freely in thinking of how to reach it.

With her new self-confidence, Mom was listening more to Fan and Belle, who regarded the house as the last straw. Particularly to Fan, who was free now to devote herself to rescuing us. She was making Mom realize that the house was not only an inexcusable dump for a man in Dad's position to stick his family in but also a clear sign that he was getting ready to leave her. She must begin to prepare for that, even take a position, make him put his cards on the table and come to a financial understanding, which Fan said that she stood ready to help her do. Then she would help us get settled nearby in Manhattan and steer Mom to a good job. Her trump card was the house, because Mom hated it so much and because it was glaring proof that Dad would support us adequately only if and when the courts made him. Mom agreed with her but was still wavering, afraid of the showdown with Dad. Fan said she would bring Belle with her. Belle, the tough businesswoman, was the only Weiss that Dad respected.

I took Fan's position wholeheartedly. Except for Latin, which would end in another month, there was nothing to make me want to stay in Roselle Park and a lot to make me want to leave. No more Coach Shaw. No more of the Brothers. I saw myself in a good New York high school, perhaps even Stuyvesant, which generally had weak teams as well as first-rate courses and teachers. Mainly, I was glad to have the whole issue taken out of my hands by Fan.

On a Saturday morning in early May, while all of this was going on, I was working at The Shop when Dad received a phone call. He asked a few questions, his voice suddenly slow and gentle. He said he was very sorry and would tell Rose. Then he walked up the three steps into the back office where I was typing and said, "Fan died last night. She had a stroke." Then he said, "I have to call your mother now. You'd better go home and stay with her."

That afternoon Mom and I went for a walk. Dad hadn't come home yet to take her to Belle's, where the family was gathering. The funeral was the next day in Lakewood. I would stay home to look after Sandy and Bobby. Mom and I were still in a daze—half of disbelief, half of realization. As we walked slowly along, deeper into Roselle Park, the alien streets seemed to second the event—strange but real and now part of my life. No one I felt close to, except Lou Gehrig, had died before, no one this important. "She thought the world of you," Mom said, as though reading my mind. "You were her favorite."

"I know," I said. "She believed in me. She was going to help me with college."

"Fan was too good for this world. She only thought of others. She and Belle had arranged to come today and talk to your father and start to break up the marriage. That may have brought on the stroke, all that pressure . . . facing Ben . . ." She began to sob again.

I tightened my hand on her arm. "We have enough to feel sorry about without blaming ourselves." Though it could have been true, I thought. High blood pressure had burst an artery in her head.

"I don't think I could manage in New York without Fan," Mom sobbed.

All that had become so remote again, as though without Fan it went back to being a fantasy.

We continued slowly along, I holding Mom's arm, as though we were at our own funeral for Fan. We were close again. It seemed to take deep trouble or deep sorrow to jolt me fully out of my condescending, impatient attitude and into the responsibility of being a good son.

"Whenever I'd read something good I would think of her, want to call her up and share it with her," Mom went on. "She was the one who started us reading." She began to tell me again the story of Fan skimping at her first teaching job to pay for the subscription to the Harvard Classics and buy her the piano.

I held her arm the more tightly, felt our kindredness the more keenly. "You and I talk about books," I said. "We'll do it more now."

The loss of Fan didn't fully register until the next day. The shock had worn off; the emptiness that had come was like a vacated room in my heart where memories and grief were gathering. Sandy, Bobby, and I were walking up East Westfield Avenue to Hahn's Diner, the rare experience of eating out shrouded by this new one. The warm late afternoon in May, the deserted Sunday streets, Mom in Lakewood at the funeral, Fan's disappearance forever, all came together in a sense of our aloneness, now that this powerful ally who had been about to lead us to a better future was gone. Even when Mom had been home more, the three of us had been like a little family of our own, semi-orphaned by our parents' personalities, bit players in their one-sided drama. Now Fan's death framed and intensified this bond.

Sandy asked if I thought Aunt Fan was in heaven now. I had to think about that because of my authority as the parent figure. I knew they both wanted to believe that; so did I. But I didn't now, not since reading a few months ago Bertrand Russell's "A Free Man's Worship," in Clifton Fadiman's anthology *Reading I've Liked*, another important book Fan had given me.

So I said I didn't know if there was a heaven or not; what I did know was that if you went on loving and remembering someone who'd died, then they went on living in you. Bobby asked how the person could do that if they're not in heaven but just dead. I said that they go on living in your soul. We had talked about the soul as the place where you go to pray. I didn't tell them about Lou Gehrig, who had vanished from my soul after his death; but I told myself that the best way to continue loving and remembering Fan was by trying to be the person she wanted me to be. I couldn't do that anymore with Lou Gehrig, but I could with her. Somewhere in the middle of this, right there on the street, I started to cry for the first time and went on doing so, off and on, for the next day. I tried to talk to her soul, but it was swallowed up in a black mist.

14 COLLEGE WAS ONLY a year away now, and I no longer had Fan's promise to help me. I set about getting a busboy job in Belmar that could double the money I'd made the summer before, and landed one at the Buena Vista, the best hotel in the area.

Though another Honey Abrams didn't turn up, I loved being away and on my own. It was flush times that last summer of the war; the hotel was jammed with well-to-do guests, and I was clearing eighty dollars a week, by the end of the season enough for a year's tuition at Michigan or Wisconsin. With a full station, I raced through the meals, deftly clearing my six tables, stacking the big service tray in scalloped fashion to the limit, then hoisting it aloft and one-handing it through the thronged aisles to the kitchen, where I picked up the "extras" and "seconds" that earned the top tips, then went back into the fray.

I was also putting a pound or two each week on my skinny frame. In the afternoon we'd have a few hours off and head for the beach, where some of us played touch football. One of the other busboys was a halfback at Montclair High, the rest of us were buzzing with testosterone, and the soft sand slowed and cushioned the body contact. So, before long, we were playing tackle football. For the first few plays I held back, once again nursing the diminished, fragile image of my body that the pneumonia had left me with five years before. But then someone on the other team took off around end on my side, and before I knew it, I'd chased him down and launched a flying block that took his legs out from under him. The crunch of the contact was delicious. I got up from the hot sand feeling like a new person, or, rather, like the rugged kid I'd once been, eager to hit and not minding being hit. My long spell of fear had been broken.

The first Sunday in August, Dad turned up in the dining room, where I was setting up for supper. He had brought Mom, Sandy, and Bobby that day to Belmar for their month at the shore, and I was pleased that he had stopped by to see how I was doing. But that wasn't why he had come. He told me to get my things together. He was taking me back to Elizabeth with him; he needed me in The Shop. His girl had left, and since Mom couldn't fill in now, he was stuck. He would try to find someone in the next week or two and then I could come back to my job if I wanted to. But I knew that even if he did hire a replacement, which was unlikely, they would never take me back here if I had to quit without notice as I was about to do, and by then the season would be almost over anyway.

On the drive back to Elizabeth I finally brought myself to ask how much he was going to pay me.

"I'll pay you fifteen dollars a week. You can also caddy on the weekends. You'll do all right."

"That'll come to maybe twenty-five a week with lunch and bus fare. I've been clearing eighty here."

"You planning to pay for your room and board when you go back to school?"

"No, I was planning to help out in The Shop without pay, same as I always have."

A bitter silence held between us for five minutes or so. When he broke it, his voice was the reasonable one. "I'll tell you what I'm going to do. I'll give you another ten dollars a week for your expenses. Also, the way you're growing you're going to need some new clothes."

I still said nothing. What was there to say?

Then he said, "Look, just because I need you to come back don't mean that I don't know how you feel, working down here, having an extra dollar in your pocket." He told me about how he had left home to work in Atlantic City and then gone on the road with the carnivals and such. "A couple of years later I was out in California, and loving it, but my father needed me in the business, so I came back. You think I wanted to?"

I guarded my silence. It seemed to be giving me leverage, something I'd never had with him before.

"I came back even though I never had a home like you have. I never had your chance for an education or even much of a childhood."

"I know," I said. I had no sympathy for him anymore. I wanted my youth, not a slightly better version of his.

"Well, then stop being so down in the mouth. We could have a pretty good time together the next week or two until I find someone. If you mind your p's and q's I might even take you to the Tavern for dinner." The Tavern was the Lindy's of the Elizabeth-Newark area.

"I'm thinking more about how I'm going to go to college next year. That's what this summer job was for."

"Well, as far as that's concerned, did it ever occur to you that you might be better off working for me?

"Even if I'm going to be a lawyer?"

That caught him off stride, but he quickly recovered. "You'll never be a lawyer," he declared. "I know plenty of lawyers, and you're just not the type. You're too scattered to get through law school, much less make any money at it."

"I guess we disagree," I said. "Fan thought I would make an excellent lawyer, and so does my guidance counselor."

"Well, listen to them then," he said. A few minutes later he again broke the heavy silence. "Of course, if you showed some initiative in the business, took your head out of the clouds, learned how to apply yourself, I might feel a little different about the matter myself." By the end of the statement his voice had grown genial; his tone and the measured sidelong look that he gave me from behind the wheel seemed to add up to a note of sincere interest in me, even an avowal that he might be more open-minded and supportive than I or other people gave him credit for.

"I'll try," I said. "You're not an easy man to please."

"I know that," he said. "You don't come as far as I have by being easy to please. Beginning with myself." He let that hang in the air for a moment. Then he said, "I'm not interested in you trying, as you put it. I'm interested in you trying as hard as you can, even sacrificing a little of your basketball and the baseball broadcasts and those books you read. You'd be surprised where it might get you. Even if you decide you don't want to go into the business."

So I swallowed my resentment, and beginning the next morning I tried my ass off. I figured that if I could cater to the obnoxious family and the phony singles I'd had at my station at the Buena Vista for the sake of going to college, I could "apply myself" at the Standard Plate Glass Co. and see if it unlocked Dad's wallet. I answered the phone with friendly, businesslike dispatch; when he wasn't there, I added, "I'm his son. Is there anything I can do for you?" I straightened up as much of the office as I dared, staying well clear of the litter of used envelopes, invoices, pencils, mail, pipes and pipe cleaners, and whatnot on his desk. I found a stenographer's pad that the girl had left and used it to keep phone messages for him in neat, chronological order. I cleaned months of dust off the picture frames, moldings, three-way vanity mirrors that were strewn about in the showroom and in the display windows that looked like they fronted a junk shop. Then I washed the windows inside and out, scrubbed the grime off the display surfaces and put back the items in an orderly arrangement. I polished all the wall mirrors in the showroom and used a dry paintbrush to get the dust out of the little crevices in their gold-leaf frames. Next, I straightened out the window glass racks in the small shop on the other side of the office area and brought in new stock from the cases in the warehouse. After business hours I attacked the linoleum floors that probably hadn't been washed since Dad moved in four years ago.

We got along that week better than we ever had over a sustained period, as though Dad was also intent on keeping up his end of the understanding. The first night back we went shopping at the Big Bear and he bought some choice cuts of beef and loin lamb chops, big baking potatoes and fresh corn and salad stuff, fruits and melons, and a fancy coffee ring and honey buns for our breakfasts. Cooking and eating together, it was as though our better days of checking out hiking trails had returned. He was pleased by my keeping busy in the front, though he seemed indifferent to my cleaning efforts and snapped at me for buying a mop bucket from petty cash when there were plenty of empty putty cans out back. Though fastidious about his person, he was oblivious to the appearance of his car, his home, his business. He was doing a lot of storefronts again, but the front of his own place was still unfinished, still covered with the black primer that had been put on to receive structural glass four years before. "The shoemaker with holes in his shoes," as Mom would say.

The Friday evening after I'd come back we were working late, getting out bills and correspondence because he was going away for the weekend, leaving me to mind The Shop with Bill, though I was supposed to be free to caddy. We were finishing up a twelve-hour day, it was already dark outside, and I was hungry, tired, impatient to be done, and also freshly resentful. I made an error of fifty dollars in the total of an invoice, taking a scrawled 6 as a 1. Dad was sitting across the desk, checking the typed bills against the invoices, then putting them in envelopes. When he caught my error, he balled up the bill and threw it across the desk. "Can't you even read a number right, for Chrissake?"

It wasn't anything that I hadn't heard a hundred times, but this time it landed against the new sense of strength I'd grown busing and playing football in Belmar. I wasn't even angry or upset. Instead a cool calmness came over me, and in it was a permission I never, until that moment, would have dreamed I had. I stood up and quietly said,

"That's it, Dad." Guided by my new tone, I walked past him and feeling very tall went down the three steps and through the office. I half expected him to grab me by the shoulder and begin to let me have it, and knew that if he did I would warn him not to, and if necessary fight my way free of him.

But he was still standing by the desk, his back to me, a slump in his shoulders, when I looked back as I left and walked out into the bleak Elizabeth Avenue night, feeling as though I were saying goodbye to that too, along with him and The Shop.

My new self-reliance was rapidly dictating to me. I'd go home, call Aunt Belle, tell her what had happened, and ask her if she could get me a job at the Lake Tarleton Club or some other hotel. Of course, Dad might be waiting for me when I got home, either to intimidate me or softsoap me, but I didn't think he would be, because of the slump in his shoulders, his staring down, as though he, too, realized that I was no longer under his thumb.

I couldn't reach Belle or Adrian, but I packed my suitcase and took the train to New York so I wouldn't have to see Dad, and spent the rest of the night on a bench in Penn Station. I knew from the New York guys at the Carleton and Buena Vista that there was a big employment agency, the Jupiter, that catered to the summer hotel trade. I was there when it opened at nine, and that afternoon was working in the dining room of the Murida Hotel in Long Beach.

Yuddy was my age but five years older in smarts. He taught me how to increase my tips, shoot craps, and almost pick up girls. "It doesn't matter what you say to them as long as you do it confidently. It's the confidence in your voice, not the bullshit, that they go for." But my nose was in my way all over again, and by the time I fought far enough through my shyness to ask a girl to have a Coke, Yuddy would already have taken her friend down to the beach and then under the boardwalk.

About a week after I arrived at the Murida the atom bomb was dropped on Hiroshima. I responded more or less as I would have to hearing that my favorite boxing champ, already way ahead on points, had knocked his opponent flat at the end of the fourteenth round. Even as the first accounts of the devastation came in, there was nothing especially horrendous about it in my mind, so conditioned had I become to taking any of our military actions for granted as necessary and just, and their civilians as the malevolent enemies who were getting what was coming to them, either for persecuting the Jews or bombing Pearl Harbor. The only civilian victims of the war were on our side; theirs belonged to a mass population of Hitler's *Sieg-heil*-ing robots or Tojo's *Banzai*-ing fanatics. One of the jukebox favorites during my senior year chortled that "it was mighty smoky over Tokyo" and went on:

> A friend of mine in a B-29
> Dropped another load just for luck.
> As he flew away, he was heard to say,
> "A hubba, hubba, hubba, yuk, yuk."

Such was the desensitization of a war that was as morally loaded as a sermon and as existentially remote as a movie. Whatever was ominous about the dawn of the atomic age was ignored in the blue skies of the war's end. After Hiroshima and Nagasaki came a progression of euphoric days culminating in VJ Day, which promised to be like New Year's Eve raised to the next power.

Yuddy and I raced through our side jobs after dinner, threw on our sharpest clothes and plenty of shaving lotion, and caught the train into the city. We were not going just to celebrate the event. "You're sure to get laid tonight," Yuddy promised. "The excitement will make them wild." As we made our way through the genial riot that extended from Penn Station up Seventh Avenue to Times Square, I took in the wanton action that girls were providing and thought that tonight could indeed be the night, that the condom I'd been carrying all summer in my wallet like a lottery ticket would be redeemed.

I lost Yuddy, found him, lost him again as he made his moves. The guys who were getting kissed and hugged and walked away with were all in uniform, and the chicks they were picking up were older women, women in their twenties. About all that was thrust at me for the next two hours were several pints of whiskey proffered by sailors whom I'd taken to thanking, for lack of anything else to do, for winning the war. It was a strange night: history being made, thousands and thousands of people around me drunk on peace, while the whiskey I was handed only made me feel all the more like the homely and lonely virgin I'd thought I was going to leave behind at the Murida for good.

I ran into Yuddy again near Central Park, from which he was returning. "Too many guys in Times Square," he said. "You should have gone to the park." He'd found a girl there from Hunter College and scored a triple. "You want to smell her?" he smiled, holding up a finger. "It's better than nothing."

As we were waiting for the subway at Fiftieth Street, a train pulled in on the uptown track. When it stopped, there in the window was a girl my age, as dark and comely and Manhattan as Gil's Toni Warren and Betty Blum—the daughter of the producer he had worked for— my longest and purest fantasy come to life. And then, as though my stare were words, exactly the right words, her beautifully cut dark eyes returned it and we gazed at each other and then she smiled. I held up my hands in astonishment, longing, God-knows-what as the train began to pull out. To which she nodded and kept smiling— nuances of welcome, bemusement, regret in the smile, as though she were the muse of life's irony, our gazes holding as gently as hands until she was out of sight.

"Hey, you know that chick?" Yuddy exclaimed.

"No, but she is the one I've been looking for."

"Too bad you didn't run into her earlier. But maybe it's not too late. Grab the next train uptown—she could've got off at the next stop and be waiting for you."

"No," I said. "She's got too much class to do that."

I didn't feel disconsolate. All the way back to Long Beach and for days after I felt lifted and clarified by her brief but unmistakable interest. Instead of cashing Little Benny's lottery ticket, life had sent the Weiss boy a renewed invitation to the feast to come.

One night, toward the end of the season, I was lying on my cot reading when one of the other busboys, an older fellow named Herb Brichto, stopped on his way back from the shower. "How come you're not out with Yuddy?"

We had hardly spoken before now. He had come to the Murida even after I had and pretty much kept to himself—a small, slender fellow who reminded me of Aunt Belle because of his Eddie Cantor look and who observed our towel fights and crap games, our boasting and preening, with the amused detachment of a missionary among the natives.

I was reading the copy of *The Grapes of Wrath* that I'd bought for the trip to Long Beach and been at ever since. When Herb asked me what I thought of it, I said that it was corny in a moving way.

"That's an oxymoron," he said, smiling.

I got my guard up, thinking he was insulting me with his term.

"Critically speaking, that is. But an interesting one for Steinbeck."

"What's an oxymoron?" I said. "I don't speak Greek."

He explained what it meant and why mine seemed particularly apt for Steinbeck's "brand of Marxist romanticism." We began to talk, he fully and fluently, I occasionally and uncertainly. Compared to Herb and his lingo about Steinback's "crude dialectic" and "Popular Front demagoguery," Uncle Adrian seemed like a piker.

I asked him how come he knew so much. He told me he was a graduate student at Columbia and a rabbinical student at the Jewish Theological Seminary.

"You mean you read the Torah and the Talmud and that stuff."

"Yes, but critically and contextually. Right now I'm reading Milton and T. S. Eliot."

I asked him who T. S. Eliot was. He said that he and his friends thought that Eliot was the most important poet and critic writing in English right now.

Almost every time he opened his mouth I seemed to learn something new. I'd been spending my nights playing basketball and gambling and chasing girls, and here only a few cots away was this genius who seemed to like talking to me. I asked him if he had some poems by Eliot. He went over to his cot and reached under it where he had several books sitting on his suitcase. He came back with a slender book in a suave blue-black binding, *Collected Poems*, and the author's name in austere type. "I'll check a few," he said. "Try them on for size."

After we'd finished talking, I read the poems he'd checked. Except for my little Latin poems, which were fun, like doing one of those puzzles where you slide letters around to make words, I'd thought of poetry as lofty feelings and language, a kind of verbal high-wire act—meter and rhyme your balancing pole. So when I came upon the poem "Preludes" I could hardly believe my eyes. It wasn't about eloquent nightingales or Lincoln's death shrouded in lilacs or ominous ravens or a soldier's blood turning a corner of a foreign field forever into England. It was about a neighborhood like Adrian's, Columbus Avenue in the Seventies, full of furnished single rooms in old brownstones, where you felt the lives of solitary people waiting out the end, the smell of their food in the hall, the beer smell coming out of their lonely corner bars, their aging, uncared-for bodies with yellow feet and soiled hands. And then, toward the end, Eliot stopped recoiling from them, and suddenly his imagination and heart went out to them:

> I am moved by fancies that are curled
> Around these images and cling:
> The notion of some infinitely gentle,
> Infinitely suffering thing.

I read those four lines over and over, fascinated by the way the ordinary end words—"curled" and "cling," "gentle" and "thing"—were lifted or dropped so expressively and precisely into place by the rhythm and the rhyme; how they suddenly zoomed into a vast feeling of compassion before the final stanza abruptly brought the poem back to its original grimness but now on a cosmic scale. I marveled at and struggled with "The Love Song of J. Alfred Prufrock," the same repugnance, sympathy, and despair attached to the other end of the social scale.

Herb was impressed that I'd read most of the *Aeneid* in Latin. He said I should try another epic poem, *Paradise Lost*, and lent me his copy. I didn't get far. By the time we finished up each night in the dining room, the lure of the boardwalk or the basketball court easily defeated the dense, archaic language and unfamiliar images and allusions of Milton, just as Yuddy was still more my speed than Herb was. On the beach after the lunch meal, he'd sit by himself and read, and for a time I could sense that he was waiting for me to join him for another of our literary discussions. During the last week or so of the season we hardly spoke at all. Yet I felt the tug of kindredness as well as guilt even then and knew that in resisting his influence I was also resisting Aunt Fan's and denying her nephew an exceptional chance to develop.

15 WITH THE WAR over and veterans pouring into colleges, the word went out to high school seniors that admission was going to be a lot tougher than we'd thought. As for the scholarship I'd now undoubtedly need (Dad and I were hardly speaking to each other), I had no chance at all unless I could make my grades rise dramatically, right to the top of the class so that I could graduate with honors.

Dad had said that if I tried hard, I might be surprised at what could happen. This time he was right. From the first day, I bore down on trigonometry and chemistry, which figured to be my weak subjects. Within a month or so I was flying in both of them. There were a few math and science "brains" in the senior class, and all of a sudden I was one of them. In the easygoing atmosphere of class at RPHS, the formulas of chemical reactions were as intelligible as Virgil's syntax had become, the proofs that had eluded me in plane geometry followed readily for the more complex ones of solid geometry.

My challenge turned out to be the formidable Maud Austin, the H. L. Mencken of RPHS: a large, rawboned, saturnine spinster in whose English class rigor, clarity, and urbanity reigned. Going from one or another of our classes into hers was like going from Chestnut Street, the main drag in Roselle Park, to Harvard Square. This had also been true of Winnie Winquist's Virgil class—they were best friends—but while Winnie was a stylish lady, Miss Austin (her first name seemed purely nominal) was a mental Amazon, so commanding was her teaching style, so strenuous her standards, so agile her mind, so cutting her wit. Even the jocks and cheerleaders were daunted by her.

My first essay, on "The Minister's Black Veil," came back with lots of question marks and exclamation-pointed criticisms in the margin, one of them "Ugh!" At the end was the comment "You seem to have an idea about Hawthorne's treatment of sin but your development of it is oafish. See me after school." I arrived half angry, half perplexed. Neither state lasted long.

She sat back in her chair, gave me a long, scrutinizing, slightly amused look, and said, "Do you have even the slightest idea what a paragraph is?"

I hadn't thought much about it. Writing, after all, had always come naturally to me. "It's a group of sentences about the same thing, I guess."

"Like a pile of pine boards."

It wasn't, but the difference made me think. "It progresses," I said. "A pile of boards just sit there."

"Sit?"

"Sits."

"Good," she said. "We're already making progress. As a good paragraph does. Let's see why yours mostly sit there."

For the next hour or so she showed me that an effective and interesting paragraph usually has a "surprising" or "complicating" element that gives the thought a "twist," while maintaining its continuity. We revised several of my paragraphs to do so. "It's like a curve ball in pitching," I said at the end. "The spin on it makes it break in a different direction."

"I'll settle for a less predictable direction," she said. "Now all you need to learn is control." So she knew baseball too.

That writing was more like pitching than throwing was exciting news to me. I worked hard on my writing assignments for her class and watched the questions in the margin diminish, some of the exclamations turn positive. As the year went along I felt that behind Miss Austin's exacting, dour manner was a warmth that offered me welcome. Once a week I would drop in on her after school, having thought up a question about Hawthorne or Melville or Whitman that would enable us to have a conversation. She became a kind of Gentile version of Fan, an exacting intelligent teacher who took me seriously and affirmed the side of me that I would otherwise blame for making me anxious, alien, unpopular.

I was still a figure of derision to several of the Brothers, the elite jocks and make-out artists in the class, and of no interest to its popular girls. I didn't have anyone to date, and the only dancing I did was at the high school mixers. My one kindred spirit was Audrey Singer, the wry girl from Elizabeth, but the passion we shared was for novels, particularly Ayn Rand's *The Fountainhead*, which ministered to an iconoclasm we otherwise didn't have much opportunity to express. She was drawn to Joe Rafalowski, star tackle, heavyweight wrestler, and master of the Brothers' revels, while I had entered a long, slow, seemingly hopeless fall for Lucy Pastor, one of the cheerleaders.

Lucy was a girl who had a lot going on. Though she held a vaunted position in Roselle Park, she was almost as much a fringe character as I was. Lithe, vivacious, high-strung, her eyes glowing like lanterns against her olive complexion, Lucy walked in a moral shadow, a sense of the potentially scandalous as firmly attached to her as athletic stardom was to Herm Herring or genius was to Belle Notkin. She was said to date fast, older guys from out of town. If a car or motorcycle roared by while we were in class, there would be a low murmur of "Lucy, hey Lucy," from some of the Brothers and their spear-carriers.

But there was more to Lucy Pastor than her siren looks and reputation. A crack math student, she had a ready wit, and a wider view of life and its prospects than most of the other seniors. Her brother had won a scholarship to Georgia Tech, and Lucy was bent on following the same path out of "this piddling burg," as she called it. Her house was on my way to school, and we would often walk there together—I contrived to be within hailing distance when she came out. As the year went along we even met a few times for lunch—hot dogs at Haps and Caps and a walk across the tracks into Roselle. I imagine that my shy, studious, ironic talk was restful to her, while she gave me back at least a whiff of the spice of life.

It remained, though, a school-day relationship, and the idea of anything sexual or even romantic was so remote that I couldn't even work up a fantasy about us. How was I to compete with the Franks and Steves, the hotrodding and motorcycling vets, who took her to the roadhouses out on Route 24?—I, who didn't even drive, not to mention my other drawbacks.

There were, of course, others whom I could work up fantasies about. The most intense involved the prettier of two boldly suggestive young women who had come into The Shop one Saturday afternoon, looked at some mirrors and picture frames, and amused themselves with my being alone there.

I sensed from the way they used their eyes and hips that they were either hookers or the kind of women businessmen "keep." Had they just passed by, looked in, seen me alone there, and decided to have some fun, or were they looking for Dad? I was too rattled by them to find out for sure. Alma, the prettier one, asked me if I would show them the warehouse in back, and when I fumbled out the excuse that I had to watch the front, she said, "I'll bet your Dad would show us around."

I didn't ask if she knew him or was just talking about men in general. I had no clear evidence that Dad played around or had a girlfriend, though at seventeen I believed that he didn't go away weekends just to ski or swim and to catch up on his sleep. As for Mom, I suppose, the relief of having him out of the house outweighed the suspicion of what he was doing. Alma and her friend did not change this attitude, but she did provide for a time an obsessively vivid and effective fantasy of what would have happened if I'd been able to swallow my nervousness and show her the warehouse.

I hoped that the added weight, strength, and toughness I'd picked up over the summer had solidified my basketball game. In Long Beach it had done so. A couple of nights a week I teamed up with two other busboys, who played for Bronx Science, and we usually held our own at the playground court where the visiting and local talent gathered. "If Coach Shaw could see me now," I'd think as I fearlessly drove the lane or muscled in for a rebound. But when Coach Shaw saw me play three months later he didn't appear to notice my stronger game, and after a week or so its aggressiveness and confidence dwindled. I made the varsity but seldom played.

About halfway through the season I developed a serious glandular infection and was out of school for almost a month. I was much more concerned about missing my classes than the rest of the games, for I had made 95s in all my courses the first semester and Miss Austin had told me I was on track to graduate with honors. It was hard to study in my weak and uncomfortable condition, my swollen neck feeling like it was in a cast. Also I was having trouble figuring out trigonometry on my own and couldn't do the chemistry experiments from bed. So when I finally returned to school, I hit the ground running.

After the season ended there was a meeting to elect next year's captain. Coach Shaw was late for it, and I was trying to catch up in one of my courses when he walked into the room. "Put that book away, Solotaroff," he snapped. "We're having an important meeting here."

His reprimand had a lot of resonance for me. When the team meeting ended, I made a point of walking out by myself, putting Coach Shaw and his team behind me, feeling the way I had the night I walked out of the Standard Plate Glass Co. to begin my own life. At present the direction of that life ran through the textbook I had been told to put away and the others with it. I knew by now my grades hadn't gotten me into a good college—I'd been turned down by Columbia, Michigan, and Wisconsin, and was left with Rutgers. My plan now was to enlist in the Navy for two years. Then, with my honors diploma and the GI Bill to pay most of my way, I'd be able to go to one of the three.

But two problems loomed before me. I not only would have to catch up but continue to excel in my courses. The other was that the Navy, and probably the Army, wouldn't take someone with a septum as deviated as mine. Where was the money for the operation I needed to come from? I might be able to earn it over the summer, but the opportunity to get the GI Bill could well have ended by then.

So I would have to go to my father. I was back to working at The Shop on Saturdays, which I thought might give me a bit of leverage. But our relationship hadn't changed since the incident of the summer. One morning he'd awakened me early to get up and shovel out the driveway after a snowstorm. I'd dozed off, and he came barreling into the room and began to pummel me.

Instead of covering up and cowering, I scrambled under the blows and out of bed. Holding up my hands in a stop position, I said, "If you ever hit me again I'll hit you back."

"Go ahead, hit your father, you miserable, ungrateful bastard."

"I won't let you beat me up anymore."

We could both see that I meant it, that I wasn't afraid of him any longer, and he snarled something about doing what I was told or being out on the street.

During the two months after my illness, when I was studying almost constantly, my father, of all people, became the person who sustained me. For, whether *he* realized it or not, I was showing him once and for all that I was going to be a man who did much more with his life than suffer. Undergirding that ambition was a principle that he had taught me by example: if you want to become someone, that is, in charge of your life, you have to work a lot harder and more single-mindedly than others do. Even though I was now trying to develop a manner that was the antithesis of his—soft-spoken, modest, gentle, attentive—I discovered that when it came to staking out and moving toward a position in the world, I was much more his son than the nephew of my happy-go-lucky uncles, Gil and Mickey.

After I'd caught up in school, I got the name of a nose specialist from Dr. Gittelman and went to see him by myself. Dr. Mamlet clucked over the condition of my nose, said that the operation would be a difficult one but that he could straighten the septum enough to get me in the Navy, significantly improve my breathing, and also give me a nice-looking nose. I asked him what his fee and his estimate of the hospital bill would be.

"I'll speak to your parents about that," he said.

I asked if he would wait a few days until I had spoken to them and told them what the probable cost would be.

"Let me get this straight, young man. You're talking to me about a major operation and your parents don't even know about it?"

I said that my mother did, and that I still had to speak to my father.

Dr. Mamlet said that his time was valuable, that he hoped I hadn't been wasting it.

"Don't worry," I said "I'm going to have this operation. How much is it going to cost?

He said that his fee alone would be eight hundred dollars and the hospital another five hundred or so.

When I left his office, it was inconceivable to me that I wouldn't have the operation. My entire future depended on it. More immediately, I could already feel the dark weight of chagrin about my appearance beginning to lift from my mind. During the basketball season, it had grown even heavier. I had only to bring the ball upcourt at the other team's gym for the jeers to ring out: "Hey, number six, is that your nose or a hose?" Now that would end. Also the idea I'd been having about asking Lucy Pastor to go to the Senior Prom with me suddenly didn't seem crazy. By the time I got home from Newark I was so excited I called her on the pretext of asking for the math assignment (I'd never phoned her before) and then told her my news and before I could stop myself asked her to the Prom. She said she hadn't planned to go, thought it over for a moment, and said, "Why not?"

My cup running over, that night I asked Dad if we could have a talk — also a first. I doubted that he would give me the money for the operation, and I knew that the worst thing I could do was to appeal to his sense of responsibility for not taking me to a doctor after I'd broken it. So I'd decided to put it as a business proposition. I told him of my plan to enlist in the Navy to pay for my own education. All that I would ask of him was a loan of eight hundred dollars, which I would pay back in monthly installments from my service pay.

"Who's going to pay for the rest of the operation?"

I said that I still had four hundred dollars saved up from the summer and that Mom had said she'd help if I needed more.

"So your mother is going to help you. All you need is a mere eight hundred dollars from me."

"I'm asking for a loan, I don't expect you to give it to me." When he didn't reply I said, "Is even a loan too much to ask of you?"

"Let me ask *you* something. What have you done to deserve it? What consideration have you ever shown me?"

"I've gone to The Shop for the past six years. That's not consideration?"

"And when I needed you this past summer? Maybe you should have thought about this operation of yours before you walked out on me."

"I'm not going to apologize for that," I said, suddenly hot with rage. "I have a right not to be shit on, which you've done all my life. I'm not going to kiss your ass for the money."

He gave me a tight, bitter smile. "My, my," he said. "Where do you get such expressions?"

That tore it. I was glad that I'd said what I'd said and had nothing else to say. After I left him sitting there, it only took me a few minutes to decide on my next move. I got on the phone and asked the long-distance operator for Trafalgar 4-1249.

I arrived at Adrian's around two o'clock the next afternoon. It was a Saturday, and his practice and kaffeeklatsch were in full swing. Aunt Belle sat me down to a slice of baba au rhum and a glass of milk and said that Adrian wanted to talk to me. While I waited, I got into an argument about Winston Churchill's Iron Curtain speech with a stylish young man from the Netherlands who was very critical of it. An attaché at the new United Nations headquarters at Lake Success, Christophe was just the sort of person I'd come to know at Adrian's who normally made me feel like I'd just jumped down from the cabbage truck. But in my new state of self-confidence and provoked by his disdain of one of my wartime heroes, I declared that Churchill was one of the two saviors of the free world and a man who knew what he was talking about when it came to Stalin. Christophe took my remarks in stride, saying that he was glad to meet an American of my generation who was so passionate about politics.

After Adrian was finished with Christophe's friend, he took me into his study. He began to ask me about Dr. Mamlet—how I had found him, what his diagnosis was, what he had told me about the operation. I told him what little I could. He said that in my case a rhinoplasty was a very serious operation and he was concerned whether I had the right man. He thought I should at least get a second opinion from a New York specialist. I was moved that Adrian, who was only tangentially a member of my family, should ask these questions when no one else had, not even Mom. But I didn't want to wait for a second opinion. I told him that Dr. Gittelman had said that Dr. Mamlet was a first-rate surgeon, and our family swore by Dr. Gittelman. When Belle came in, they talked quietly for a moment and then she wrote the check and tucked it in my shirt pocket. Each of them gave me a big hug and a tender look, as though I were their son.

After leaving Adrian's, I walked down Amsterdam Avenue to Verdi Square to get the subway to Penn Station. As I was going though the little street park there, who should I run into but my father's sister, "Crazy Aunt Sophie," as Sandy, Bobby, and I called her. She was no longer married to Leo, he having fathered a child elsewhere and married the child's mother, and Sophie seemed a little farther around the bend each time we saw her, which was rarely. Sandy had stopped taking lessons from her because of the wear and tear on her nerves, and since we'd moved to Roselle Park we hadn't seen her at all.

She seemed to have aged ten years, to have turned into one of those refugees from their better days that you often saw in the cafeterias along Broadway, who lived alone in one of the thousand furnished rooms like the woman in "Preludes."

Sophie thrust her face at me as though she were accosting rather than greeting me. "How's my brother?" she demanded.

I said he was all right.

"Are your foolish sister and mother still studying the piano?"

I said they were and that they weren't foolish. I didn't want to talk to her. I was getting upset.

"What are you doing in the city by yourself?"

The phrase "by yourself" did it. The stress of taking the operation on myself, of the pitch and yaw of hope, despair, and gratitude, of pride and self-pity, of going from Dr. Mamlet to my father to Belle and Adrian during the past twenty-four hours, was suddenly too much to bear. Standing there on the sidewalk, my Solotaroff aunt clutching at me, I raged at her, said she was "crazy like the rest of your family" and then broke down. I heard her telling someone about her "brother Ben and his ungrateful children." "Don't listen to her," I shouted and sobbed. "She's all wrong. Wrong, wrong, wrong." The Verdi Square regulars sitting on the long bench that fronted the park went on looking back and forth at Sophie and me, as though trying to determine who took the cake for nuttiness in this family.

On a beautiful Memorial Day morning two weeks later, Mom and I were sitting on the top step of the front porch. Past us on East Westfield Avenue walked little groups of recent and older veterans in uniform, kids from the high school band in theirs, cops and fire-men and other marchers, all heading toward the high school, the staging area for this first big parade since the end of the war.

I imagined Lucy out there with the three other cheerleaders at the front of the school band, her smile flashing, her eyes widened as she took in the crowd taking in her. I wasn't sorry I'd be missing her swan song. We were about where we had been before the Prom, or perhaps a step back, since the few illusions I'd been growing had died that evening, her scented body so close and yet so far.

I could hardly blame her. The photograph of our table of eight at the Zanzibar, the famous New York nightclub, had sunk my heart; for all my primping beforehand, there I still was, as photogenic as a baboon, my swarthiness emphasized by my white dinner jacket, my fierce beak by my shy smile, my ears even more protuberant than usual. Lucy herself looked a little pop-eyed and frantic, as though she were knocking herself out to have a good time. At the end of the evening she'd given me a quick kiss on the cheek, her hand already on the doorknob. The foxiest girl in Roselle Park—but not for me. What with the rented tux, the corsage, the nightclub, it had been an expensive exercise in magical thinking and teenage conformity, the only real thrill that of listening to a silky-smooth new group—the King Cole Trio.

But my face, and perhaps luck, was about to change. Mom and I were sitting together for a few minutes before I headed off to Newark to put myself in the hospital for the operation.

As always when my health was involved she was very much pres-ent. But then she made one of her wayward remarks that we called "Momisms."

"I know the operation will be successful, but I feel that I'll soon be losing you."

Both parts of the sentence annoyed me, also that the first part seemed less important than the second. "Okay, I won't have the operation. I'll call it off. 'Hello, Dr. Mamlet. Don't bother showing up tomorrow. I'm calling it off. My mother's afraid of losing me. I'll get back to you in ten years or so. Bye.' And then I'll stay home with this dumb nose, work at The Shop, and we'll live miserably ever after."

She put her arm around my shoulders. "You know that's not what I want," she said. "It's just that you've been my son for seventeen years, my firstborn, my male companion."

"True," I said. "So what?" Sometimes, as now, I hated her way of leaning on me. With the war over she was no longer working and had fallen back into her former scatteredness and dependency. I knew I was again belittling her, even her love for me. To cover myself I blamed her for something else. "I don't see why you're not worried. At least a little. I am. Adrian said that he's heard of cases where a surgeon doing this kind of operation damaged the optic nerve."

"Of course I'm worried. I'm trying not to show it." Then she said, "I wish you'd let me go with you, get you settled."

So we went through that again. The two-hour bus trip there and back. The greater need I'd have for her to be there after the operation. The truth was I wanted to go by myself, the truth was that I was on my way out of her life as we had known it. I resented even her arm around my shoulder, as though it were trying to hold me back.

"Sometimes," she said hesitantly, "I think you still blame me for the abortion. I think maybe your going for this operation is bringing that back."

That, too, was Mom: one putt all the way off the green; another, no less unexpected, dead center. "No, I don't," I said quickly and even more irritably, for as soon as she said it, I knew she was right. "Let's just lay off our feelings, okay? This isn't exactly the right time to talk about them." For emphasis, I pushed her hand off my shoulder.

She stared out at the street, each eye bright now with a tear. "Someday you'll understand. I know that. But it's hard now, particularly with Fan gone. Who else do you think I have? What do you think I live for besides the three of you?"

My special dilemma again. Her neediness and my ambivalence, half of me sympathetic, half of me cold. I put my arm around her. "Not out here, Mom," I said. "Let's go in the house."

Where we patched it up again, me holding her at the end but looking into space over her shoulder, wishing I felt more clearly and strongly what I was supposed to feel. "Look, I said. "If you want to come with me it's okay. I can understand why you want to."

She opened her arms, stepped back, and gave me her other smile, the steady, brave one. "No, you go yourself. You've done this on your own. You're becoming a man. I'm very proud of you." Then, moving closer again, she said, "Now give me a real hug and let me take one last look at that face."

16 THE NIGHT BEFORE graduation there was a baccalaureate ceremony at the high school, my first public appearance since the operation. The shiners and other facial bruises from the operation had all but faded away, and though my nose was still swollen it was straight and seemed to me half the size of its predecessor. The stir of interest when we arrived at the school and the favorable comments and curious questions of my friends and even the snide looks of my critics turned me into a one-night celebrity—as positively self-conscious (itself a great change) as though a spotlight were trailing after me. Miss Austin came over to Mom and me, gave me a long appraising look, and said, "Handsome is as handsome does."

The main event of the ceremony was a talk by Reverend Williston, the most influential clergyman in town. Toward the end he began inveighing against the pernicious ideas of the thinker who had been responsible for fascism. Just as our older brothers and sisters in the armed forces had saved the world from its evil dominion, so we, the class of 1946, should dedicate ourselves to saving our spiritual heritage from the fascists' atheistic father—something like that. It seemed strange that Reverend Williston could get so worked up about this Jap philosopher Neechi, which is how his name and identity lodged in my mind. But then I saw he was defending Christianity against Neechi's charge that it was a religion of the slave mentality when it was clearly, as the war had shown, the religion of the free and the brave. Conjoined to keep the world safe for Christianity as well as democracy, we were sent forth into the future. On the way out, Belle Notkin, Audrey Singer, and I exchanged shrugs.

The following day was Senior's Day at school, which we mostly spent autographing our photograph in one another's yearbook. Rapport and sentiment reigned, a shared past (many of the seniors had been together since the first grade) coming upon a sharply dividing future. The word had gotten around that I was one of the four students who would graduate with honors. Again, I was floating upright through the moment, surprised and touched by many of my classmates who congratulated me and asked me to sign their yearbooks—the "in" crowd as well as the kids with only one or two activities like Sewing Club or Photography Club in their caption. Some signed my book perfunctorily but some warmly, as though I had come to matter to them.

As some of them, I realized, had come to matter to me. Emil Kleinert, the wrestler and trombone player, who had introduced me to Fifty-second Street in New York and taught me how to listen to serious jazz. Bob Tuohy, the football tackle with a sly wit and inquiring mind, whom I had taken to walking around town with late into the night and deep into the questions serious seniors think about. Jean Forrest, the lively daughter of the biology teacher and another of the "brains," who all along had made me feel welcome and even understood.

They and others, I was beginning to realize, had enabled Roselle Park High to "work" for me, to bring me out of my prolonged tailspin in Elizabeth, to "straighten up and fly right," as one of the songs of the day advised. It wasn't just the effort I'd made that had done it. I'd needed the easygoing atmosphere of RPHS to relax my anxious mind, to restore the confidence in it that I seemed to have lost somewhere between junior high and the Standard Plate Glass Co. How strange and paradoxical that I should find the acceptance and confirmation I'd lacked, except from Honey and my Weiss aunts and their circle, in a Gentile community, an outcome that belied the ethnic facts of life that even my mother took for granted. But the more I thought about it, the more it tied in with the changing spirit of America that had been fostered by the war. American democracy was at work, right inside my own life.

I tried to indicate my belated gratitude to my classmates as I went from yearbook to yearbook. There, looking down and away, set in its bleak, outcast expression, was the face and perhaps the attitude I'd left behind. There, too, was the visible evidence of the recognition, in both senses, that the past two years now signified. Under the photograph was the caption, "Trust Ted to throw light on the subject," that one of the editors of the yearbook, Jean or Belle, had written.

The groove I was in continued to the evening graduation ceremonies, and then suddenly grew even wider when, after the procession of the class to our places on the stage, I saw Dad sitting with Mom in the audience. He had never come to anything I was involved in before, not a play or a basketball game or even parents' night. But now there he was at the very event I would have chosen, the climax of my life so far. When the honors certificates were awarded, he would see for himself that in my own sphere I could work as hard, could apply myself as effectively, as he did in his, that I could come out on top. And at no one else's expense.

The ceremony dragged along through the welcoming remarks, the musical performances, the valedictorian's speech, the class president's speech, the class adviser's speech, and on finally to the awards. By the time my name was called I was so wound up with nervous anticipation that I seemed propelled from my chair, past the legs of the other S's, down the steps of the stand, and onto the stage. To calm down and then to milk the moment of its triumph, I sort of sauntered up to Mr. Brown, the principal, and when he handed me the scroll, all of the fulfillment it represented welled up and I kissed it. The wave of laughter that broke out was not what I'd intended but it reactivated the ham in me, and I waved the scroll in triumph as I made my way back to the stand.

The following morning I was trying to rouse myself from my first hangover when Dad walked into the bedroom and then stood there glowering. "What the hell is the matter with you?" he declared as if for once he didn't know.

"I got a little drunk last night," I replied. "Celebrating." Then I thanked him for coming to the graduation. "It really meant a lot to to me."

"Well, I want to tell you I've never been so embarrassed by you as I was last night, seeing you walk across the stage in that schlumpy way. And what did you have to kiss that award for? I mean, they were giving it to you for being a good student, not the class clown, for Chrissake."

I got sober very quickly, by the time he was finished. If I wasn't going to take the physical pummeling anymore, why take the mental? "You've made your point," I said. "Now you can leave."

"What're you talking about, 'I can leave'? What kind of answer is that?"

I got out of bed and drew myself up to my full height, facing him, steadied by the three inches I had over him. "You want an answer? Okay. Last summer I walked out of your life for good, which you confirmed last month when you wouldn't help me with the surgery. Now I'm asking you to walk out of mine, to lay off me from here on. We have nothing to do for each other or say to each other, so let's not do any more harm."

He gave me a long stare, which I returned. His hard, nasty look cooled. "You've got a point there," he said. "You've never understood me, and maybe I don't understand you." Then he said, "But I know you're going to have a very hard life. Unnecessarily."

"Perhaps," I said. "But I've had plenty of training for it."

He shrugged. "Who hasn't around here?" he said. "When are you going in the Navy?"

"As soon as I can."

He nodded, giving me another level look. "Well, take care of yourself," he said, as though he meant it, as though a little concern had broken through.

That day I stopped going to The Shop for good. During the following two weeks before I left for bootcamp, Dad and I hardly spoke, but he was on my mind a lot. My final declaration of independence gave me some detachment, enough so that I was bemused as well as embittered by his attack. No matter what he said about my behavior on the stage, he couldn't change the fact that I had triumphed, which meant, in the moral code I still thought in, that he was a sore loser, someone who couldn't see the other guy win without knocking the outcome to maintain his own superiority. But it was his own son who had won. Why couldn't he maintain his superiority with that? After the ceremony the auditorium had been full of parents hugging their kids just for graduating, particularly the Italian parents who probably hadn't finished high school and so were all the prouder. Perhaps Mom and

Adrian were right after all—his fault-finding was more to be pitied than scorned, though I still had plenty of scorn on tap.

The other thought that my detachment opened up was that I was following in his footsteps by joining the Navy not only to get an education but to see the world, just as I had knocked around the past two summers trying to make money, as he had at my age. Perhaps that's why he had calmed down at the end, and even said, "Take care of yourself," which he had never done before and coming from him in almost a caring way seemed like as much of a blessing as he had to give.

PART FOUR

FOOTSTEPS

1 I ENLISTED WITH a group from Roselle Park, three of the Brothers and I ending up in the same company at Bainbridge Naval Station. They took to service life and quickly made a strong place for themselves in the company. I didn't and quickly made a weak one. I hated the regimentation, hated the abusive company commander, hated taking stupid orders. I had been demeaned and jerked around all those years by my father; now I was being treated so again, even more derisively and arbitrarily, by the preening, sadistic old salt whose notion of authority was "When I say shit, boot, you squat and strain." I didn't do much better with the squad and platoon leaders from our own ranks. By a kind of social tropism, the company of 160 divided into the many who fell into step and the few who did-n't—the fuckups, the sensitives, the scoffers—who stuck out like jug ears on a face with otherwise regular features.

I had a particularly hard time with my platoon leader, who seemed to single me out for reprimands and shit details. Harlow had had a year or two at Bowdoin, was bright, literate, and haughty. In other cir-cumstances we might have become friendly or at least tolerated each other, but at Bainbridge our similarities exacerbated the different view we took of his authority. The tension between us mounted and finally spilled over when he took away my canteen privilege for a week to show me he could. In a fury, I seized the only recourse I had, which was to challenge him to a grudge match in the ring.

It was the regulation way for boots to settle differences and scores, but in my case an extremely foolish one, as I realized a moment later and for the next six days, since my new nose hadn't fully knit, and I had been warned to stay out of contact sports for six months. By the time Saturday afternoon came I was in a high state of anxiety, and when we got into the ring and began to duke it out, I immediately lost my head and rushed at Harlow, slugging away. Sure enough, I was popped squarely in the nose and, distracted and dismayed, was then knocked down.

So there I was, on the canvas, the fight hardly begun, the rest of this round and two more still destructively ahead. I couldn't quit for the same reason I had to go through with the fight. But though my nose hurt, it wasn't bleeding. I was sober now, even in place on the deck, knowing what to do—Kid Galahad at bay. I got on my feet and then up on my toes and began to box, beating Harlow to the punch with my jab, then dancing away. I got through the round with no further damage, the tide turned in the next, and Harlow gave up just before the end of the third. Which was well, since by then I could barely hold up my arms. After I had showered and dressed, a group of mostly Catholic guys from New York took me over to the canteen, bought me a quart of ice cream, and made much of my comeback. For the first time, I felt I belonged.

The next morning I took my swollen nose to sick bay and was told it was broken again. A doctor reset it—much as he might have turned a wing-nut. When the swelling went down there was still a twist in the bridge. Otherwise it didn't look that bad. From then on, Harlow laid off me, but he had no further cause not to. The fight was really my enlistment. Because I'd stood up for myself, I was no longer one of the misfits, an available butt. I did more readily what we had to do and cut out the clowning and griping that had kept me from fitting in. I scored fifteen percent higher on the intelligence test than I had on the one we took at the recruiting station, which led to my being recommended as a fire-control striker or apprentice—the high-tech branch of naval ordnance.

My first ship was, oddly enough, the USS *Hyman*, a destroyer that had been badly damaged at Okinawa and was only now returning to active duty. The crew was divided between the wartime sailors, the chiefs and petty officers who were making the Navy their career, and the peacetime recruits, most of whom were using the Navy to go to college or to get out of Wilkes-Barre or Cabin Creek for a couple of years. The latter group, who were mainly on the deck force or in the engine room, soon got their sea legs or at least shore legs, since for most of the fall the *Hyman* sat in the Charlestown Navy Yard in South Boston. The college-bound, usually referred to as "cunts" or "pogues," tried to talk the salty, macho, routinely obscene lingo of shipboard. Most of us, though, didn't take as readily to the "regular-

Navy, fucking-A" ashore walk of getting smashed as quickly as possible to facilitate the chances of getting laid or into a fight. I felt as much out of place in the sailor joints in Scollay Square and Charlestown as I did sitting over the communal trough in the morning and trying to move my abashed bowels while the gunner's mates and torpedomen and the other strikers in the Ordnance Division chatted as they pooped and tooted away.

Since I was sending sixty of my eighty dollars a month to Aunt Belle to repay the money I insisted on regarding as a loan, I often didn't go on liberty and spent the evening reading and smoking in my rack and taking advantage of the deserted and less odoriferous head. Occasionally I would pick up a girl at a dance. One was a fiery Portuguese with whom I thought I was all set, but by the time we got to her place she said I was too nervous for her. Another was a sweet, sad girl who worked in a laundry, whom I felt too sorry for to try to con into bed.

I wasn't doing much better in O Division. Not even knowing how a car engine worked, I didn't have a clue about the hydraulic, electrical, and electronic systems and devices that moved and aimed the five-inch guns and antiaircraft batteries, and I couldn't make sense of the manuals we were given to study. Mostly I was assigned to painting the fire-control shack and after that chipping, wire-brushing, and painting the turrets that housed our tracking and firing gear. By then winter winds were coming off the water, and I was cold most of the time from working on the turrets and standing watch on the dock. I seized any opportunity to get warm; even applied for an NROTC program because I saw a line of men waiting in a heated passageway to be interviewed. I lied through my teeth about wanting to be an officer. From my second day on the *Hyman*, I was counting the days to my discharge.

The few friends I made were with the strikers in the Communications Division—the quartermasters, radiomen, radarmen, yeomen. Though I had hardly led a sheltered existence, I was out of my league in the Ordnance Division. It was known for its crack mechanics, binge drinkers, berserk bar fighters, and intimidating poker and pinochle players. If the *Hyman* had been a football team, O Division would have been the linebackers—the smart and the violent.

One of the wildest of them was a third-class gunner's mate, Bill Nelson, known as Nelly, a short, barrel-chested fellow with an impish grin and golden curls. He had been a frogman during the war, someone who swam five miles into a Japanese naval base, attached an explosive to the hull of a ship, and managed to get away. In peacetime, he carried out his daredeviltry by other means. A few weeks after I came aboard, he won a twenty-dollar bet by jumping from the ship's bridge forty feet or so into the November water in order to go ashore and get properly drunk. I'd joined the Navy hoping to sow a lot of wild oats, but alongside guys like him I seemed to have hardly any on me.

But the service creates strange bedfellows. Nelly's rack was directly across from mine. (We slept in stacks of four bunks with perhaps a foot between rows.) Effervescent and garrulous, he liked to gab with me, and since he had an imagination and wit as far out as the rest of his personality, I began to let my own rip and riff with his. We developed a routine of parodying the tales of prodigious sexual adventures that sailors tell, and went on from there to the other types of sea stories. Nelly loved not just the laughs but the chance to bounce language around, turn Navy jargon into surreal imagery. Along with his manic temperament was an original mind on a prison break. He'd been raised in an orphanage, could barely read and write, but his taste for language was keen. At the time I was reading Thomas Wolfe in a rush of enthusiasm for the rhapsodic imagination that made him the Jack Kerouac of my bookish generation. One evening lying in our racks Nelly asked me to read him something from the novel that was shaking me up so much. So perched above the nightly pinochle game, the pop music from two or three radios, the shouted to-and-fro complaints and insults that passed for conversation, I read Nelly "A stone, a leaf, a door," one of Wolfe's most vaulting meditations. From then on, I gave him updated reports on whichever Wolfe novel I was reading. I told him that I didn't know what the Great American Novel was but that I was pretty sure Thomas Wolfe had written it. Nelly was thrilled to be put in touch with that fabulous creature.

In return for my book reports and reading performances, Nelly taught me in two minutes how to tie a bowline — a complicated, necessary knot that I had been struggling with. From there we went on to the other knots and then to the machinery I needed to know. He explained how a range finder worked and how hydraulic action simultaneously moved his quad 40 gun mount on a horizontal axis and the gun barrels on a vertical one. Together we would pore over the manuals that I had to master to qualify as a firecontrolman.

Once or twice we went ashore together. He took me to the Charlestown waterfront dive that the *Hyman* had made its own, where there were a few sorry semaphore flags on the walls, sawdust on the floor, a jukebox full of syrupy country music and polkas, and women who seemed as crusty and salty as bosun's mates. I'd nurse a beer or two, watching him knock back boilermakers as he continued his role as my "sea daddy," telling me how to watch out for myself in places like this and in our compartment if I didn't want someone to "tear you a new hawsepipe." I'd get him to talk about Subic Bay and other dangerous places he'd operated in, and this would get him to wishing for another war soon with the Russians or whomever so that his life could have some meaning again instead of being spent tearing down his quad 40 every couple of months and hanging out in miserable places like this one.

In the late fall the *Hyman* made two shakedown cruises to Guantanamo Bay, Cuba, to see how the rebuilt and refitted ship performed. In between the two cruises, Nelly fell in love. It came out of nowhere and didn't make much sense—Sabu the jungle boy meets the aging wallflower. She was the sister of a girl one of the strikers was banging and was said to be five years older than Nelly and looked ten, a teacher somewhere. Nelly wouldn't talk about her, and if anyone else did, even one of the heavyweight gunner's mates, he would shut him up with a few words and the look in his blue eyes of a man who would keep coming at you with anything he could get his hands on.

About a week after he met Magda, he missed the two-a.m. curfew and was caught trying to slip aboard near dawn by climbing a mooring line. He was then discovered by the entire O Division to have a big patch of blood on his shorts, which furnished enough laughs and barbed questions to last the second cruise to Cuba. But they all rolled off him now; he was in another place, one of utter longing and despair, because missing curfew had cost him his Christmas leave and our squadron would be pulling out of Boston right after that for a year of duty in the Mediterranean and Red Sea.

I was about the only one Nelly was talking to during this time. He wanted me to think up a reason for him to get compassionate leave and then to write a letter to the base chaplain. But compassionate leave was for serious illness or death in the family, not for falling in love, though seeing Nelly pacing the narrow aisles between the foot-lockers or springing into or out of his rack every ten minutes drew compassion even from the cutthroat gamblers and bar fighters. He was like a man deprived of animal protein all of his life, who had been fed a couple of sirloin steaks and then summarily sent back to his rice and fish heads. I had the standard teenage notion that falling in love made you soft and sappy. But there was nothing sappy about Nelly in love; it was primal and cruel.

Finally, he jumped ship and was gone for three days. As it happened, I was standing dock watch when the Shore Patrol brought him aboard. He looked dazed, was still bleeding from his forehead. He was handcuffed, his skivvy shirt, which was all he was wearing in the December cold, half torn off him. Coming up the gangway, he suddenly revived, even broke free for a moment before they clubbed and manhandled him aboard, the two men on deck watch both aiding and trying to calm the SPs, Nelly screaming in pain and rage.

The image of that beating, that constraint, sank in. Until then, my sympathy for the underdog, the downtrodden (beginning with myself), had extended outward mostly to the Jews and to their Gentile counterparts—the working stiff in the1930s, the Brooklyn Dodgers, GI Joe and Willy during the war. Now there was Nelly, a much more specific and affecting figure to focus and inspire my sympathy and respect. The pilot light of his spirit that the orphanage, the frogmen, the peacetime Navy, the heavy drinking had not blown out and that his love for Magda had now turned up so strongly made him a walking example of what those in authority ignored or oppressed. A few years later I read Rousseau's statement that man is born free and is everywhere in chains; that was Nelly being forced up the gangway of the *Hyman*.

Service in the peacetime Navy was an abrupt, prolonged immer-sion in the working class, in its crudity and cruelty, its noise, crowdedness, and stinks, its narrowness and dullness. Also in its modes of adeptness, shrewdness, perseverance, its gregariousness and laughter, its loyalty and courage. The first of its lessons was the iron law of necessity that governs most workers' lives: on the job, you do what you're told, however stupid or demeaning the order or its giver. This was exaggerated by service discipline, but that only made the lesson the more obvious. Either you gave the orders or took them, or else you became as autonomous as possible, which meant, at the very least, a college education. Before I'd wanted to go to college to excel; now I knew I had to if I was to stay out of the hands of life's executive and petty officers. At the same time, the Navy spiked my hostility to class prerogative and privilege. We were still in the era when the blacks on the ship were steward's mates, when the executive officer mustered the entire crew one morning at sea to tell us that we were a sorry lot and that he gave the orders because he not only had a better education than we did but also had been brought up better.

The Navy's officer caste system made more obvious the unfair way society distributed its power and status, goods and comforts. So, though O Division was telling me that I didn't belong in the working class, I felt an affinity to its situation from my attachment to Nelly. I was going through the typical liberal phase of the times, but I was also developing a mind-set that had deep roots in my early life and would continue to affect my later one.

All of which said, I was still a novice helmsman venturing into the crosswinds of aspiration and experience. During the voyage to Europe, the chief firecontrolman was told that he had too many strikers and to transfer his least promising one to the deck force, the manual laborers of the ship's company. For all of my sentiment about the working class, the deck force of a destroyer in the mid-Atlantic in January was the last group I wanted to belong to. I couldn't go topside without holding on to something against the pitch and roll of the ship, without turning away from the bone-chilling spray, without getting even more seasick. How was I to work there chipping and painting the bulkheads, along with all the other crap jobs that fell to the "swabbies"? How was I to get along with guys who were even cruder than those in O division and half as smart? For 546 more days.

So I did what I had watched my father doing over the years when he was in a tight spot. I stalled and finagled. At sea, the fire-control strikers stood wheel watch, steering the ship by gyrocompass on the course the navigation officer monitored. One of them was the officer who had interviewed me for the NROTC program, and on our night watches together, alone on the bridge, we'd chat about books and sports. I told him what was happening and asked if he could help me to transfer to the Communications Division. I said that I could type much faster than I could chip paint or haul anchor chain. He laughed and said he'd see what he could do, that he thought they might need a striker in the radio shack.

I asked one of the yeoman I knew to sit on my transfer order for a day or two, told him that I was probably going to C Division and he could save himself some paperwork. Instead of moving my gear to the deck force compartment, I hid out in the tiny radar room I'd been assigned to during gunnery exercises. I needed to avoid the chief firecontrolman and also one of the boatswain's mates, who was itching to get his hands on me. It was a tense twenty-four hours in which I was skirting a captain's mast or worse for not obeying my chief's orders. But just as I was about to give up the ghost of my chance, I heard the blessed words on the intercom, "Seaman Second Class Solotaroff report to the radio shack." The chief there gave me a sample dispatch to type, and I was home free. A few hours later I moved my gear to C Division, the closest the ship got to the middle class. Whatever regret I had in leaving Nelly or in being cut from the macho glamorous O Division or in evading my loyalty to the down-trodden—all of that dissolved in a great sense of relief in being where I belonged.

2 THE SECOND NIGHT after the *Hyman* docked in Naples, our first port of call in Europe, I went ashore with a carton of ciga-rettes in the sleeve of my peacoat and a momentous curiosity that I hoped would turn into wild oats. Two of my bunkmates and I were quickly taken in hand by a boy of six or seven who told us he had

three beautiful sisters. He then led us through a series of dank alleys, past scabrous tenements with missing doors and windows and little cottages that seemed more infested than inhabited. Elizabeth had slums, but nothing like this. We thought he would take us to a dance hall or café to meet his sisters, but he opened the door of a one-room hovel and motioned us in. A large family was sitting around a table. Without a word they got up, put on whatever they had for coats, and filed out into the cold. The boy collected his cigarettes and left too. A short, lively-looking girl of about eighteen came toward us.

"Seesters?" one of us asked.

She shrugged and indicated there was just herself.

We consulted. We'd been had, and there was nothing to do. We were from C Division and didn't make trouble. Besides, we all felt guilty about driving out her family She was affable, even sexy in a squat way. So we threw fingers to create the batting order. I went second or maybe it was third. I hardly remember anything except a patch of round belly, her rubbing and then inserting my sheathed, unenthusiastic member, and her face turning impatient as she urged me on.

Though this first erotic experience was about as thrilling as blowing a stuffed nose, the social one was intense and continued to ache. Instead of my sexual innocence, which was still pretty much intact, the girl removing none of her clothes, I had lost my political innocence. The little boy's precocious pandering, the family getting up and shuffling out into the cold, the stag line of jittery, joking young Americans produced a troubling image of mutual degradation. It capped those of the blackened bombed-out harbor; the flocks of children waiting on the docks for our squadron to put out the garbage, which they would then swarm over like human flies; the forlorn piazzas where vendors sat like mourners behind tables with a few cans of Heinz beans, or a scattering of old bicycle and radio parts, or a manikin wearing only the jacket of an old suit; a little restaurant with its smell of garlic over sewage; the still-blown-out windows in almost all of the tenements near the port—all of this and much more had begun to teach me what our great triumph was still inflicting on innocent people. With my own vision now of some infinitely tender, infinitely suffering thing, I stayed away from the pimps and spent my time ashore looking for a beautiful eighteen-year-old girl to befriend, who would want me for my own sake rather than the three or four packs of cigarettes, the few hundred lire, it took. Also I was selling my cigarettes on the black market to accumulate enough lire for an original Italian oil painting to bring home to my mother and redeem all of the times I had been a sullen, halfhearted son.

Nelly came along, thinking he might buy a painting at some point for his beloved. He too had lire to burn, for he was determined to stay out of the clapshack. So having sold the last of my cigarettes, we got a horse and buggy driver to take us to a "galleria pictura, capeesh?" We were taken to a dealer who laughed at us for thinking I could buy a classical oil painting for seven thousand lire, but he could let me have a nice contemporary for ten. I chose a lively blue-and-green landscape, which he said was of Capri. Then Nelly and I scraped together eight thousand lire and he finally gave it to me for that.

There was still the buggy driver to pay. When I asked Nelly about it on the way back, he said, "Fuck 'im. We've given them enough dough already. We'll get the driver to take us near the gate and run for it." I said we couldn't do that, the poor guy probably had a wife and six kids who were starving. Nelly said that what he probably had was half the money I'd paid for the painting. The issue became moot when the cab stopped and Nelly jumped out and yelled, "Come on." Close behind me came the driver, screaming curses and swinging his whip. He was surprisingly fast for a man of his girth and age, and I was slowed by the rolled-up canvas I was clutching. But Nelly ran like a quarter-miler and was already at the gate, explaining the situation to the Marine guard, when I got there. Once the Marine stepped forward, his hand on his holster, the driver quieted down. It was his word against Nelly's and mine as to who had been cheated. He was in the right, but we and the Marine were on the winning side and he was on the losing one. So that was that. I was glad to be American and ashamed of myself.

About a month later when we were cruising in the Persian Gulf, I took the painting out of my footlocker. I could barely unroll it, and when I did the view of Capri and its blue sky was so many blobs, streaks, and naked patches. Probably the intense heat in the compartment, 110 and up during the day, had caused the paint to decompose and stick to the back of the canvas. Just as the sentiment of buying it for my mother had decomposed and stuck to my conscience. Both heart-sore and relieved, I took it topside and dropped it into the Red Sea.

Shortly thereafter, my checkered Navy career moved to its next square. I'd picked up Morse code quickly under the threat of the chief radioman to ship my ass to the deck force when he found out about my maneuvering. Though I got along well with some of the younger officers, I had trouble with most chiefs. The officers saw in me a clever, well-spoken kid they could converse with; the chiefs, who took a more functional view of character, saw a wise guy.

I proved to be a good radioman and soon was assigned to stand the Fleet Broadcast watch. This was important but tedious duty; I had to take down fifty minutes of Morse code every hour, much of the broadcast not even in words but in coded units of five letters. To pass the four-hour night watches, another radioman and I devised a way to split the earphones so that the Fleet Broadcast from Port Lyautey came in on one earphone and Radio Stuttgart, which played classical music or jazz through the night, on the other.

One dawn I came back from my ten-minute break to find the chief radioman glowering at my desk, holding my headphones in his hand. The Fleet Broadcast hadn't begun its next hour, but Radio Stuttgart was still on the air. The chief pulled the splitter from the receiver and shook it in my face as though he wanted to gouge out my eye with it. I didn't try to explain that the music kept me more alert. I waited for him to finish reaming me out and then tell me I was on my way to the deck force. Instead he told me I'd be explaining my way of standing watch on the ship's main line of communication with the Seventh Fleet to the Old Man. Which shortly came to pass at a captain's mast, where I received twenty-four hours of extra duty.

Though I remained with the radio gang, the sentence still turned out to be severe. Extra duty was administered by the chief boatswain's mate whose supervision I'd evaded, and he delightedly told me I'd be spending all twenty-four hours diving the bilges. In two-hour ordeals, down I went into the bowels, literally, of the *Hyman* with a bucket of seawater and rags and a caustic disinfectant to clean up what the pumping system didn't. This was an odious task under any conditions, but in the heat of the Persian Gulf it bordered on the horrific. A destroyer is called a "tin can," and in the Persian Gulf it is a tin can in an oven well into the evening. At six p.m. when my stint began, the bilges were like a steam room in a sewer. Wearing as little as possible that would cover as much as possible, I crawled my way forward, breathing through my mouth, scraping and wiping and wringing for 120 very long minutes, crawling back every ten or so to change the water and the rags and to draw a few breaths of clean and relatively cooler air. When I emerged on deck after the two hours, I was not someone my shipmates wanted to be near. I couldn't take a shower, because fresh water was turned on for only two hours a day at sea, and so I had to make do with a salt water hose and Navy laundry soap, which left my skin raw without completely doing the job. I had come to be known on the *Hyman* as Arab (pronounced "Ay-rab") for my darkly tanned skin, but now, as I was frequently told, it took in my odor as well.

I had done six hours when the ship returned to the Mediterranean and docked in Alexandria. I was watching the other C Division guys getting ready to go on liberty in that fabulous city when one of the yeomen came bouncing down the ladder into our compartment, grabbed me, and announced, "Ay-rab's getting sent Stateside. Ay-rab's going to be a fucking officer."

I could hardly believe it myself. The interview that grim afternoon in Charlestown Navy Yard had led to my being one of the three on the ship selected to take a College Board–type exam. It was sprung on me after we'd reached Gibraltar, the first thing in the morning after I'd tried to match a group of British sailors beer for beer. Barely able to see, much less think, straight, I'd taken three APC tablets, done what I could, and thought no more of it.

I didn't want to spend another four years in the Navy after college and I already had the GI Bill. But orders were orders, and there were no bilges waiting for me at Great Lakes, the base I was being sent to for orientation and assignment to the college of my choice. I had to take my orders around to be signed by my superiors; when I handed them to the chief radioman, he looked at me as though I'd stolen his wallet and gotten away with it.

By the next night I was in Rome, having been flown there on a Navy cargo plane that the following day would take me to Port Lyautey, where I'd catch a ship to the States. The only Italy I'd seen was Naples, Trieste, and Pompeii, which nothing I had learned even from Winnie about the Roman Empire had prepared me for. Among the many such tourist attractions was a wall painting of a small figure holding his toga up and his cock on a scale. "What's it say, Ay-rab?" my mates wanted to know. I didn't recognize one of the words, but it was easy to extrapolate its meaning. I told them it said that a big cock is worth its weight in gold.

Pompeii seemed like an ancient version of Naples without the poverty and tears. And now I was in Rome, the capital of that lascivious empire. From the stories that Ernie, a high-living crewman of the cargo plane, told me, the sexual revelry was in full swing again — classy chicks in nightclubs rather than dispirited girls and women in their wretched dwellings. And though I didn't have a big cock, I had four cartons of Chesterfields in my seabag, which Ernie assured me was all that I needed for the nightclub he was taking me to and for the girl he would fix me up with.

Her name was Elena and she was from the central casting office of my fantasies — a curvy, dusky ash blonde in a green dress that matched her eyes and with a pleasant, intelligent manner. A secretary for an import-export company, she spoke enough English for us to converse. While I was dancing with her, Ernie came by and said I had the pick of the litter. Elena asked me what that meant, and when I tried to explain, she said that she didn't like to be thought of as a kitten or a puppy. Instead of going back to the table where Ernie and the copilot of our plane and their two ravishing girls were sitting, Elena took my sweating hand in her cool one and steered me to a little table of our own. A waiter appeared in nothing flat with a bottle of sparkling wine in an ice bucket and two glasses. I asked how much it was. Six thousand lire, more than half of what I had for the whole evening. Elena said not to worry, that I would still have enough to make her a small gift. We raised our glasses. "Happy days," I said. "And nights," she added with a little sparkle of her own.

We danced to a black combo who played American dance tunes and ballads. We got along better and better, our bodies moving closer and closer. It became easier to ignore that she was a club girl by night who expected "a little present," and to imagine that I was dating the smart secretary she was by day. It also became easier in this expensive place to realize that I was now officer material, whether I went through with it or not. From the bilges to a Roman nightclub in forty-eight hours. And the topper was still to come.

The hotel the crew and I were staying at was only a few blocks from the club, but Elena didn't want to go there, and we walked to her place. I began to be concerned about the midnight curfew for American servicemen and also about being back at the hotel at 0700 to leave with the plane crew, but she said she would make sure I got back to the hotel after dawn when the curfew lifted.

The scruples I'd had about bought sex in Naples had dissolved in Port Said, and then in Musquat, Aden, and Abadan, where the poverty seemed to be an eternal given, and a dirt floor, a bare, buggy mattress, a soiled shift, and bad breath and other strong odors spiced rather than dashed desire. These ports had introduced me to kif, which uncovered in me a voracious appetite for thin girls with lascivious black eyes, skin as dark as my own, and moves and ways that left no sense or erogenous zone unstimulated. The squalor in which my partner worked or lived spoke to my revved-up sex drive rather than my turned-down social conscience, and I'd pay her gratefully instead of guiltily.

Elena's room was at the top of an old house, once the servants' quarters. It was clean and orderly, touching in its brave effort to create a modern look that almost overcame the gloomy beams, the ancient fixtures, the primitive toilet in the hall. When she took off her clothes, Elena was no less pretty, appealing, and effective in obscuring the basis of my presence there. She even let me kiss her for a moment or two before she said, "As you say in your country, let us get down to business." But my business was half vacant as I undressed, haunted by her phrase and by a photograph on the credenza of a nice-looking guy in horn-rimmed glasses, with a scarf furled around his neck, student-style.

"Who's that?" I asked, hoping it was her brother.

"Someone, I know," she said in a tone that told me he was not up for discussion, that he belonged to her other life that was not for rent.

So I tried to focus on her nice breasts and what was inside those bottle-greenpanties and with her help managed to run my flag up from half-mast and put its cap on. But the fucking was pretty desperate on my part and minimal for her, and when it suddenly and prematurely was over, she quickly moved me off her.

"That wasn't so nice," she said. "What is the trouble?"

"With me?"

"Who else is here?"

Well, her boyfriend for one. But I couldn't say that, and besides he was only part of a wave of disheartenment that swept over me. The falsity of my staying there in her bed began to mount. I got up to take off the condom and then kept going, pulling on my shorts and pants. Elena asked if I was crazy.

"No," I lied, zipping up the flap of my bell-bottoms even more desperately than I had let her unzip it. "I have to get back to my hotel," I said. "I'm worried about missing my plane." She reminded me that I could stay, that I had paid for it, which made me want even more to get away from her and the photograph and the brave room that belonged to another life that was properly closed to me.

She gave me instructions for getting to the hotel, but once in the maze of streets around the piazza, I panicked. There were no street signs, only names here and there on corner buildings, and I couldn't tell one from another. I ran up to people still in the streets to ask if they knew where my hotel was. I got only blank looks; no one spoke English. No one. How could that be? Was I even remembering right the name of the hotel? It was already well after midnight, the curfew was in effect, I soon would be picked up by the Shore Patrol or MPs. My unlikely story about being transferred to an NROTC unit at Great Lakes would only make things worse. My travel orders were back at the hotel I didn't know how to get to and whose name I wasn't even sure of. I'd be a thrown in a brig until morning and miss my flight, the new turn my life had taken already over. I'd return to the *Hyman* in disgrace and go right back to the bilges and the chief radioman's leer.

I took off my white hat, stayed out of the little light there was. I tried this street and doubled back along that one, berating myself for recklessly letting my new Officer Cocksmith illusions lead me into this fix. Growing more crazy by the minute, I turned a corner into a boulevard and there, somehow, was my hotel. Flooded with relief, I ran low, like a thief, across the broad avenue and up the steps of the hotel as if they were the boarding ramp of the last plane out of Casablanca.

But my disturbance wasn't done with me. Once I'd gotten

undressed and into bed, I jerked off to my fantasy of the way it should have been with Elena. Which ordered up a fresh shipment of depression, and soon my panic in the streets returned in another form. According to the training films, a condom wasn't enough protection, particularly with a hooker. In Naples and the Gulf towns I'd gone directly to a prophylactic station or back to the ship to scrub my genitals and then smear them with the prescribed ointment. This time there was no station or ship to go to. The Navy lore was that you got the clap or worse from the girl you'd least expect to, and Elena certainly qualified for that. By the time I got to my ship in Port Lyautey it could be too late, the gonococcus germs or the corkscrewlike spirochetes already boring in. Instead of coming home with an original Italian oil painting, I'd arrive with a dose of the clap or the dreaded syph. Either was contagious—you could get it from a toilet seat.

Still needing to tear at myself, I may have only half believed that I and even my family were at risk, but then my dismay grew as it became attached to the unassailable fact that I'd become a whoremaster. My mother had raised me to have ideals, and one of them was not to take advantage of women, that a gentleman was just that. "Gentleness is true manliness. I want you to always remember that." And now look at me. In Port Said I'd really gone berserk, having won sixty dollars in a crap game and then spent almost all of it to smoke kif with, ogle, and fuck and worse, hour after hour in the back room of a tea shop, a sixteen-year-old named Alya in a little red shift whose breasts were just big enough to fit in my mouth—probably not sixteen at all, probably fourteen, probably twelve! And what about the other young whores I'd gone for in the oil ports, trying to repeat the first maniacal orgy.

I was now in a state of moral panic, every bit as trapped as I'd been in those dark, labyrinthine streets. There was no getting away from it, I was no better than my father, who I was sure now went away weekends to fuck, who probably even fucked those two young whores who had teased me in The Shop. Like father, like son. Little Benny, deep down and permanent. No wonder I couldn't get enough of that precocious little whore in Port Said who'd been corrupted by sailors and tourists like me. Self-hatred rose up in me like bile, thick, bitter, and sickening. I began to pummel my lascivious, heedless head with my fists, giving it the beating it deserved, shouting, "Freak! . . . You're a total freak," until someone in the next room pounded on the wall.

When the fit was over, I lay there weeping. The image of my mother drew near, and gradually my misery found my other voice, my other sense of myself. I told her how wretched I felt, how ashamed I was, how unlike any son of hers, any Weiss. Even Gil, who'd fucked around but wouldn't have gone with a whore as young as Alya. Then I promised her I would never go with a whore again, no matter what age. But after I said it I realized she wasn't a strong enough sanction for keeping this vow, for I'd made many promises to her I hadn't kept and the world was too full of slim dark girls with a wicked look and twitch. It was like asking an angel, a creature of goodness who had little power, to keep me to my word. The only one I could count on to do that was Fan. Whether she was in heaven or not, she was now in my mind, her face as stern as the Jewish God's.

"Aunt Fan, please help me," I prayed. "I have been taking after my father and don't want to. No one else is strong enough to keep me on the path of righteousness and restore my soul. Help me to be a Weiss and not a Solotaroff. Anytime I want to go with a whore, I will think of you. That's a promise. Wherever you are, please follow me all the days of my life and keep me to this promise and also help me to be a better person like you. Amen."

Something like that, the words as spiritual as I could make them. When I was finished the anguish receded and my spirit felt cleansed, clarified, forgiven. All that I would have to do to maintain this state was to stay under Fan's influence, a Weiss for good.

3   ANY INCLINATION TO remain in the NROTC program, immediately evaporated when I arrived at Great Lakes, weeks later than most of the others. Two were to go to each of the sixty colleges and universities in the program, and the only two slots left were at Rice Institute and Tulane. Harvard or Columbia I might have considered, since it was unlikely I would get into either of them on my

own. But going to college in Louisiana or Texas for four years and then having to serve another four with the fleet seemed like a new version of my worst dream come true, so alien did these schools seem to me, so alienating was the South itself. Boot camp had confirmed that—half my company seemed to be rednecks, swallowing hard at seeing a negro or two in the barracks, worse yet at their table in the mess hall, vowing the Navy wouldn't have changed their minds one itty bitty bit once they got home again.

But in the NROTC detachment at Great Lakes, even the marines from the South were literate, ironic guys who soon made me realize that when it came to wit and language, storytelling and even literary taste, they made us Yankees seem like John Wayne and the posse. "Thomas Wolfe?" one of them chortled over my enthusiasm. "Ted, Thomas Wolfe is a baby alongside of William Faulkner. He's all just fifty-cent words, can't tell a story worth a damn." Another Marine, also a Rebel, nodded and drawled, "Ol' Wally's right. *Look Homeward, Angel* got more shit in it than a Christmas turkey. And that's his best one."

"What other Southern novels have you read?" Wally asked me.

The only one I could think of was *God's Little Acre*, and that was only because almost any high school kid who could read had read it.

"We'll have to educate this boy," said Wally. "He's like someone who knows about the North from reading Walt Whitman and 'Archie.' "

A few days later he checked out a Modern Library copy of *The Sound and the Fury* from the base library. "Read this," he said. "You'll see what I mean."

I read it in four or five evenings and long into the nights, sitting in the head after lights out, rushed along like a rafter in white water. I had only to make the initial connection between the golfers and Benjy to see the difference from Wolfe, who left nothing implicit, nothing flashing on its own between the poles he fixed in your mind. I'd read enough Hemingway by then to appreciate implication and suggestion. But Hemingway was the clear stream with the smooth pebbles of his words, as Malcolm Cowley said, and the shadowy trout of his meaning. Faulkner was the Colorado River, full of shoals of language and snags of syntax, the meaning a play of sun and shadow but with a current of narrative that picked up everything it came to and carried it along. How did a writer get such an idiosyncratic but commanding voice, such a huge grasp of life from all sides, such imperious nerve? I asked Wally about it. "Genius," he said. "Genius, Southern storytelling, and lots of bourbon."

I became tight with Wally Beatty—a handsome devil in the clean-cut, dark-haired Southern mode—think of Jack Nicholson in *Easy Rider*—who had made corporal in less than a year. As was true of most of his circle of Southerners, Wally's civility and cultivation coexisted with a hard-playing, hard-drinking masculinity. He said he'd "played a little basketball in high school," but once a game started, his casualness and geniality disappeared and a warrior emerged. We took each other, and I could feel the force of that relentless, impersonal will, fixed on the ball and the play to make and nothing else, least of all himself. It was my missing ingredient, and it forced me to recognize why he had starred in high school and why I had ended up on the bench.

I spent most of the three weeks I was at Great Lakes with Wally and his circle of mostly Southern Marines and sailors. They didn't make me change my mind about going to Rice or Tulane, since, like me, most of them were riding the easy duty and planned to resign as soon as the NROTC contracts came around. Still, it was a treat to be dealt into their conversation, the cruising, the binges, and to be given an almost continuous lesson about another piece of the American Puzzle.

For one thing, the Northerners in the country-club class, such as those I'd caddied for, were typically aloof, not only toward me but toward the world around them. Not so these well-bred Southerners, whose down-home consciousness of their community was as broad as it was genial, with a taste for character that belied the prejudices I'd been led to expect. I'd never met Americans whose culture was so intensely local and tolerant, who told stories about their family members as though they were special friends and about people in their town as though they were family. Jews came up in the stories without any of the usual tags clinging to them. But what really floored me about Wally and his friends was that they talked about negroes in the same way they talked about whites. In fact, they were the first group of whites I'd ever known who were on intimate terms with negroes, who regarded them as familiarly and individually and impartially as they did anyone else.

There were hardly any negroes in Elizabeth, and the only one I'd known at all was Hilton Davis, the son of a prominent dentist who produced a family of crack tennis players, culminating in Hilton. To know him was hardly to know the brutalized, victimized people that I read about in *Native Son*. Which did not stop me from having strong views about race, but the truth is that they were formed mainly in opposition to my whole family's view of the *schvartzers*, which seemed to be that they were either dangerous or foolish except for their wonderful cleaning woman — Bigger Thomas or Amos 'n' Andy or Hattie McDaniel. I had developed my own counterimage of the noble negro — a meld of Mark Twain's Jim and Jackie Robinson. Meanwhile, Southerners like Wally, who were supposed to be still standing directly on the backs of negroes were the only people I'd met who talked about them as individuals rather than racial items. This was true of Faulkner too. No other American writer I knew of created freestanding black figures like Dilsy and Luster and the visiting preacher. Nor had an any of them, not even Richard Wright, come within miles of Faulkner in portraying the character of bigotry, inside and out, as he had in the person of Jason Compson.

As far as I know, Wally and his buddies didn't become writers, but when I got to college and found that the South was rising again in the literature of the time, I felt that I'd seen the preview.

The curtain came crashing down at Great Lakes before I could bring myself to take up with Wally the touchy paradox of race in the South. One of our cohorts told the authorities that most of us intended to resign from the program when this phase ended. An angry review board was convened to listen to our lame second thoughts about becoming officers, and the next day we were sent back to where we'd come from. Since the *Hyman* wasn't due back for another two months, I was sent to Norfolk for reassignment.

Sailors spoke of Norfolk as Shit City, U.S.A., because of its enmity to them. It was supposed to be the only liberty port where the sailors had to be protected from the civilians. I had few chances to check that out. In the evenings I was either working a double shift in the "grease pit" —

the section of the huge galley where the cauldrons were scoured—or recovering from it. Perhaps an irate officer at Great Lakes had stamped PAYBACK on my traveling orders; in any case it came out that way. The one or two times I had liberty were Sunday afternoons, and what I saw was the chilling fact of segregation not only displayed on all the public facilities but in the hurried, eyes-down way most negroes seemed to move through the downtown streets.

The onerous work in the galley and the bullying of the cooks went on for three weeks, after which I was given a new set of orders and a Pullman ticket to Newport, Rhode Island. Go figure. Duty at the small, almost pastoral naval base there was nearly as good as it had been at Great Lakes. I made friends with two other transients who were college-bound—a gentle blond wrestler named Eric who hoped to study classics at Dartmouth, and a third-class electrician's mate, Jack Carter, who was the most impressive man I met in the Navy.

Jack was the first negro I'd come across since boot camp who was not a steward's mate. He came from Flint, Michigan, where his family had lived for several generations and his father was an assistant shop steward in an automobile plant. This interested me on several counts. Since coming back to the States in June, I had been following the intense political struggle that would culminate in Congress's overriding President Truman's veto and passing the Taft-Hartley Act. This major assault on the labor movement quickly channeled my free-floating idealism of the common man into the cause of trade unionism, so much so that I decided to go to Michigan, if I got in, work summers in Detroit on an assembly line to familiarize myself with labor conditions, go to law school in three years, become a labor lawyer, and then work for the political action committee of the CIO. I'd come across an article on A. Philip Randolph, the leader of the Brotherhood of Sleeping Car Porters, who had revolutionized working conditions and job benefits for its members and enabled them to lead middle-class lives and even send their children to college. Now Jack could fill me in on all these matters.

That I had hardly a clue about my new career choice became quickly clear. I thought a shop steward was like a steward's mate, someone who worked in the cafeteria or brought coffee around to the workers on the assembly line. We were digging a flower bed together, and he leaned on his shovel and chuckled. "Remind me not to bring you home with me," he said, "if we meet up in Ann Arbor." He then set me straight. Chagrined, I let a day or two pass, but then went back to pumping him about the labor movement. My questions, often prefaced by what I had been reading or thinking or imagining, tended to be a lot longer than Jack's answers, but he'd hear me out and tell me what he knew. At one point I threw in my opinion that Southerners like Wally and his friends and William Faulkner seemed to understand negroes much better than Northerners did. Jack said he didn't know much about Southerners and went on digging.

"How about the ones you've met in the Navy?"

"Varies," he said. "But the Navy's not the South."

"That's true," I said. I told him about my impressions of Norfolk.

"Maybe you can see then that having a man's balls in your hand isn't the best way of knowing him."

He said that in the calm, offhand way he said almost everything, but it pinned my question to the mat. Squirming, I brought up A. Philip Randolph and his union and how unionism in my opinion was the best thing that had happened to negroes since the Emancipation Proclamation. Jack went on digging for another minute or so. Then he said, "Let me ask you something. Are you trying to get to know me or are you trying to get to know a Negro?"

"You," I said.

"You sure of that? Because I don't believe you." For all of his calmness, something was gathering in him that I didn't want to be in the way of. I tried to waffle, but he cut me off.

"Let me ask you something else. If you were trying to get to know Eric, I don't think you'd spend much time trying to get him talking about the white race."

Jack turned away and started digging again. "I'm sorry," I said. "I see what you're getting at."

He nodded and said no more. Neither did I. After that I soft-pedaled my curiosity and my self-congratulatory liberalism. What I began to learn from Jack was self-respect and good judgment, about being different and yet fitting in, the first pair enabling the second. The more time I spent with him, the more I tried to emulate his way of handling himself. Since I was starting almost from scratch, my effort was often transitory, but over the next month or so certain changes did occur. I stopped counting the days to my discharge. I cut down on boasting about things I had done, such as being an honors student, and lying about things I hadn't done such as playing on the first team. I also got into the habit of asking myself, "How would Jack handle this?" when I got into a stressful situation.

Such situations were not long in coming. The same day I left Newport and Jack's influence I was standing on a dock in Charlestown watching the *Hyman* approach and tie up, and there on the forecastle was the chief radioman looking down at me, as though I were the reason he was glad to be home.

4 WHILE I WAS in Italy, Mom was hospitalized again with what was confirmed to be rheumatoid arthritis. During the time she was away, Dad stepped fully into the breach, astonishing everyone. He brought flowers and chocolates to the hospital, visited almost every day, even offered to take Mom away with him for a weekend when she'd recovered. At home, he was as loving with Sandy and Bobby, either making dinner or taking them out to eat, supervising the household, even doing the laundry. When he bought Sandy a corsage for St. Patrick's Day, she thought, "It's as though I woke up one morning and had a real father."

But then Mom came home from the hospital, and soon he was putting her down again, staying away evenings, and blew up the one time she reminded him of his promise about the weekend. Around the time I came back to the States, she found a fancy condom in one of his weekend outfits, which he claimed a friend had given him to try with her. For once she didn't swallow his explanation, and she grew even more distraught the following weekend, when she couldn't find her diaphragm. So beside herself by the time he came home that she could stand up to him, she accused him of using it with his weekend friend. The next day she developed alarming symptoms. Wild with fury and panic at his giving her a venereal disease, she rushed to

Dr. Gittelman, only to have him find the missing device during his examination. The discovery came too late as far as Dad was concerned. Complaining that her crazy suspicions had poisoned his feelings for her, he packed his suitcases and moved out.

In Boston, restricted to the ship, I followed the crisis by phone and letters. Dad's maneuvering began almost immediately. He said that with two residences to pay for he couldn't afford to send them to Belmar for August and that she and the kids could go to Lakewood and stay with her brother Harry's family. When I finished serving my time in the bilges, I managed to get a two-week leave and join them in Lakewood. They were staying at an old hotel that took in summer boarders. The dilapidation and torpor of the mostly empty Levy's Paramount and of the town, a winter resort hibernating through the summer, seemed to go hand in hand with the family situation, their life reduced and in abeyance as they waited for Dad's next move.

I expected to find them anxious and forlorn. But this wasn't so. It was more like visiting the Samsa family on holiday after the last of Gregor's presence had been removed. Mom looked better than she had since her job at American Typefounders. She was taking an Ethel Cotton correspondence course in self-improvement, doing exercises to firm up her face and figure, her self-confidence, even her elocution. Because they didn't have a car, they walked everywhere, and this too had helped her regain her figure. Even her arthritis seemed to be taking the summer off in the hot dry piney air.

Sandy, too, had become visibly happier. She was a loner in Roselle Park and had been going through an ungainly early adolescence. But she, too, had grown tall and lithe, blossoming overnight in Lakewood. Swimming and sunning every day at the lake beach and being noticed by the boys there, she had found her way into the teenage set and was going on her first dates. Bobby, an ebullient imp at ten, was even more so in Lakewood, where his mother and sister and now his big brother provided a steady audience for his pranks and witticisms. Since I'd been away he'd developed into a baseball fan with virtual total recall of the record book and much of the lore. I'd be swimming along and there suddenly would be my kid brother thrashing up to me and sputtering, "What did Ty Cobb hit in 1915?" One day while we were hiking in the words, Sandy stopped short and said in a stage whisper, "There's something in the brush." To which Bobby immediately piped up, "Maybe it's a hare." On the beach I drilled him in the moves of pass receiving—Gil and I ten years later.

Though I could see men giving Mom the eye again, she was stuck in a kind of brave distraction. Her eyes, like her mind, would drift past them and everyone else as she persevered through another day of her "new life," which, as I soon saw, was undercut by her old habits of denial and wishful thinking. After he'd moved out, Dad had come once in a while to the house in Roselle Park for dinner, and she hoped he would visit them in Lakewood so that he would see how well she was doing, thank you, on her own.

I tried to make her see that so far she had only gone from the fire into the frying pan. As we walked through town, she drifted back to scenes of her life there as a young woman not much older than me, with her own dreams and plans before she was swept off her feet by the smooth-talking Ben Solotaroff, which I mustn't let happen to me. I said there didn't seem to be much chance of that, and besides I was the one who was supposed to do the sweeping. "Yes," she said. "You're too considerate to waste a girl's time." I let her non sequiturs pass and returned to my theme of her facing reality. There were a number of such talks, because in between them the points I made tended to disappear like pressure applied to a pillow.

"The marriage is over. You have to accept that and act on it."

"It'll be twenty years in October. Do you realize that?"

"What does that have to do with it?"

"He came back before. He always came back from his weekends and ski trips."

"Mom, this isn't the same situation. Moving out isn't the same as going away for a weekend. It's over, finished, kaput. You have to make your own plans now. For Sandy's and Bob's sakes as well as your own."

"I know that. I'm trying, believe me. But if he wants a divorce so much, why doesn't he offer me a reasonable settlement and be done with it? He still comes to visit us, you know. One night he came while I was sitting on the porch and before long he gave me that look of his."

"For the tenth time, Mom, I don't see why you let him hobble you this way. How many people need to tell you he's bad news? You know yourself now that he's unfaithful. Visit? He visits like a bear does."

"So you think I should move to New York."

"Yes, also for the tenth time. I don't understand why you're balking. You were almost ready to do it five years ago when you were still living together. You were even more ready to do it when Fan died. Now you have all the more reason."

"And you don't think he'll try to stop me."

"How can he stop you? He's moved out. You're separated. S-e-p-a-r-a-t-e-d."

"It's such a big step to take. Breaking up a home like that."

"The home is already broken. As far as I'm concerned, it's always been broken. Now we finally have a chance to have a real home, one that works."

"Suppose we move to New York and then your father decides he wants to come back?"

"You can tell him to go to hell. And if you don't I will."

"And you think you can force him to give us the money? It's very expensive to move, and New York is much more expensive than Roselle Park. I don't have to pay rent there."

"As I've told you, it's not his say. We'll get a good lawyer and the court will tell him what he has to do. In the meantime, Belle has offered to help you."

"He can't stand to part with a dollar he doesn't have to."

"Mom, will you face the facts? It's not a question of what he can stand anymore. He doesn't have a leg to stand on. He's moved out, deserted you."

Sometimes I wanted to take her by the shoulders and shake her, as if that were the only way to dislodge him. Even when I could get her to contemplate living in Manhattan, even when she would begin to fill in some of the positive details herself, she would soon lose her volition. All of our discussions went around in a circle, because they always came back to the same thing or, rather, person.

Sandy and Bob weren't as troubled by the separation and apprehensive about the future as I'd expected them to be, but I worked at assuring them that I was on the case now and that they would soon have a better life in New York than they'd ever had before. I reminded them of the interesting people we'd met on the roof of the Franklin Towers and said that they would be living in a place just like it, maybe even in it if there was a vacancy. To Sandy I sang the praises of Music and Art High School, which she would be sure to get into, and maybe even into Juilliard. I told Bob about the Manhattan schools where kids were not only brainier and learned much more but also were smarter ballplayers. I painted a rosy picture of a city in which Carnegie Hall and the Met, Yankee Stadium, the Polo Grounds, Madison Square Garden, and Ebbets Field were only a subway ride away. It would be easier to make new friends in Manhattan than it had been in Roselle Park, because so many more kids were Jewish and came from families that shared our interests.

They listened to my description of their future in a detached way, as though I were describing a movie they'd like rather than the life they would soon lead. "Where will you be while all this good stuff is happening to us?" Sandy asked. I hadn't thought of that, but I immediately made up my mind. "I'll go to Columbia or NYU instead of Michigan," I said. "So I'll be nearby. I'll be looking after things."

Then Bob piped up. "And you really think that skinflint Dad will give Mom enough money so that I can go to Yankee Stadium whenever I want to?"

"He'll have to," I replied. I explained how alimony and child support worked, how a judge looked into the man's financial situation and made him adequately support his family.

"That's if he tells the truth about how much money he has," Sandy said.

"He has to," I said. "Our lawyer will make him."

"I'll believe it when I see it," she said.

"If he has to pay a lot of money to us, he'll probably just move back in again," Bob said.

Which is what he did a month later.

I spent the late fall and winter in Davisville, Rhode Island, a small, bleak naval station inhabited mostly by the North Atlantic winds. Four destroyers from our squadron were deactivated and moored there, their ships' companies reduced to skeleton crews to maintain them until they could be decommissioned. I was sent to a sister ship, the *Dickson*, and put on the deck force.

This time basketball came to my rescue. Each of the ship's crews moored there as well as the station personnel had a team, and the normal enmities between crews and between sea-duty and shore-duty personnel were funneled into the basketball games as well as the usual cursing matches and bar fights. So the basketball league soon became a big deal, and the games were almost as fiercely attended as they were contested. We had only six or seven players, but they were good ones and we won most of our games. Two inches taller than I'd been in high school, fifteen pounds sturdier, and benefiting from what I'd learned about concentration from Wally Beatty and about calmness from Jack Carter, I played without my former high tensions and became a mainstay of the team. As with summer ball in Belmar and Long Beach, I usually did better the farther away I was from home.

The coach of the *Dickson* team, Lieutenant Bailey, was also the deck officer. He came by one arctic afternoon while I was chipping paint, one hand in my foul-weather jacket.

"You're supposed to use both hands on that thing," he said.

"I know, Lieutenant. But if both my hands are frostbitten I won't be able to shoot very well tomorrow night."

"It doesn't seem that cold to me."

"Well, I've been a radioman, sir. We're not used to working outdoors."

I was soon given the assignment to paint the aft washroom and head. This may seem like a humble, even onerous task, but in January in Davisville, Rhode Island, this was the deck force equivalent of a commission to paint a mural in Rockefeller Center. So, at least, I went about doing it. Never were bulkheads and overheads and decks scraped and wire-brushed, primed and painted more meticulously; even the invisible areas behind the sinks and troughs got second coats of zinc chromate and enamel. Weeks went by, the areas often closed during working hours once the painting began. "Ay-rab, why is this fucking place taking so long to paint?" my shipmates would complain.

"For the same reason you're here. Because it's warm," I'd reply.

Late one afternoon when I was making my usual production of cleaning my brushes, Lieutenant Bailey stopped by. "Looks good," he said. "I've never seen showers and crappers painted so lovingly."

We talked for a while in the semiregulation, semi-ironic way we used. He knew that I'd turned down an NROTC appointment, which piqued his interest. I told him about my plans to go to either Michigan or Columbia.

"Have you thought about applying to Yale?"

I said I hadn't. I said I thought it was out of my league.

"You should apply," he said. "Let me know if you do. I might be able to help you."

So I applied. Yale would get me home for weekends; also it tweaked my curiosity. In the following months I was accepted by Michigan and Wisconsin, was turned down by Columbia, and forgot about Yale. But in early spring I received a cordial letter from the assistant dean of admissions, asking me to come to New Haven for an interview.

I arranged to do so from home, so that I wouldn't have to go in my uniform. Men's fashion in Roselle Park at the time favored a loafer jacket—mine was powder-blue—slacks with pegged cuffs, a dress shirt with the collar points tucked under, and a knit tie with a broad Windsor knot. Mom thought I should buy a nice dark suit. I was riding high and paid no attention to her.

My only contacts with Yale, except for Lieutenant Bailey, had been the Frank Merriwell and Dink Stover books and "The Whiffenpoof Song," which seemed to me the anthem of Ivy League sentiment. My walk through the imposing campus set a fantasy going that revolved around a beautiful, gentle girl from Vassar whom I would take away from some frivolous young scion. We would met at Morey's, where I waited on tables when I wasn't studying to stay on the dean's list or playing on the basketball team. I would win her by my down-to-earth ways and my high ideals. She would wait for me summers, doing something artistic in Greenwich Village or at her family's mansion in Duchess County while I worked in automobile factories and maybe even a steel mill to familiarize myself with the working conditions of my future clients and prepare to follow in the footsteps of Lee Pressman and Walter Reuther.

The assistant dean of admissions who came into the waiting room seemed a bit startled to see me. He was all in charcoal gray and looked like Sonny Tufts, one of the blond gods of Hollywood, playing a banker. "You're Mr. Solo . . . you'll have to help me with your name."

"Sol-o-tar-off," I pronounced. "It's in trochees," I added, trying to make the best of it and me.

He said, "Hm," and then led me into his office and indicated a chair across from his desk. He tried my name again, wrapping his voice around the syllables as though he were learning a new language. Then, after giving me another quick scrutiny, he picked up my application, glanced through it, and came halfway out of his shell. "You have good College Boards," he said.

I saw I needed to do something else impressive, so I played the prospective veteran's hand. "I was more relaxed when I took them than I was in high school," I said. "Having been in the service, I'm much more mature than I was or than the high school seniors I'm competing with."

He said that the selection process wasn't a horse race, that students were chosen not only on their individual abilities but on how well they would fit in as Yale men. His tone suggested that I was pretty far back in the second qualifying heat.

I'd known right away that I'd dressed all wrong for the interview, and I sensed even this early that it was becoming a formality. I'd prepared myself to play it in Jack Carter's cool way. But the imp of outspokenness in me now broke loose and decided to make it interesting. "As I understand it, the few spots for Jews at Yale are intensely competitive."

"There are no "spots" at Yale for this or that religious or minority group," he said tightly. His mouth twisted out the word "spots" as though I'd been referring to those of lepers.

"Well, that's its reputation," I said. "It's not just Yale's, of course. It's supposed to be true of many private schools, particularly in the East. The 'gentlemen's agreement'?"

"I can only speak for Yale," he said. "And I can assure you it doesn't apply here. We try to be gentlemen, but we're often in disagreement." He smiled at that as though he'd reminded himself of his usual charm, which made me feel all the more patronized. Then he said, "Perhaps we could get around to why you want to come to Yale."

"I'm not yet sure that I do," I said. "I've already been accepted at Michigan and Wisconsin. When I got your letter, I decided to look Yale over just like you're looking me over."

A secretary knocked on the door and said that someone needed to see him. While he was gone, I reached across the desk and picked up my application. I wanted to see my College Board scores, but what immediately caught my eye was the recommendation from the principal at Roselle Park High. It was three sentences long. The first was "Theodore is a hardworking student of Jewish extraction."

After the interview I spent a while taking in the campus, knowing that I wouldn't be seeing it again. It was around five o'clock and the walks and avenues that connected the fabled colleges and buildings of Frank Merriwell's time were still there, thronged with students, many in sports jackets or ski sweaters, the glamour of white-shoe confidence and privilege and status abroad in the young spring air. Even so, not everyone looked as if he were on his way to a squash game or Morey's or the place where Louie dwells, or dying to get into Skull and Bones. I saw some distinctively Italian, Irish, and Slavic faces, mostly with heavy-duty bodies, and even a number of distinctively or possibly Jewish ones. But I didn't see a single loafer jacket or a pair of pegged pants. Even if I hadn't worn mine, I knew I'd still feel like the kid looking through the fence at the Elmora Country Club tennis matches.

But beyond that, something had formed in my mind that told me that both the opportunities and resistances of Yale were beside the point of what I wanted to become. The point didn't have to do with aspiring Jews and privileged Gentiles anymore but with an America that was as ample and remarkably diverse as my Navy experience was proving it to be, where the Bill Nelsons and Wally Beattys and Jack Carters and Ted Solotaroffs found common ground. With all my heart now, I wanted to go to Michigan, because it appeared to be, ever more clearly the school where I could best activate and educate the person I wanted to become for the role in society I wanted to play. As it was to prove to be, though in ways that I had no idea of at the time. That afternoon at Yale stands out in my past as one of the defining moments of my identity, the place where I first touched the Ariadne's thread that, several times dropped and found again, would guide me through the maze of my career.

5 TOWARD THE END of April I was transferred to the Philadelphia Naval Station and, thanks to cutbacks in the military budget, discharged three months early. On the bus ride to New York, I saw signs for Trenton and then Hightstown, and realized that I probably was only a few miles from Cream Ridge. I had revisited it

once, seven or eight years before, when Dad still took us for car rides on Sunday. By then the Weiss property had been taken over by a Zionist group that used it to train young people to become farmers in Israel. The Old House had recently burned down and the hotel and grounds looked badly neglected, as though Poppa's religious freeloaders had returned en masse and taken over. When we drove up to the place, Mom gasped. She told Belle that evening, "It was like dropping in on an old friend and finding her at death's door."

Which was where the Zionist farm school proved to be. During the war it was abandoned, like much else of the Jewish situation. I wondered if some of its pupils were working now in one or another of the places that the Solotaroffs had helped to colonize—forging another of the ironic links between the two family stories of Jews returning to the land.

Soon now the main one would be broken. I was coming home just in time for the definite breakup of the marriage. Dad's moving back in again had lasted only a few months, and now he was asking for a divorce, or rather telling Mom that he was, in effect, divorcing her and, as usual, he was calling the shots. She would receive two hundred dollars a month and the use of the house. His lawyer would take care of everything. Well, we would see about that. The new man of the house was about to weigh in.

Later that week, I phoned Leo, Aunt Sophie's former husband, the one source of reason and clarity in the Solotaroff family. Though we hadn't seen each other in years, I knew that he was still close to Sophie, so that he could probably tell me what was going on with my father as well as advise me how to deal with him. As Mom said, "Leo is the only person alive who understands Ben Solotaroff." He greeted me less like a nephew he hardly knew than like a long-lost son. When I told him the purpose of my call, he said that he had "a few useful things" to tell me and invited me to come to his office in Manhattan so that he could take me out to dinner.

He took me to the Hickory House, ordered me a martini, my first, and we sat back and beamed at each other. He was a small, genial man with a puckish mouth and eyes that missed nothing. The last thing he looked like was a chemical engineer, someone who had just come back from the atomic energy facility at Oak Ridge. "Your dad can come later," he said. "Tell me more about yourself."

I told him of my plan to become a labor lawyer and work for the CIO.

He smiled and said, "What else could you do, being your father's son?"

I said that I didn't get him, that such a career was about the last thing my father would have wanted, that he hated unions.

"Of course," said Leo. "The last thing he wants is the first thing you do. And vice versa. You've got a lot to rebel against just to stay sane, much less to have a life of your own."

"Stay sane . . . ?" I hadn't thought that it was that bad.

"You come from a pathogenic family. Take it from me, I've seen a lot of them and I know the Solotaroffs firsthand." He ticked off the names of four or five who had been institutionalized, including Sophie, and ending with my cousin in Elizabeth, who he said had recently had a lobotomy. Leo spent part of his summer vacation with his brother, who was the head of a mental hospital upstate, so I felt I was receiving a professional opinion, which made it all the more troubling. I asked him what "pathogenic" meant.

" 'Path' as in 'pathology,' 'genic' as in 'genesis'—conditions that breed disease. In this case schizophrenia. It's commonly found in families like the Solotaroffs where terror, fear, and delusion reign supreme, where hate is called love, falsehood is truth, tyranny is parenting, and so forth. Contradictions are maintained that eventually can tear a mind apart."

That was a lot to grasp and digest, but "the brilliant Leo," as we called him, was in full flight. "Or short of that, there are other personality disorders that lock into relationships. Your father grew up in a family in which a masochist was married to a sadist, which he has been replicating with your mother. The children may become either the one or the other or, more likely, will internalize both tendencies like Sophie and drive themselves whacko with fear of their own rage and their guilt. Most of this is unconscious. Do you follow me?"

I did, somewhat. It did and didn't seem to fit my situation of Little Benny and the Weiss boy. We talked about that for a time. When Leo told me that the Weiss boy was a "healing illusion" and Little Benny the "self-destructive" one it was trying to overcome, I decided I'd had enough psychology for one evening. I asked him to tell me about what was going on with my father.

"I haven't talked to your dad recently but I gather he has a girl-friend he is serious about. Some highclass executive secretary. I feel sorry for her, because Ben is basically a misogynist, but that's her lookout. You can tell your mom that I think she's well out of it. Also that I'd be glad to talk to her. She'll probably need some help now that Ben has pulled the rug out from under her."

I asked him what I should do in dealing with Dad in her behalf, and he advised me not to deal with him. "He's going to be sore as hell when he finds out he's not going to get his divorce so easily. He's used to having his way. Let a lawyer handle him. Find a good, tough one."

A day or two later, at my urging, Mom called him at The Shop and told him that Leo and I wanted her to get her own lawyer. "I don't have time for this nonsense," he said and hung up.

Ten minutes later he called back. I picked up the phone. "I have a few words for you." His voice was trembling with rage. "Listen to me very carefully. If you try to stand in my way, if you try to prevent this divorce, I'm going to come to the house with a gun and kill you all and then myself. Do you understand what I'm saying?"

The thought went through my mind that I was the one who'd fired Colt .45s, not he. I said, "I hear you, Dad, but I don't understand you. You're not going to kill anybody. You'll get your divorce, but it will be in the normal way, with Mom having her own lawyer defending her interests."

"Of course she'll have a lawyer defending her interests. What're you talking about?"

"But it won't be your lawyer," I said.

"So you get her a lawyer. What difference does it make?"

"The difference is that we'll be asking for a good deal more than two hundred a month and the use of the house."

"Ask for what you want. Ask for a thousand a month and a pent-house in Manhattan. See what you get."

"Good," I said. "We'll see what we get."

The next afternoon I went to Newark to see Dr. Mamlet about my nose and to register for a ten-week economics course at a night school there, a head start for my prelaw program at Michigan, which I would cram into three years. When I returned home, Mom told me that a divorce lawyer had phoned and offered his services.

"I can't imagine who referred him," I said. "I hope you told him to get lost."

"He was nice," she said. "Businesslike but understanding."

"Did you expect him to be awful and obtuse? Probably that's what we should be looking for. A real slugger. Just what did you tell him?"

She gave her head a little shake, which she did when she was being headstrong. "I'm not going to drag your father through the courts," she said. "I'm not that type of person."

It was so much like Mom, unflagging consideration for everyone except herself and us. "It's not a question of dragging him through the courts like he's Tommy Manville or Charlie Chaplin. We're just asking him for a settlement that will enable you and the kids to live in Manhattan. We need the right lawyer to do that, because it's going to be tough, and not someone he already has in his pocket. We don't have to put up with his tricks anymore."

"What makes you so sure I want to live in Manhattan? Manhattan is very expensive."

"That's true," I said. "Precisely my point."

"I love the greenery and peace of the suburbs." Then she said, "I'm a country girl, you know. Not sophisticated enough to be Mrs. Ben Solotaroff."

"Like the greenery around here. We even have our own fruit trees. We can just stay here, like he wants us to, admire the greenery when the cattle cars aren't going by, and live on sour cherries and wormy apples."

"Don't make fun of me. I'm thinking of Westchester."

"Someplace like Scarsdale or Larchmont? From Roselle Park to Scarsdale with Ben Solotaroff's lawyer."

"No, some place more modest. I don't have my head in the clouds."

"Mom, you're all over the lot. We started out talking about this lawyer."

"Well, I said that we would come to his office as he suggested. Then we can make up our mind about him. We can always say no."

And so we did. We went to an impressive law office on East Jersey Street, and there we met a youngish lawyer whom I'll call Dick Berman. I half expected to be greeted by some Walter Pidgeon type whom Dad's lawyer had set up for us, but Dick Berman was cut from the local Jewish cloth, one of the sleeveless-sweater high-marksmen from Elmora twenty years later.

Right off the bat I said that I would need some convincing that we should take on someone who had come to us through my father's lawyer. He said that my attitude was understandable but naive, that a divorce case, if there wasn't a custody issue, was essentially a negotiation and that a lawyer often referred the other party to an attorney he'd worked with before to facilitate it. Then he went into his line about collusion and losing his right to practice, and sat back, awaiting our business, as though he'd made up our mind for us.

I wasn't done. I began to tell him about Dad's initial ploy to make Mom use his lawyer.

"Why don't you let your mother tell me about her needs? We can get around to your father later, though it's his ability to pay, not his schemes, that I'm interested in."

"It's not that simple," I said. "He's a very tricky customer about money, about hiding his assets."

"Ted," Mom put in, "I know what he's worth. I've kept his books. Let's let Mr. Berman take us through this."

He did so in the me-chief-you-Indian manner of Irwin Taubman. I didn't like him, but I figured that we'd need all the arrogance we could get.

A few weeks later, the three of us met again at the office of Dad's lawyer. We'd all been sitting there waiting for twenty minutes or so, no surprise to Mom and me, when Dad hove through the door of the conference room dressed in old pants and shirt as though he had just climbed down from a truck. This too was no surprise, though it was hard to know whom the penurious act was for. The postwar boom was in full swing and he was doing storefronts up and down Broad Street.

Dad's lawyer, whom I'll call Joseph Schwartz, was an older man, very *haimish*, smooth as glass. He distributed us around a large conference table, lifted his hands momentously as though we were about to carve up Poland, and began by saying that such meetings were hard on everyone but if we approached the issues in an objective way and were sensible about each side's concerns, we should be able to work out an agreement that both parties could live with. He looked directly at me. "I know that you've been instrumental in bringing us this far, and though I can understand that your Mom's welfare and Sandra's and Robert's are your primary concern, Mr. Berman and I are counting on you to help us steer between Scylla and Charybdis. I know that you're a crack Latin student, so you no doubt appreciate the motto *Respice finem.*" He stopped, waiting for me to translate.

But my mind was still racing from the realization that Dad—who else?—had told him that I was a crack Latin student. My father? Meanwhile everyone was looking at me. "I don't know . . . 'look for the end'?"

"Close," he said. "Consider the end."

Mom was beaming. "Like mother, like son," she said. "I was a prize Latin student myself. Is that from Cicero?"

"It could be," he said, "now that you mention it."

"Let's get started," said Dad. "You three can entertain yourselves with your Latin, but I still have a business to run. If you can call it a business."

Mom, led by Berman, went through the monthly expenses she would have. Dad sat there, hunched forward, heavy with potential energy that seemed to swell his big, tanned arms—a line-smasher on the bench waiting for the other team to hand over the ball.

When Mom had finished he snapped, "What's this hundred and twenty-five for rent or mortgage payments? She's got the house."

"Mrs. Solotaroff doesn't want to live there," Berman said. "I thought that was understood," he said to Joe Schwartz.

"Ben has two concerns," he replied. "One is that Rose not get beyond the means at his disposal. The second is that she not sell the house and move to Westchester until the children are grown, so that he can be available to them and they to him."

"I don't believe this, Ben," Mom said in a choked voice. "Even from you. You know how much I hate that house."

I was boiling even more but called on my new self-control. "What my mother is saying is that it's hard to believe she and my sister and brother are supposed to stay in the wretched dump they're living in alongside a railroad track so that my father can see the children he hasn't visited since he's moved out and hasn't paid any attention to in years."

"I didn't ignore my children," Dad said stiffly. "I couldn't reach them. They were turned against me by my wife and oldest son. Mr. Big Shot here."

"That's just total baloney," I said. "What about your phone call? What about your threat to kill us if you didn't get your way?"

Joe Schwartz stood up and said, "Ben, let's have a word outside."

Once they had left the room, I turned to Dick Berman. "Now maybe you see what I mean."

Mom was saying, "I won't live in that house. He can have his freedom, but not at our expense. I need to be able to hold my head up again. Also it's cold and damp and very bad for my arthritis. I didn't tell you but I have a serious form of arthritis."

"Rheumatoid, the worst kind." Then I said to Berman, "What're you going to do?"

"I'm going to make sure that your mother doesn't have to spend one day longer in the house than it takes to wind this up and sell it. But you aren't making it easy for me."

It felt like Irwin Taubman and me all over again. He knew the score, I didn't. He was rational, I was emotional. Would he, too, betray me and Mom?

6   I HAD A second nose operation about a month after I was discharged. As Dr. Mamlet clucked sadly at the "beautiful work" I'd partly undone, he had said, "You know, you should get those ears tucked back too." Since they were now the main bane of my appearance and since the VA was picking up the tab, I thought, why not?

My self-image, still shaky, smiled at the prospect. I also liked the idea of further recreating my face as I would soon be doing with the inward me in Ann Arbor. Though I didn't know of William James's concept at the time, I was bent on becoming one of the twice-born.

By the time all the bandages came off and the swellings went down, it was late June. When I went to the agency in New York to get a job at a summer resort, the only jobs left were for two "staff waiters" at the Lido Beach Hotel—the Ritz of the Jewish ocean resorts, just outside of Long Beach, where I'd worked two summers before. I then talked a friend from my Elizabeth days, Jeff Levitt, to come with me. In the restaurant and hotel business the best tippers are the people who work in it. I told Jeff we'd clean up from the waitresses, busboys, bar waiters, and bellhops at Lido Beach.

As we soon found out, most of them were not professionals but college students who were saving everything they could for the coming year, and not much money flowed our way. Also we did little more for them than serve the food, chowline-style, and keep the coffee and iced-tea pitchers on the tables filled. Still, we stayed on, because there proved to be other inducements. In his off hours during the day, Jeff, an accomplished golfer, had a whole beach on which to practice his bunker shots; and in the evening he had a whole new field of women to play. Jeff was my friend Yuddy from two summers ago with twice the finesse. He was nice-looking but no more so than several other guys at the hotel who were visibly and mostly unsuccessfully on the make. Nor was he particularly charming. But in his eyes and in his voice was the discreet message "I'm your night to remember this summer," and most of the women, both young and mature, he chose to send it to seemed glad to accept it.

I hadn't been with anyone since I'd managed to pick up (as much as be picked up by) a large, attractive book designer, nearly twice my age, in a bar on MacDougal Street toward the end of my Navy career. Being literary, Lee had given me confidence as well as a fluent "line"—the surprisingly articulate and well-read young sailor. I'd surprised myself by the *savoir faire* with which I made my moves. Until, that is, she took me home with her, where I lost the *faire* part once we were undressed. She had a nice body, but its sudden bigness when she removed her girdle made me small. I remained so, though she took it in stride, said it often happened to guys the first time, and taught me a lesson in lovemaking by other means. My face in her full breasts, my hand between her legs, I found myself on a wave of bliss I'd never experienced so before. But the next morning Lee sent me on my way, saying I needed to be with someone my own age. I was grateful to her, even a little in awe of what she had done and where she had taken me, but in the clear light both of day and of reason, she really was twice as old as I. Also my impotence troubled me, and I was relieved to get away from the situation and the new questions about my manhood it posed.

Then along came Jeff to pose them in a different way. My recrafted nose and inconspicuous ears were not making much of a difference with the waitresses at the Lido or the local girls on the boardwalk and in the bars of Long Beach. As I watched Jeff operate or listened to his conquests, it was rather like watching him hit precise wedge shots or talk about his near-par rounds. From my caddying days I thought I knew how to hold and swing a club. But when I tried his sand wedge I hit either sand or the ball or both to little purpose — my coordination honed in other hitting sports had vanished. So with girls; when I tried to score, I felt inept, unreal — my normal ability to connect with people had vanished. Instead I'd struggle with some "line" that was as uncertain and ineffective as my golf swing on the beach.

I was as tongue-tied with the prettiest waitresses at the hotel as I was with the secretaries and beauticians I'd try to pick up in town. Once I had some rapport with one of the other waitresses, the shyness vanished — up to a point. The point was when things got sexual. Then I'd feel anxious or guilty — anxious that I wasn't virile enough or guilty that I was "wasting the girl's time." That was Mom's phrase. We almost never talked about boy-girl matters, but the message had come to me that the worst thing I could do, short of rape, was "waste a girl's time." I knew this was old-fashioned and even silly at my age, but there was a residue of it in my system. Unless I was at least half in love with a girl, as with Honey, or paying for the girl's time, as with the Arab ones, I was nowhere. And even paying could break down, as with Elena.

In the midst of this nagging hang-up, life again intervened. I became friendly with a busboy who was also going to Michigan in the fall, though as a junior. His name was Murray Gitlin, a chubby fellow with a rich baritone voice, radical convictions, and a love of the theater in all of its modes, from opera to dance. He was the nephew of a prominent opera singer, and though he was a prospective psych major, his heart was backstage when it was not with the Young Progressive Socialist League.

As the like-minded among the large dining-room staff found each other, a group emerged that shared one or both of Murray's passions. There were two modern dancers, Alice and Doris; a cultivated theater director named Sloan, who was working as a bar waiter, the elite staff job; Marcia, a witty English major at Michigan; a bold-looking poet named Ellen, who lived in Greenwich Village and was a girlfriend of a poet with the strange name of Delmore Schwartz; and several others, either from the arts or the political barricades. Soon two projects were afoot to register our opposition to the Lido Beach Hotel as a sweatshop resort and a citadel of warmongering greed. The first was to organize a strike of the dining-room staff to increase wages, which were nominal, and decrease the hours, which were three meals a day, seven days a week, so that everyone would have one day off a week (though no one would be off Sunday, when the guests forked over the weekly tip). The second was to put on a play that would force the *nouveau riche* clientele, most of whom were probably profiteers in World War II and now in the Cold War, to confront the wages of their greed. Finally we settled on a stage adaptation of Dalton Trumbo's antiwar novel about a basket case, *Johnny Got His Gun*. The unsuspecting management gave us the use of a Quonset hut with a stage—left over from the war, when Lido Beach was a naval station—where we began both to rehearse the play and discuss the strike.

So began my revolutionary period, in which all that was solid in my mind melted into the air, just as Marx and Engels said it would. The viewpoint of Uncle Adrian's circle, which in the Navy I'd dismissed as effete anti-Americanism, returned now with redoubled force and up-to-the-minute relevance. Instead of the old Communist saws about the United States and other arsenals of capitalism supporting the White Russian armies or driving Stalin into the pact with Hitler, there were now the forceful explanations from Murray and his cohorts of how the United States had started the Cold War.

The Truman Doctrine abroad, the Taft-Hartley law and the House Un-American Activities Committee at home: they formed what Murray and his YPSL friends called "an amalgam." I was shown how everything connected to everything else to create the renewed national and international conspiracy against the toiling masses. At home, it was already happening in Hollywood against writers like Dalton Trumbo. The witch-hunts that had followed World War I were resuming. Did I know about the Dies Committee, which President Truman had been a member of? Had I heard of J. Parnell Thomas? Where had I been? Couldn't I see that this reactionary menace was using a few isolated radicals to get at and root out the New Deal values of social justice and freedom of expression I cherished? That was what the presidential campaign of Henry Wallace was all about. He knew. He had been inside the Roosevelt administration and had seen at first hand how the capitalist class had been biding its time and was now on the march with Truman as both its dupe and it's accomplice. Even my heroes Walter Reuther and Lee Pressman were part of the witch-hunt.

My catch-up education in the realities of American policy and power extended to other areas in these hectic weeks of rehearsing and talking late into the night. From Sloan, the director, I learned about the persecution of a poet I'd never heard of named Ezra Pound. Sloan had visited him when he was in the Army in Italy just after the war, when Pound was beginning to be harassed by the military authorities because he had made a few addled broadcasts against finance capitalism for the Mussolini government. For this he was declared a traitor and driven insane, and was now in a mental hospital in Washington, D.C.

Sloan was impressive, a tall, well-built fellow with a smooth manner and an esoteric mind that made him seem older than he was. I had no cognate for him; he was off my charts. He was a man of the theater, but of a theater that I had never heard of. Who was Brecht? What was the *duendo*? How could the most important contemporary play be about "the absurd," the principal philosophical question that of suicide? Though Murray told me that there was much more to the Ezra Pound story than Sloan let on, that Pound was an out-and-out fascist, I didn't question Sloan about it. I felt too much like a hick in his presence.

I also became friends with another bar waiter, who wasn't part of the radical crowd, was very different from it. Bud Harris was twenty-five or so, had been an air force navigator, and had recently graduated from Clark University. He was tall, thin, with a narrow fine face, a cap of smooth black hair, relaxed ways, and a quiet wit that made him, like his name, seem more Gentile than Jewish. A few years later I would read Salinger, look at his photograph, and think of Bud; they not only resembled each other physically but seemed to be cut from the same urbane cloth, to have the same rapport with vulnerability and oddness, so that they looked at people they liked with the charmed empathy of a big brother.

We got to know each other one afternoon on the beach. He came by and said he was wondering what I could be reading so intently each time he saw me there. Then he said he'd tried *The Magic Mountain*, but some of it was over his head. I said that it was over mine too but it kept me climbing. "It's kind of a magic mountain in itself. Also I'm in love with Clavdia Chauchat. She's my oxygen."

"I see," he said, laughing, and asked if he could join me. "The only things I see you looking at as intently are a couple of the waitresses. Are you looking for the Clavdia in them?"

"No," I said. "Clavdia would never be a waitress. If she was here she'd be married to one of the tycoons and having an affair with a handsome bar waiter like yourself and breaking my heart."

We began exchanging the usual information. Before long, I was telling him that my parents were getting divorced and why I was so involved in it. He said, "So, you're arranging your parents' divorce. That's quite a feat for a nineteen-year-old."

I hadn't talked about my parents before to anyone outside the family. Once started, it was like letting water out of a dam, my new friend's thoughtful questions and responses opening the locks.

At one point he said, "Even though you can stand up to your father now, you seem to have bought some of his view of you, and even there you're probably mistaken. You think he despises you, but I'll bet he really envies you and has been jealous of you all along."

I was startled. "Envies me? The *schlemiel* who can't even walk across a stage?"

"That's how he wants you to think he thinks of you. But I'll bet the truth is that he's jealous of you. That's why he behaved the way he did after your graduation."

"I thought he was just being mean and rotten. Taking a last whack at breaking my spirit."

"No one is just mean and rotten. There's always a deeper reason. What did you say your father most regrets?"

"That he didn't have a proper education."

"Well . . . ?"

It was like Edgar Allan Poe's, "The Purloined Letter." All my life it seemed I'd been trying to figure out why my father had it in for me, and here was the answer, at least a good part of it, right there in his own words in my ears. "Always with your nose in a book."

Bud wasn't an intellectual or even ambitious; in the fall he'd try to get a job in advertising or public relations so that he could live in New York, where there were good French restaurants and decent theater. I, who was brimming with ambition, didn't get him. How could you study psychology at Clark University, the very place where Freud had given his American lectures, and be able to figure out my father so quickly, and still want to go into advertising? But I loved talking to him, because he was so attentive and insightful in his quiet way and also had a flair for living. He reminded me of the people on the roof of the Franklin Towers and made me realize that being bourgeois wasn't as simple and negative as I was hearing elsewhere on the staff beach.

Until I got into Murray's group, I hardly noticed Doris. She was not one of the luscious chicks who sashayed past on the line and gave me a little spurt of desire or hope when they joshed with me for a nicer piece of chicken or a second vegetable instead of the mashed potatoes. There was nothing coy about Doris. She looked like what she was, a keen-minded girl from Vermont who wanted to be a dancer—the strenuous Yankee countryside meets Greenwich Village. She and her friend Alice were usually together, absorbed rather than aloof; in the afternoon when everyone gathered on the staff beach, they would usually be off on their own in the distance, doing their exotic stretching and bending, votaries of a different life than ours. Though you wouldn't suspect it from his heavyset body, Murray, too, was a dancer and would sometimes join them—a nimble elephant and two gazelles.

When we began to meet at night to plot the strike and to choose the plays, Doris showed up too. We decided to also do a one-act play about a summer resort that had a 1930s edge to it. That was the one Doris and I were in. Playing opposite her, I began to notice the character in her face and bearing—how her strongly molded chin and mouth set off the delicacy of her cheekbones, how her eyes, set too close together for beauty, were a soft warm brown alight with feeling, how the taut curves of her dark hair drawn across her temples, dancer-style, were at one with her lithe, small-breasted body. What had seemed austere and angular about her turned subtly feminine in my opened eyes.

There were no dates, nothing erotic. Because the dining-room people didn't finish until nine-thirty or so, the group met and rehearsed late, and so we were all either together or catching up on sleep. The only time I spent alone with her was a gray afternoon when I happened to meet her coming out of the hotel and we ended up going for a walk on the beach.

By then the plans for the strike were lagging, because the professional waiters and waitresses, about one-third of the staff, were dead against it, saying that a bunch of Commie college kids had no right to screw up their livelihood. Some of the other college kids who had been interested were becoming skeptical or bored. Murray and the hard core wanted to persist, because there was always a "retrograde element" in the working class that had to be fiercely resisted. I asked Doris what she thought. She said that since everyone was making good money and had only the ten-week season to make it in, she hadn't thought there would be a strike. "Sloan calls it a classic case of infantile leftism," she said. "I think it's more a case of Murray and the others wanting to do some practicing on us."

"What about the plays? I asked.

"Oh, I don't think they'll come off either. People will decide they're too tired to rehearse or have something better to do. But it'll be fun while it lasts."

"That's disappointing, "I said. "I don't have much reason for sticking around here except for being involved with the group. My friend Jeff is already talking about leaving."

Doris said that everyone wondered why "two smooth guys" like us had ended up dishing out food to them.

"Jeff's smooth," I said. "I'm not."

"You're just smooth in a different way."

"How so?"

"Well, Jeff, of course, is a smooth operator. You're more complicated and unpredictable. No one can quite figure you out."

I felt both flattered and uneasy. I hadn't thought anyone was paying much attention. "Neither can I," I said. "I've been sort of at loose ends since I got out of the Navy. But then I was at loose ends in the Navy too."

"How old are you?

"Turning twenty," I said, giving myself the benefit of a few months. She probably wasn't much older than I was, but she already had her own place on the Lower East Side, was studying dance with José Limon, was leading her own life.

"Then you're right on schedule. You're just more in-process than most people. If you keep feeling at loose ends, that's a good sign. It means you've left who you were and are in the process of becoming who you're going to be. I'd like to be around to see how you turn out."

"You would?" I said, startled, elated.

"You have to believe in your process and go where it takes you."

"How do you know when you're on the right track?

"By the excitement you feel and by the conviction that this is where you belong, what you need to do."

By now I was thrilled to be with her, thrilled by the conversation, even thrilled by my own ease and fluency. We were walking barefooted along the smooth margin where the incoming waves hurried in like a long line of masons, filling and leveling the little craters made by the suck of the outgoing ones. "The toiling masses of the sea," I said, pointing out what I meant.

"Where did *that* come from?" she said with a sweet laugh.

"Who knows? Maybe I'm going to be a poet instead of a labor lawyer. Maybe I'm becoming my next thing right before your eyes. You won't even have to wait to see it happen."

"You are a strange one," she said.

I guess my face dropped. "Don't fret," she said. "Poets and dancers are supposed to be strange. When we like a new piece we say, 'That's *really* strange.' Strange is good." She took my hand. "Come on," she said. "Let's join the toiling masses." And we began to run through the surf.

Toward the end of July, Jeff decided to leave. He said that he could make more money hustling golfers and have fun doing it. The summer was going fast, and I wasn't making anything like the money I'd need to supplement the hundred dollars a month that the GI Bill paid for living expenses. I tried the hotels in Long Beach but couldn't come up with a waiter or busboy job. So I quit when Jeff did and said my goodbyes on the staff beach that afternoon. As I turned to leave, Doris got up from the group and walked a little way with me. I said that I would like to stay in touch with her. She said that she'd like that too. I held out my hand; she took it and squeezed it. It felt almost as exciting and promising as if we'd kissed.

By the next evening I was working as a busboy at a good hotel in West End, New Jersey. I had a full station and served drinks in the hotel's casino on Saturday night, and the money rolled in. But I was like a Hans Castorp who had left the Berghof before his time. At the Lido Beach Hotel almost every day had been significant, almost every relationship had mattered. Now very little affected me. I went on reading Mann, but I began living interiorly on memories and fantasies, mainly of Doris.

They weren't just to cuddle with, though there was plenty of that. They helped me to realize that I wasn't a defective Jeff or Yuddy, as I'd been casting myself, but more like Hans Castorp, "life's faithful problem child," a young man whose sense of being wounded came from his feelings and ideas being under cultivation and therefore often raked over. When conditions were right, as with Honey and Lee and Doris, I knew my ground and flourished. I was the Weiss boy but growing up in my own way. Because I hadn't realized that and wanted to be like Dad on his weekends, I was bound to fail because my confidence and heart weren't in it, and also bound to screw myself up. It seemed so clear and heartening that I read in the evenings instead of dating or chasing and kept the fantasies of Doris chaste.

I waited a week or so to write to her. Usually I just sat down, pulled the chain, and the words came out, but this letter took a lot of time and several attempts and then revisions to strike the right note of friendliness with an undertone of ardor.

The Saturday-night entertainment in the casino was the standard Borscht Belt routine—a derisive comedian followed by a schmaltzy singer—but one show was different. Its featured number began with the singer, a baritone with a cantor's ache in the upper register, singing one of the melodies to a text from *Lamentations* in memory of the Six Million. As he came to the final keening phrase, a clarinet began to play very quietly, almost distantly, a series of syncopated phrases that slowly gained momentum in the rhythm section and then burst out in a joyous tune. It was an Israeli song of celebration, "Tzane, Tzane" ("Stand up, Stand up, join the celebration . . ."), and it lifted everyone out of his seat and onto the dance floor to join in a hora circle. The sequence was corny, the effect was overpowering; I put down my tray and got into the dancing and exultation.

I hadn't thought seriously about being Jewish for a long time. The Holocaust had faded into a subcategory of World War II's horrendous side of the ledger. A few weeks before I was discharged, the state of Israel had come into its imperiled existence, and I'd toyed with the thought of going there to fight—my version of Spanish Civil War heroics. The success of the Israeli army had allowed me to forget the idea. Now the show number had joined the Holocaust to our brave new state, a connection I had not grasped until then, which actualized both of them in a surge of emotion and a burst of significance. Apparently I could bring myself to relate to the mass murder of my people only when I could turn to it from this new vantage point of rebirth and pride.

After the evening was over, I tried to figure out my previous insensitivity. That the Israeli forces were proving to be so tough and resourceful as well as strategically smart had relieved and elated but not surprised me. It meant that the other Jews, the ones who belied the stereotypes, had gone into action—the Israeli counterparts of the clever lightweight boxers and quarterbacks, ball handlers and pivot men, the *shtarker* handball players and boxers, the medicine-ball throwers and weight lifters from the YMHAs of my youth—and they were showing the world as well as the Arabs that we knew how to handle ourselves. That was my frame of reference, and seeing it play itself out so dramatically revived the early attitude implanted by my Weiss uncles (the six-year-old me telling Judge Waldman, "I'm a Jew and proud of it").

At the same time, it neutralized what I saw now as a sense of shame about the Holocaust, that, deep down, it had reinforced my own stereotypes of weak, helpless Jews. One of the jokes that had stuck with me told of two Jews about to be shot. The officer offers each of them a blindfold. One of them says, "Keep your rag, I want to die with my eyes open." The other says, "Jake, take it. Don't make trouble." Israel was showing the world what I and everyone else badly needed to be reminded of, that we weren't only bargainers and victims, that many of us were like the first Jew in the joke, and given half a chance we could fight back and fight for and prevail. Assured of this that evening, I could begin to imagine myself in the death camps as well as the Negev, begin to mourn as well as exult as a Jew.

I didn't hear from Doris for two weeks or so. By then I was so dependent on the memories and images of her that I decided I was, for the first time, in love. I'd wake up in the morning and begin singing to myself "The Very Thought of You," and continue through the day. At night I would try to write a poem that captured the serious/playful mood of our walk on the beach, which kept ending up as a mish-mash of Keats trying to sound like E. E. Cummings, whose poem "i sing of Olaf" had bowled me over when it was proposed for the anti-war show.

Doris's reply to my letter was little more than a note, but each word was riveted to my mind by her presence behind it. After telling of her pleasure in hearing from me and giving me a bit of news—Murray had been fired, they weren't putting on the two

272 / TED SOLOTAROFF

plays but were thinking of putting on a Staff Night show—the letter wound up:

> We all miss you. Your talent and wit would have come in handy as we put together the show. Speaking for myself, you, too, have been a special person in my summer and our walk that day is part of my permanent memory of it. I'm sorry you'll be going off to college so soon after the season ends, but I hope we'll stay in touch with each other and I'll try to be dancing in something in December that I can invite you to.
>
> Fondly,
Doris

I kept going back to the final paragraph and the final word. In my sensible moments they expressed an interest in our getting to know each other; aloft in other moments, I thought they might be saying "I'd like you to come here." In between I tried to compose a response without knowing what level of feeling to pitch it at. Days went by and then a week of torn up-starts and whole versions of a letter. In twelve days the season would be over. It was no longer a question of what her note was saying but of who I was—an ordinary guy with a crush or a young poet in the throes of his first great passion. That proved easier to resolve. I wrote to Doris that I wanted to be in the show and would find a place to stay in Long Beach and probably a job for the Labor Day weekend. Then I told the headwaiter I had a family crisis, worked through the weekend so that he could get a replacement and I could collect my tips, and left on Monday for Lido Beach.

One of the first people I saw at the hotel was Bud Harris. The season was already over for him. He'd been ill for the past week or so with a nasty virus and was leaving for home the next day. We went for a walk on the beach during the dinner meal. Though I was highly keyed up at the prospect of seeing Doris in another two hours, the atmosphere of the hotel had lost its charge for me, or, rather, what had been so fraught with interest and implication in my memory during the past month was now simply a summer resort at the end of the summer.

Bud looked worn and glum. He put his hand on my shoulder.

"You didn't come back to be in some staff show," he said. "What's up?"

"I'm in love," I said.

"With who?"

"With Doris."

"The dancer? You scamp. You never even told me you were seeing her."

"I wasn't," I said. 'It happened just before I left. It mostly happened since I left . . . I mean . . ."

Usually he made me feel older, but now I felt nineteen again or maybe sixteen. As we trudged up from the beach, I told him about being in the play, the walk on the beach, the two letters. It seemed pretty flimsy in the telling. We sat down on a cabana lounge chair. Finally Bud said, "Does Doris know you're in love with her?" The question seemed to give him pain.

"I just said I was coming back to be in the show. But I imagine she suspects something."

He seemed about to ask me something else but didn't. Instead he said. "Well, lots of luck. It's certainly been an interesting summer for you."

It was a strange remark or rather tone—distinctly unenthusiastic. But after he went away to pack, I went back to my former state of tense dreamy expectation.

An hour later I was dancing with Doris in the staff canteen. She was wearing pale yellow beach pajamas and looked terrific, the deep tan of her face and arms set off by the fabric. She hadn't been this stylish before, and she also seemed rounder, softer, the dancer receding into the woman. We hadn't danced much in the past, but there was a difference there too, though it went in the opposite direction. When I tried to draw her closer, she looked at me in a careful, gentle way and said, "Did you come back partly to see me?"

"Mainly," I said.

"Then there's something I'd better tell you. I've been seeing Sloan for the past two weeks."

The blow was softened by her evident feeling for me. Also, as soon as I heard it, it seemed inevitable. They were right for each other—two New York theater people.

"When I got your second letter, I wanted to tell you that. But I only got it Friday."

"It's okay," I said, trying to be manly, mature, though I felt like sixteen again. "These things happen."

"Perhaps I should have tried to reach you by phone. But it seemed a little presumptuous. You said you wanted to be in the show."

"Sure," I said. "I can see that."

A little while later, Sloan came into the canteen as if on cue. His big, fair face was also aglow, his bearing even more magisterial than I'd remembered. They clearly were both flourishing. We exchanged a few pleasantries, he asked what I had in mind to do in the show (I hadn't really thought about it), and then he organized several of the others into a move to the beach.

That's where we ended up, with blankets and sweaters and a driftwood fire. There was a lot of hilarity and wine-drinking and New York talk that I didn't find to be as exciting as I had a month ago. Mostly I watched and listened and drank more than my share of the wine. Doris and Sloan were very much a couple. Every now and then I'd see her looking at me and I'd try to smile in a not too shit-eating way.

When it broke up, the people who were sleeping together went off down the beach, the others went back to the dorms. There were just the three of us left. Doris asked where I'd be sleeping, and I said, "Right here if I can borrow a blanket."

"I'll get you one," she said.

I thought of going for a swim to wash away my disappointment and chagrin. But the wine was getting to me, and I was already half asleep when I felt Doris put a blanket on me; then she knelt and kissed my forehead.

"Will you be around tomorrow?" she asked.

"I doubt it," I said, standing up, feeling woozy.

"I'm really sorry about what's happened. I care for you a lot."

I believed her. It took the pain away but doubled the regret.

"Stay strange," she said after we'd hugged goodbye.

"I'm giving myself every opportunity," I said.

I left the Lido the next morning, accompanying Bud into New York, where I would help him transfer to his train for Springfield—the foolhardy lover taking his leave as the Good Samaritan. On the way in I asked him a bit stiffly if he'd known about Sloan and Doris getting together.

"What you're really asking," he said, "is why I didn't tip you off. Spare you the embarrassment. What would you have done in my situation?"

"I'd have tipped you off. That's what friends are for."

"Not grown-up friends," he said. "You'd have told me because it would be an exciting, dramatic situation for you, which you have a taste for, and not because you'd thought it through."

"Thanks a lot."

"You're wounded and wish you'd been spared, right?"

"I thought we were friends . . ." I began.

"Friends don't spare you the consequences of your mistakes. That's not being a friend, that's being a bad parent."

His thin face was still looking pale and pinched but no longer frail. "Also there was Doris to consider."

"Doris?"

"How would you have felt if you'd been in her shoes and I'd tipped her off?"

I hadn't thought of it that way at all. Once I did I saw what he was driving at. I would have felt meddled with, unfairly cornered by Bud. I would have wanted to tell her myself, in the caring way she told me.

"Also, what difference would it have made to you if I had told you. You still would have had to face the situation, and I doubt that it would have hurt less."

I thought it over, running his points through my head and heart, sifting and weighing their import. The truth was that Bud had given more thought, serious thought, in the few minutes he'd had to make up his mind not to tell me than I'd given in the nearly two weeks of trying to make up mine by reading and rereading between and behind the lines of a friendly note. In the end I'd thrown away a week's tips that I could have lived on for a month in Ann Arbor and put my feeling for Doris ass end up because of a romantic image of myself. I'd acted impulsively, foolishly, and called it being a poet. No wonder I'd felt like the teenager left behind by the two adults at the end of the evening.

I looked at Bud, who wasn't a romantic, wasn't even literary, who would probably end up very bourgeois but who had just taught me more than had all the others combined that summer. "You've just helped me begin to think like a *mensch*," I said.

"It's a long process," he said. "Believe me."

7 I SPENT THE rest of the week in Roselle Park, shopping, leave-taking, reading, daydreaming about the various new opportunities at Michigan but also noting the signs of problems in the family. The house was in its usual disarray. Mom had received Fan's bedroom set when her estate was settled, and she and the kids were now stripping it of its gray paint and staining it walnut. Bobby was working on the dresser in the bedroom we shared, and one of the new shirts I laid out to pack developed its own walnut stains. Freed from Dad's iron control, everything was done freestyle and without precaution, a kind of fairy-tale anarchy. The orderly ways I'd picked up in the Navy were easily defeated by it, which gave me another reason for feeling that I couldn't wait to leave.

Which, in turn, gave me another reason for feeling guilty about leaving. Focused wholly on Ann Arbor, I had ignored my good intention of going to a college closer to home and stepping in at least as the weekend head of the household. A man in this house was clearly needed, for Mom was not the only one who needed support. In Roselle Park, nervous about starting school again, Sandy was not the blossoming girl she had been a year ago in Lakewood. She was lonely an easily irritated, particularly by Mom's nagging her about her work at the piano, which had become more a burden than a bright prospect to her. I said that I'd tell Mom to lay off before I left.

"When you went into the Navy, it made a big hole in our lives," she said. "Now you're going away again."

"You'll be going away too in two years," I said, the only thing I could think to say.

"On whose money?"

"Dad's. I'll make sure of that."

Bobby, too, was in emotional flux, in high spirits one day, morose the next. He said that he had begun to have trouble doing his home-work, my precocious kid brother who at four had vowed the people on the roof of the Franklin Towers by his ability to add large sums in his head and to wield the vocabulary of a child twice his age. When I asked him what the trouble was, he said, "I have only one more year to be happy."

"How do you know that?" I asked. "Are you a fortune-teller?"

"No, a preadolescent," he said.

What then to do to stop feeling like the grown version of little Benny for abandoning Mom and the kids? Since nothing had moved on the divorce settlement over the summer, I picked up the phone and called Dick Berman.

He confirmed what Mom had told me. "Your father's being very stubborn about alimony. He says that he'll only increase the monthly payments for child support. That would leave your mother with fifty-five dollars a month once the children are grown."

"She has rheumatoid arthritis," I said. "She could be crippled by the time Bob turns twenty-one. That's only ten years from now."

"He also wants the child support to end at eighteen."

That made me even angrier. "How are my sister and brother to even think about going to college? Can't we put any pressure on him? He's the one who needs the divorce."

"What do you mean by pressure?" he replied testily.

"Tell him that we'll withdraw the divorce consent. That we'll sue him for abandonment or desertion or whatever it is."

This produced the long pause in which Berman liked to let me stew or cool off.

"I think it's advisable for you to let me handle this. We've in effect told him that he can't have the divorce until he makes a more reason-able offer."

"So why is he stalling?"

"I can't speculate about his motives. I can only respond to his offer and wait for an improved one. Anything else?"

"Perhaps I should try to talk to him," I said. "I'm going off to col-lege and don't want to leave things hanging this way."

"I wouldn't advise that," he said.

"Why wouldn't you?"

He wouldn't say, but we both knew that judging from the meeting in the other lawyer's office, I was right at the top of Dad's shit list. On the other hand, what did we have to lose? Also I wanted to test what Bud had revealed were his true feelings about me.

A woman answered the phone in a pleasant professional way. The charming Gladys, I wondered, the executive secretary Leo had told me about? Could he have roped her in already? When he came on the line, he said in a civil, even lightly concerned voice, "Where you calling from?"

"I'm home," I said. "I'm going off to Ann Arbor right after Labor Day, and I'd like to come by around six or so and say goodbye to you."

"You don't say," he said. "What a surprise."

I'd prepared myself to deal with antagonism, not irony. "It has been a while," I said.

"Oh, what's three years of almost total silence between a father and his oldest son? It happens in the best of families."

"Perhaps it's time to end it," I said, a sudden gust of emotion in my throat. "I'd like to," I said. I'd prepared to decoy him downfield, and here I was, tripping myself in my own backfield.

"I'll tell you what," he said. "Come here around seven and I'll take you to the Tavern. And Ted . . ."

"Yes, Dad?"

"Dress nice."

"I dress nice these days. I'm grown up."

"I heard about your fiasco at Yale," he said. "You wear those kind of clothes on the street corner with your pals, not at a place like Yale. No wonder they turned you down."

This was more like it. Jab and parry—his jab, my parry. "Well, I got into Michigan, which is where I wanted to go anyway."

"What're you talking about? There's no comparison between Yale and Michigan in terms of what it can do for you."

"We'll talk about it," I said.

But we didn't. Over shrimp cocktails and filet mignon that almost did "melt in your mouth," we talked about the glass business. He had more storefront and insurance replacement work than he could handle. "I once wanted to be the biggest glass contractor in the area, so now I am and I can't wait to get out. Between the manufacturers and the competition and the union I can barely make a dime." He explained that the veterans had taken over the local and not only had driven wages sky-high but were also demanding benefits. A number of other veterans had come into the business, some of them former union glaziers, as contractors. "They work fast and cheap and smart. The sons of bitches never worked for me like that."

"It's called free enterprise, Dad. You can't expect people to work less hard and smart for themselves than you did."

"Well, I hope to be selling to them soon instead of competing with them." He stopped for a moment, gave me a long, confidential look, and went on. "But that's my other problem. I'm going to be very short for a while, probably the next few years. Distribution means inventory, and you don't get paid for your inventory. You pay the interest on it. Every month. It's costing me close to four thousand dollars a month to open the door in the morning, and it's going to get worse as I make the change."

The food was turning less delicious with each mouthful; the feeling of well-being—Joe College and his well-heeled father dining out at the Tavern—was gone; so was the curiosity and hope I'd brought with me. Nothing had changed. He was just trying filet mignon instead of the threat of a gun.

"What you're telling me is that you can't afford to pay Mom four hundred dollars a month."

"I'm trying to explain something to you," he said, as calm as he could. "What you and your mother don't understand is that I have to look down the road. In another two years your sister is going to be ready for college. And she's not going to have that GI Bill of yours. Then there'll be Bobby. At the same time, five years from now, I expect to be much better off and in a better position to help your mother. And maybe you when you're ready for law school."

"Let's look at it another way," I said. "The difference between what you're offering and what she needs is maybe one hundred fifty a month. That's what? Three or four percent of your overhead? It's not going to make any difference to how you run your business or how you and your new wife live."

He didn't respond, so I knew I'd scored. In stride now, I went on, "There's also the need to improve the alimony part. Mom can't live on fifty-five dollars a month after the kids are grown."

"Of course she can't. We assume she'll be working or remarried. Your mother is still an attractive woman."

"She has rheumatoid arthritis, Dad. It's a progressively crippling disease."

Again he went silent. He called the waiter to clear away the dinner course and then asked about the desserts. "Try the nesselrode pie," he advised me, then said to the waiter, "My son here is going away next week to the University of Michigan. We're doing a little celebrating."

While we were driving back to Roselle Park, he said. "You've given me something to think about."

"Thanks," I said. "I'm glad I got through."

"You may think I'm a peasant . . ." he said and then stopped.

I didn't know what to say. I'd never heard him say anything remotely like that before.

"Not even a tenth-grade education . . . Well, I'll tell you something. I'm going to be living with a very civilized person and I'm going to make the most of it."

"I'm glad for your sake," I said. Talking with him in this way was an exercise in mental balance—responding to what he was saying, while thinking about what he didn't say or even get, and trying to negotiate the difference. "Mom is a very civilized person," I said. "I don't think you ever gave her her proper due. I hope you don't make that mistake again."

"Your mother," he said slowly, "would cut off her arm for me, but she was not someone I could take anywhere or have an intelligent conversation with."

"Well, we'll never agree about Mom and don't have to anymore. But I think that she was never the hick you kept telling her she was. She lacked confidence with you, and there's plenty of reason for that."

"I couldn't wait for her, that's true," he said. "She couldn't even smoke a cigarette in public without getting ashes on herself."

"That's not lack of sophistication, that's nervousness. I'm not talk-ing about waiting for her to develop. I'm talking about encouraging her instead of discouraging her. I'm talking about not—"

I was about to say "squelching" but he cut in. "Well, maybe I never understood her, any more than you'll ever understand me."

"Me understand you?" I couldn 't keep up anymore with the turns his mind was taking.

"I'm a self-made man, " he said. "You'll never understand what that means because you'll never have to go through what it takes. You don't begin to know . . . and you should be grateful that you won't have to."

For all of my disapproval of him, I did understand. I even felt clos-er to him right then, objectively closer, than I ever had before, even on the hikes, even the week we were together before I walked out of The Shop. But I couldn't tell him that I was beginning to know about being self-made. That it wasn't just nose jobs and reading the right books and finding a way to pay for your education so that you could help humanity. That it was about not going to Rutgers, or even trying to go to a better school close to home like NYU. That it was about not letting anyone stand in your way or change your course, about following, in that respect, in his heedless, blinkered, self-centered footsteps. How could I tell him all of that when I could barely begin to tell myself?

The divorce agreement was finally hammered out the following spring. "Hammered" is the right verb. By then Mom was so beaten down by Dad's stalling and duplicity about his ability to pay, and she so much needed to put the house on the market and be gone, that she succumbed rather than settled. In return for the right to sell the house and keep the proceeds, she agreed to the pittance of $280 a month in alimony and child support, the latter to end in eight years. If I'd stayed on the case and found a lawyer who would have demand-ed an audit of my father's assets, it all might have been different, but I was in Ann Arbor and more or less lost by then in my new dream of becoming a fiction writer and in my first love affair.

Aunt Leah, who was at the final hearing as a pro forma witness, told me that when the terms were read out by the judge, she gasped at their meagerness. "It was so sad," she said. "Ben with all of his power and money on one side, and she and Sandy on the other. It wasn't justice that was being done in that courtroom, it was a crime being committed. But then your mother signed the papers, put on her brave smile, and walked out with her head up. That was your mother. She put up with so much and still kept her head up."

With the proceeds of the sale of the house, Mom got a mortgage on a decent house in Teaneck, New Jersey, and though it took up almost half of her monthly money from Dad, she was able to swing it by getting a job as a bookkeeper. When I came home for Christmas vacation the following year, they had settled in and the three of them had more or less reconstituted the Shelley Avenue look of taste winning by a length over shabbiness and disarray.

The morning after I'd hitchhiked home, I came downstairs to find her reading the book I'd traveled with, Oscar Williams's *Little Anthology of Modern Verse*, the canon of my new literary faith. In the back were the rows of austere little oval head shots of the patriarchs, heroes, and heroines of modernism, and it was these Mom was gazing at, as I so often did to personalize the movement that was changing my life.

"Archibald MacLeish is as distinguished-looking as his name," she said. "But I don't like his poem, 'Ars Poetica.' She turned back and read a few lines. " 'A poem should be palpable and mute / as globed fruit. As dumb as old medallions / To the thumb.' It's pretty language, but what kind of poem would that be?"

I tried to explain to her about the hermetic notion of poetry that I was trying to grasp and believe in myself. "Poetry makes nothing happen, like Auden says. It's self-contained. That's why MacLeish winds up saying, 'A poem should not mean / But be.' "

"I don't see how anyone who writes as beautifully as Archibald MacLeish could say something as silly as that. I can understand art for art's sake but not art for silence's sake."

Until then such an opinion from her would have exasperated me. What could *she* know with her meager and out-of-date literary background? But there was a self-confidence in her voice now that I'd been waiting half my life to hear. Also deep down I still agreed with what she was saying rather than with what the New Critics were. I thought what a clear, firm mind she suddenly seemed to have, and was reminded of Dad's telling me Mark Twain's remark that when he was sixteen he thought his father was ignorant and was surprised at how much his old man had learned by the time he was twenty-one.

But there was more to it than that. I looked around the living room at the familiar prints—Renoir's *On the Terrace*, the Degas of a woman in blue, the Albert Ryder corral of horses, a lovely etching of small bears—looked at them as though for the first time, the film of familiarity suddenly wiped from my eyes. So, too, the Harvard Classics she had rescued from Cream Ridge tumbling on the shelves of the secretary, the piano scores, ragged from use, heaped on the piano. These were the icons of our household, of her faith in taste and culture we had been raised in, however haphazardly and indirectly amid the deprivation, fear, and sorrow.

A month after I'd begun college she'd sent me a copy of Keats's poems as a birthday present. "That's nice," I'd said to myself and thought no more about it, even though I was so infatuated with Homer and Herodotus and Aeschylus that my ambition to become a labor lawyer was already headed for the door. I'd put the book on the shelf where I kept the remaining humanities texts I couldn't wait to read but made no connection between Mom's gift and my passion, which I'd thought was new and all my own. I could see now that it was neither, that it had come with her milk and been sustained by her spirit, her taste, her ways, particularly her way of being somewhere else as the practical world went by, which was now manifestly mine.

'I just realized something," I said. "How much I owe you. It's no accident that I want to become a writer. It's your footsteps I'm following in.

She took it in, blinked a tear or two, then said, "I've always hoped you would scale the heights."

Scale the heights, another Momism. "It's more than your hope. It's your values. Your example."

"Oh, my example hasn't amounted to much. *Potchkeeing* at the piano. I haven't had an artist's life like Sophie has."

"That's not what I'm talking about. For all her nuttiness Sophie was free to lead her own life, and she's always had Leo's support. You've had no freedom and no support. On the contrary. But you have more of an artistic nature than she does."

"I guess that I didn't want to struggle the way she has, the way you'll have to. Not knowing where your next dollar is coming from."

"Well, you've taught me how to live with that."

"Oh I always knew where it was coming from. I just didn't know when. I still don't. His monthly checks are never here at the first of the month. Sometimes not even the fifteenth. I've had to send Sandy to Elizabeth."

We talked for a while about why he did that and what I could try to do about it. There seemed little point in calling Dick Berman. I said that I'd go to see Dad myself and put it to him man to man. The sluggish, futile feeling of the permanently oppressed had taken over the tone of our conversation, which had started out so freely and freshly. The heavy bear who goes with me, with us, I thought.

"I've been looking at that etching of the bears," I said. "Remember when you told me your mother's remark about marrying her best daughter to a bear?"

"That's what she said. Momma knew." Then she said, "I've always liked that etching. A little sentimental, but delicate and warm."

"Well, there's a poem in that book I've been wanting to show you. It's also about a bear. It's by a great poet named Delmore Schwartz." I found the poem and began reading:

> "The heavy bear who goes with me,
> A manifold honey to smear his face,
> Clumsy and lumbering here and there,
> The central ton of every place."

As I read on to the end, her attention was so strong that I felt I could have walked on it. When I finished she said, "Read that again about the show-off."

> "—The strutting show-off is terrified,
> Dressed in his dress-suit, bulging his pants,
> Trembles to think that his quivering meat
> Must finally wince to nothing at all."

"That's what I've always thought about him," she said. "A lot of his behavior is a pathetic need for attention."

"Of course, Schwartz is not writing about Dad or anyone. It's mainly about his own body. But a lot applies. Particularly the ending." I read again:

> "Stretches to embrace the very dear
> With whom I would walk without him near,
> Touches her grossly, although a word
> Would bare my heart and make me clear,
> Stumbles, flounders, and strives to be fed
> Dragging me with him in his mouthing care,
> Amid the million of his kind,
> The scrimmage of appetite everywhere."

"Let me read it myself," she said. After she had done so, she read the last two lines aloud and said with her new assertiveness, "See, he's not that unusual. There are a million like him. I just want to forgive and forget, put him behind me."

"He won't let us," I said. "He'll have to die first."

After a moment, she suddenly shrugged and smiled warmly. "What name are you going to write under?"

"I haven't thought much about it. I don't like 'Theodore.' "

"I've been thinking of changing our last name to Del Sola. It's an old Spanish, Sephardic name."

"It's very musical," I said.

"Theodore Sola," she intoned. "Sandra Del Sola. Robert del Sola." She was beaming now, almost lost in the sounds, as though she were playing our new names as a melodic phrase on the piano that was taking her to her other place. "Rose del Sola. It's a breath of fresh air already."

"Rose del Sola," I said. "That's the best one of all."